STALKING THE ELEPHANT KINGS

STALKING THE ELEPHANT KINGS

In search of Laos

Christopher Kremmer

A Latitude 20 Book
UNIVERSITY OF HAWAI'I PRESS
HONOLULU

To Marlene and Ted,
for everything

Copyright © Christopher Kremmer, 1997
Photographs © Felicity Volk

All rights reserved. No part of this book may be reproduced or
transmitted in any form or by any means, electronic or
mechanical, including photocopying, recording or by any
information storage and retrieval system, without prior permission
in writing from the publisher.

Published in North America by
University of Hawai'i Press
2840 Kolowalu Street
Honolulu, Hawai'i 96822

First published in Australia by
Allen & Unwin
9 Atchison Street, St Leonards NSW 2065
Australia

Printed in Singapore
Set in 10/12 pt Garamond by DOCUPRO, Sydney

Library of Congress Cataloguing-in-Publication Data

The Cataloguing-in-Publication Data has been applied for.
ISBN 0-8248-2021-5

Contents

Acknowledgments

I am indebted to many Lao people who helped me in writing and researching this book. Among them are members and officials of both past and present regimes, exiles and stay-behinds, numerous members of the royal family and former re-education prisoners, and both Lao and foreign diplomats who have served in Vientiane and abroad. My thanks must go to the Lao government for facilitating my travel in the country. My appreciation also goes to the Lao exile movement, which provided a great deal of historical background. My wife, Janaki, provided unstinting support, and help with translations from the French was provided by Jean-Gabriel Manguy and Christophe de Neuville, and from the Lao by Teng Teng Kinnavong. My thanks also go to Martin Stuart-Fox, who advised me on aspects of Lao history but who is not responsible for my interpretations of it, and to Julio Jeldres for access to the Sihanouk archives. The staff of the Siam Society and the *Bangkok Post*'s clippings service also provided invaluable help and quiet corners in which to escape the clamour and pollution of Bangkok. The staff of the Australian Archives in Canberra gave their time and resources, albeit on a user-pays basis. Felicity Volk provided some of her captivating images of Luang Prabang, and Patrick Gallagher was generous with his time and experience.

Dramatis personae

Savang Vatthana

The last King of Laos, forced to abdicate in 1975 by the Pathet Lao and later incarcerated in the north-eastern province of Houaphan. A devout Buddhist and lover of French literature, he tried unsuccessfully to remain above the political fray during the Civil War. He succeeded his father, Sisavangvong, in 1959, but his refusal to undergo a formal coronation until his kingdom was reunified meant he was never formally crowned.

Souphanouvong

Dubbed the 'Red Prince' for his royal blood and communist views, he waged an ultimately successful 30-year struggle against French and American intervention in Laos whilst allowing Vietnamese forces to operate on Lao territory. Born into the lower branch of the royal family, he inspired his followers by forsaking the privileges of his birth and living in a cave for ten years to survive American bombing. He supported the abolition of the monarchy and was named the first President of the Lao PDR after the abdication of his cousin, the king.

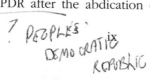

ix

Souvanna Phouma
Leader of the 'neutralists' and several times prime minister, he sought a genuinely independent, non-aligned Laos free from domination by its neighbours and the great powers. The half-brother of Souphanouvong, he was seen as an unreliable ally by both camps during the Cold War, and eventually capitulated to the victorious Pathet Lao.

Vong Savang
The last crown prince of Laos. He served his father, Savang Vatthana, with dedication but lacked the intellect and guile of his communist rivals. His wife Mahneelai still lives in the former royal capital of Luang Prabang, whilst most of his children live in the west.

Kaysone Phomvihan
General Secretary of the Lao People's Revolutionary Party and its precursors from 1955 until his death in 1992. In close consultation with Hanoi, he directed the Pathet Lao struggle from the caves of Houaphan province, and led the country from the installation of a communist regime in 1975. Towards the end of his life he abandoned socialist economic policies and embraced Buddhism.

Sisavangvong
At the time of his death in 1959, the longest-reigning king on earth. He survived the French protectorate and a nationalist uprising at the end of the Second World War to stay on as a constitutional monarch. He had twelve wives and at least 24 children.

Prince Boun Oum Na Champassak
Descended from the family which once ruled southern Laos as a separate kingdom, he served as prime minister in a pro-American royalist government. Renowned for his corruption, he escaped to Thailand and died in Paris in 1984.

Soth Phetrasy

The Pathet Lao representative in Vientiane during the Civil War. After 1975, he was sent to Houaphan province to take charge of re-education of members of the former regime, despite his expectations of a senior post in the government. He later served as ambassador to Moscow and now lives a quiet life in retirement in Vientiane.

Sisana Sisane

Chief propagandist for communist forces during the Civil War. After many years fighting against French and American involvement in Laos, he became the first Minister of Information in the new regime. In the early 1980s he was sent into internal exile for political errors but was later rehabilitated and given the task of writing the official history of the Lao revolution, a task he has yet to complete.

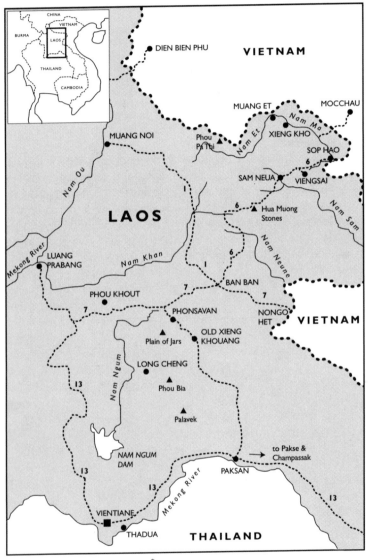

VIETNAM

DIEN BIEN PHU

CHINA
VIETNAM
BURMA
LAOS
THAILAND
CAMBODIA

MOCCHAU

MUANG ET
XIENG KHO
Nam Ma

MUANG NOI

Phou
Pa Thi
Nam Et
SOP HAO

6

VIENGSAI

SAM NEUA

Nam Ou

LAOS

6
Hua Muong
Stones

Nam Sam

Nam Khan

6

Nam Neune

Mekong River

LUANG
PRABANG

1

PHOU KHOUT

7

BAN BAN

7

PHONSAVAN

NONGO
HET

VIETNAM

7

Plain of Jars

OLD XIENG
KHOUANG

Nam Ngum

LONG CHENG

13

Phou Bia

Palavek

NAM NGUM
DAM

to Pakse &
Champassak

13

PAKSAN

13

Mekong River

13

13

VIENTIANE

THADUA

THAILAND

3
NAM = RIVER

Prologue

The Chinese-built aircraft had to bank hard before slamming onto the airstrip, the only straight line in the province. Disembarking, we trudged up a slope to a shack where uniformed men wielding rubber stamps asked to see our *laissez passer*, the document permitting travel outside Vientiane. In those days, even Lao citizens needed them, so paranoid and bureaucratic had the place become. It was quiet and sunny. People smiled, and their smiles said, 'Leave us alone!' My rucksack landed with a thump in the tray of a *tuk-tuk*, whose driver smiled and squinted against the sun. He drove like they all drive—madly—an anarchy of bumps and dust as he charged across the ridges of the iron bridge over the Nam Khan like a kamikaze.

The dawdling streets of Luang Prabang, with their shuttered shopfronts and opaque people, formed a still eye in the typhoon of Indochina's history. It was October, the dry season, and people carried parasols in the sun. The black night skies were embedded with stars. You might hear the occasional song of a woman, unseen beyond a balcony; the monks' quiet chatter; the steady gurgle of the river. Life revolved around the morning alms-giving to the monks, the market, and the afternoon snooze. At the former royal palace, guides conducted the odd tourist along polished wooden corridors, through halls hung with portraits of kings and queens, heirs to something called the 'Kingdom of the Million Elephants and the White Parasol'—the elephants representing power, the parasol sovereignty. But the kingdom was gone and the heirs were missing.

Back in Vientiane, inquiries with laconic government officials about the fate of the Lao royal family were met with quizzical looks and embarrassed silences, even the odd giggle. The king, they said, had 'gone to the north'. Was he still alive? The most common answer was: 'We don't know.' It seemed the only people with sufficient authority to answer such questions were dead. The late revolutionary leader, Kaysone Phomvihan had said something on a visit to Paris in 1989: 'I can tell you now that the king died of natural causes. He was very old. It happens to all of us.' It happened to Kaysone three years later. His words were not reported in Laos, and the government has never given detailed responses to questions about the royal non-persons.

In 1994, the *laissez passer* was abolished, and travel became easier within this war-damaged, land-locked country, without ports or railways, slowly emerging from its socialist cocoon; I began stumbling over clues to a past which officially no longer existed. The proletarian veneer of the People's Democratic Republic crumbled into dust wherever you poked it, revealing an ornate society which for 600 years had been ruled by the 'sacred and inviolable person' of a king. Like neighbouring Cambodia, Laos had strayed into the path of war and ideological upheaval. It was less barbarously damaged, but damaged it was, and few people seemed able to face up to what had happened. They turned their faces optimistically towards the future, or painted the past in primary colours of good and evil. Access was difficult, unless you confined yourself to innocuous subjects like the sleeping bombs the Americans left behind, or economics.

This book is essentially a travelogue which may help the reader better understand the context of contemporary Indochina. But the secret history of Laos—as obscure and dangerous as those unexploded bombs littering the countryside—lies across even the most remote trail. I have traversed the country from Houaphan in the north to Champassak in the south, crossing its land borders from Thailand and Vietnam, crossing myself anxiously aboard propeller aircraft, and perching on the back of logging trucks. At times I was shown only what the government intended me to see, at others I thought I might never again feel so free.

Those who govern the four and a half million citizens of Laos have introduced a measure of economic freedom, but are yet to embrace political change. Average annual income is a paltry $US350 per head, and life expectancy is only 51 years. Living standards trail those of Bangladesh and are just ahead of Mozambique's. According to my rough calculations, I spent about five months in Laos from 1993 to 1996. Each journey was complex and wonderstruck, at times deeply worrying and at times fun.

Where possible, I have tried to avoid judging people whose lives and actions happened in the context of war. Where attributions might prove dangerous for the individuals concerned, I have fudged identities. Where the facts have proven too slippery, I have said so.

Laos sometimes seems more like a family than a nation. The word for 'family'—vong—is embedded in many names. Surnames were considered unnecessary until 50 years ago, when the government made them compulsory. Had it not been for the involvement of the great powers, the civil war in Laos would have remained small and intimate, a family squabble. In a part of the world where the direct approach never works, and indirect methods scarcely do better, I conducted many interviews but found conversations more useful. And given the luxury of time, I found, Laos does open up to you, even on the most sensitive of subjects.

Christopher Kremmer
Melbourne, January 1997

1

Luang Prabang

Wattay airport, like all airports in Laos, was painted washing-powder blue. Decades of war and communism had regimented the colour scheme, if nothing else about the country. You could count the available tints on one hand. There was the electric lime of Vietnamese Green; Revolution Red—that angry offsetter of stars and sickles; and Wattay Blue, the colour of skies and airports. A sign above the x-ray machine commanded embarking passengers to 'Show All Weapons', so I handed my ballpoint pen to the security guard, who inspected it earnestly, then returned it with a smile as torpid as the heat.

Weeds sprang from the cracked tarmac, where a Chinese-built YUEN-12 awaited. The other passengers included a fretting mutt standing in the aisle, and a box of singing sparrows in the luggage rack. The emergency instructions stapled to the bulkheads were in English and Chinese. The Lao, it seemed, had already made their peace with the gods of flying. With engines grinding furiously, we careered down the runway, and leapt into the greater Wattay Blue.

'No sweat. No sweat,' said Boun Kham, my one-eyed companion and guide, wiping his profusely perspiring brow.

'When I was in the air force I flew in Laos many times. So many times. No sweat.'

The plane wove a path through the tapestry of the Lao landscape, flying blind through cloud banks and at times barely clearing the tops of the slashed and burnt hills. Then we lost altitude, and I saw it. Luang Prabang. A finger-point at the confluence of the Mekong and Khan rivers, bristling with coconut palms and ringed by mountains.

'Here,' said Boun Kham, shouldering my backpack for the hike uphill to a breezeblock shack which functioned as the terminal. 'You follow me.'

The habits of leadership were deeply ingrained in the old bloke—he had been a colonel in the Royal Lao Air Force, and spent 13 years in detention after the communist takeover. From 1975 to 1988 he'd belonged to a chain gang which ranged across northern Laos, building roads from village to village, and public buildings in the settlements thus connected. It was in these camps that he lost his eye, damaged by a spring which bounced out of an engine he was repairing. The commandant had refused permission for him to be flown to Vientiane for surgery. He had told me that story the first time we met, at a soup stall on Samsenthai Road, and we had been firm friends ever since.

The flashy, welcoming smiles of the *tuk-tuk* drivers waiting outside the terminal dissolved as we boarded the minibus of the Villa Santi, a small hotel which, it was said, had once belonged to the royal family, and been 'donated' to the state after the revolution. Now it had been given back to the original owners, and large pottery urns bearing triple-headed elephants and the words 'Royaume du Laos' flanked the colonnades. After helping unload my bags, Boun Kham slipped away to cheaper lodgings and old friends, leaving me surrounded by short, solicitous young men and women with hands raised prayer-like to their foreheads in the *nop* of greeting. They seated me in the airy lobby of the whitewashed villa, with its old teak furnishings and hand-woven coverings, to await my host.

Santi Inthavong was 34, and had grown up mainly in France. His surname meant family of Intha, a corruption of Indra, the king of the Vedic gods in Hindu mythology, who rode a white elephant and commanded thunder and rain. In the late eighteenth century, an Inthavong had ruled in Vientiane, but during the revolution in 1975, the hitherto-powerful family had split—spreading its risk, cynics said—with some supporting the communist Pathet Lao, and others fleeing the country. Now, after a lost decade, attempts at socialist levelling were being abandoned, and the old families were again coming to prominence. The Inthavongs were in hotels, and Santi's father was chairman of the powerful Economic Planning and Finance Committee of the National Assembly. On his return from France, Santi did what young princes have always done. He took a wife from another old family, though one whose power had long since faded. Sawee Nahlee, or 'Tin', was the grand-daughter of Savang Vatthana, the last king of Laos. Now, surrounded by his success in the lobby of the Villa Santi, Santi Inthavong seemed comfortable, almost secure.

'My God!' he exclaimed in French-accented English. 'My uncle from France is here and for the past three days it's been nothing but drinking, drinking, drinking.' He wore a faded denim shirt and sunglasses and affected the harried air of the successful bourgeois, his cheeks constantly ballooning and deflating in the Gallic gesture for 'What can you do?'

A young woman wearing the traditional silk skirt, the *sin*, and carrying a brass tray, glided into the room in silence and served us with coffee.

'So what brings you to Luang Prabang?' Santi asked me, as a ceiling fan barely stirred the languid air.

I told him I needed a rest after the stresses of life as a foreign correspondent in Hanoi.

'A rest, *oui*, but I expect you will also find many stories in Laos. And for somebody like you, these are the best kind of stories—the ones that have never been told!'

He hid a smile in his coffee cup.

Through the tall open windows I could see the sunny

street, and a group of women daintily covering their noses as they crossed an open sewer. Another minivan unloaded a party of European men, some of them wearing jungle greens, their hair in ponytails, and carrying suit bags. Soon the lobby filled with the flutter of French and the thick perfumes of mosquito repellent and sun screen. Their baggage formed a small mountain on the floor.

Santi said he himself had an 'untold story'. It turned out to be a routine tourism operator's complaint: the delay then affecting Luang Prabang's listing on UNESCO's register of world heritage sites.

'It's a great pity, because it will protect the city and bring in a lot of money,' he said. 'We have tried to preserve it. To revive it. Much more needs to be done.'

He spoke of his efforts not only to restore the villa but to revive the arts in Luang Prabang, which had declined without royal patronage. The communist authorities were supporting his efforts but were ambivalent about how far to indulge tourists' interest in the royal past. They had, for example, asked him to change the original name of the hotel, Villa de la Princesse. Then they had recalled the fine brocade dancers' costumes, heirlooms of the royal family, which had briefly clothed Santi's dancing troupe.

'We have good relations generally with them,' said Santi, making light of his problems with the local government. 'They're worried about the costumes being damaged. In the time of the king, the dancers might perform once or twice a year. Now it's once or twice a day. They'd like to put them in the museum.'

'And the name Princesse? What was wrong with that?'

He shrugged.

'You know, they asked me to join the party once,' he said, squinting through his cigarette smoke. 'It was after the war with Thailand in '88. I was wounded and given a medal, and then they said, "We need patriots like you." I was quite touched. But I said, "No! I couldn't possibly accept such an honour!" From what I hear, being in the party is worse than being a monk!'

He was interrupted by the arrival of Tin, his big-boned wife. I jumped up, offering an elaborate *nop* for the princess in blue jeans and flip-flops, her thick black hair cut in a bob. But she was not interested in me. She had come for her husband, and they drove off in a beaten-up blue Corolla. In the coming days I would see her around town, usually riding a motor scooter. I asked a well-connected person what this princess did with her time.

'Nothing,' was the reply. 'She goes to Vientiane.'

In the late afternoon, I went walking on Rue Sakarine, named after a king. The evening was scented with incense and spice, and the droning of the monks at prayer spilled from dozens of temples. Further along the road, as it bent to follow the river, a pair of formidable stone cats with pink-tipped penises guarded a grand staircase tumbling from Wat Xieng Thong down to the water. Before a Lao prince could become King, he must descend this staircase, crossing the Mekong to another temple, Wat Long Khoun, there to spend several days in meditation. I decided it would be a suitable first excursion from the royal capital.

The following day I stood on the steep right bank, groping in my pockets for the few hundred *kip* a boatman would ask to ferry me and Boun Kham across the swirling waters. The river was another shade of brown today, a different consistency. On some reaches it formed the border with Thailand, but here it was Lao territory on both sides. We made our way across the bank, between the ashes of the previous night's fires, to a pirogue moored there. The passengers were mainly stocky, barefoot women wearing T-shirts over their sarongs, rocking the boat as they embarked. The boatman smoked as he waited, yawning and adjusting his Mao cap and jacket, bailing bilge water or fiddling with the engine. When every seat was taken, we set off in a long, sidling arc across the river. On the swollen Mekong, the strength of the south-rushing current meant it took twice as long to travel upstream.

as to go in the opposite direction, and direct crossings were less straight lines than enormous, elastic Us. Closer to the opposite shore the current weakened, and we were able to zip north in the shallows until the boatman—exercising an artist's judgment—cut the engine and allowed the pirogue to drift slowly to the chosen spot onshore.

Boun Kham led the way through the vegetable gardens that lined the riverbank. As the river contracted in the dry season, the farmers would follow it, replacing the wet-season overflow with neat, square plots, sprouting in order of planting, from the top down. The soil here was fertile, but a few hundred kilometres upstream in China, the first in a series of dams with names like Manwan, Daozhan, Xiaiwan and Nuozhadu had begun to regulate the river level and hold back the rich silt. The dams would reduce the variation in the river's height between the wet and dry seasons, and might even force these riverbank farmers to change their age-old planting system.

The track rose steeply to the village of Xiangmen. At a wooden bridge we passed a young girl whose eyes were blighted by cataracts but who gave us a ringing '*Sabaidee*'. There were stilt houses and marigolds, and we passed a bonze carrying a saffron umbrella which afforded little shade but made him look radiant. Less than a kilometre from the capital of northern Laos, the economy was based on growing vegetables and rice and cutting wood from the forests. Every time we passed someone, Boun Kham would mumble a few words of greeting to them—cautious, staccato phrases delivered under the breath with a thrifty laugh, as if smoothing the path whilst checking for obstacles ahead. He said the people did not own this land but paid rent to the government. There were signs of modernity—toothbrushes for sale in the shop stalls that lined the path—along with pungent delicacies like minced pork on a stick, fried fish and sticky rice. Boun Kham bought an 'elephant's ear', a stuffed vine leaf.

'Inside it's meat,' he said. 'Meat! Sour, with ginger.' He pronounced 'ginger' like 'zha zha'.

'What sort of meat?'

'Buffalo.'

'Then shouldn't it be called 'buffalo's ear'?'

'Don't worry,' he said with his mouth full. 'It's named after the leaf, not the meat.'

Lizards rustled the undergrowth and butterflies hovered above the path, which ran alongside a plantation of mango, tamarind and frangipani. Villagers said the land had recently been leased by French interests and a resort was planned. An arching bridge led into Wat Long Khoun, a compound of whitewashed buildings with steep, tiled roofs sweeping low to the ground. A novice asked us to remove our shoes and led us inside the coronation room. He pushed open the wooden shutters and light poured in on kings, lovers and the massed armies of the Ramayana, the Hindu battle epic. The murals leapt out from the walls, recalling a passionate people who fought, thought, negotiated and celebrated, inspired by angels and terrified by demons. Statues of Buddha were arranged at the end of the chapel, averting evil, making peace and asking for rain. They were very fine, more than a metre tall, and had been dressed in *pukhai*, the monks' orange robes. I had seen people washing and dressing similar statues during *Pimai, the Lao New Year,* in Vientiane. They handled them gently, more as if washing a baby than an idol. It was reverence with affection and a touch of melancholy.

In 1905, King Sisavangvong, then a prince, had washed his spirit here. He donned the *pukhai*, lit incense and chanted the mantras given to him by the monks, resting and taking meals in the open gallery of the *sim, or chape*l. In the afternoons, he listened to the breeze rustling the leaves of the banyan tree, and contemplated the junction of the Khan and the Mekong, where the water is brown and boils. In the late 1950s, the monks at Long Khoun began to prepare for a new royal visitor, repairing the stairs and distempering the walls. Sisavangvong was dead, and his eldest son, Crown Prince Savang Vatthana, had been confirmed by the King's Council as the new king. He would rule for sixteen years but he never made the ceremonial procession to Long Khoun, and the coronation was never held. The monks and novices told me they couldn't remember the old kings and looked forward to the French resort's opening, because it might increase their income.

Leaving the *wat*, we took the path back to Ban Xiangmen via the abandoned temple of Chompet and its 100-step staircase. From the top we had a panoramic view of the river and Luang Prabang. The *wat* was in a terrible state, the stucco cracking and red clay bricks tumbling out. A carved floral motif above the locked entrance door had survived, but the wooden lintels were eaten away by termites. At the rear was a *stupa*, almost toppled, containing the ashes of one of King Sisavangvong's many wives.

A few hundred metres downstream was the old royal cemetery, known to the locals as Sala Tam Passar Luang. There, an open pavilion—a concrete platform shaded by a corrugated iron roof supported by pillars—had once been used for ceremonies and rites. Some of the white plaster pillars bore reliefs of skeletons. Others had been vandalised, or defaced with charcoal drawings of skeletons with penises. Beyond the pavilion stood the charred brick pyres on which the bodies of royal family members were cremated. Behind the pyres, some smaller tombstones were almost overgrown by vines. I sensed that Boun Kham was getting impatient—or was it uneasy? Soon we hurried away, as if there was a curse on the place.

Six months before my arrival in Luang Prabang, the town had been placed under curfew following a rebellion by a Hmong army commander called Boualy. It was a convenient little rebellion, satisfying a variety of prejudices. Those looking for an anti-communist uprising depicted it as such; those looking for stability said Colonel Boualy had been disgruntled at being forced to retire at 60 and dissatisfied with the size of his pay-off. Whatever the truth, the former royalist officer had gone into the hills and formed several rebel companies, who shot at policemen, Vietnamese road workers and government emissaries. They had staged hold-ups on Route 13 north of Luang Prabang, and made off with half the weapons in the local garrison and 700 sticks of dynamite. The government had responded by imposing a curfew and trucking thousands of Hmong, mainly women and children, into the town, housing them temporarily in schools and temples. Again, some said this was for their own protection, whilst others said the families were hostages. Whatever the truth, soldiers patrolled the streets of Luang Prabang. Eventually Colonel Boualy had surrendered, and as usual, his whereabouts in custody were a secret. Military operations were reportedly still under way in Sayaboury province to mop up after the rebellion, and foreigners had been banned from venturing outside Luang Prabang.

The Hmong villagers in Luang Prabang's Dala market hardly seemed rebellious, browsing at stalls offering papaya, pomelos, and black water chestnuts. Their black pyjamas fringed in blue distinguished them from the more cosmopolitan Lao Loum, the majority group. Ethnic minorities make up almost half of the country's population and include the Red, White and Black T'ai, distinguished by costume and language. Tired of the domination of the Lao Loum, many supported the Pathet Lao. Most Hmong, however, never accepted the communists' claim to represent the minorities. Many had died for their defiance and some were still living in refugee camps in Thailand.

The sticky-rice-eating, lowland Lao could not be indifferent to the Hmong, whom they regarded with a mixture of wonder and dismay. They admired their toughness, but felt their lack of education made the hill people inferior. Boun Kham said all *tuk-tuk* drivers in Luang Prabang were Hmong who'd bought their vehicles from the proceeds of trading in opium, but I had learned to take anything the Lao Loum said about the Hmong with a pinch of *padaek* (the pungent fish paste which, along with sticky rice and the *khene* bamboo pan pipe, was a Lao Loum cultural marker). The push now was to settle the Hmong, on the grounds that their nomadic slash-and-burn agricultural practice was environmentally unsound. The government logging companies were felling more timber in a day than the Hmong would in a year, but the smoke-filled valleys of the burning season, and the resultant scorched hill tops, were more obvious. The Hmong were considered nomads, but in fact each small group moved only within a small farmstead area. When resettled in the valleys under government aegis they often succumbed to malaria, a rare ailment in the hills.

Before leaving Hanoi I had been given the name of a foreign aid worker who'd been living in Luang Prabang for several years and was knowledgeable about the town and its surrounds, a sort of Lord Jim with a loyal following and even a motor-launch on which he visited remote upper reaches of the Mekong. Clive Rankin was an Englishman who spoke fluent Lao, and he'd agreed to show me the grave of Henri Mouhot, the nineteenth-century French explorer who'd made it to Luang Prabang before expiring of brain fever on the banks of the Nam Khan. The restrictions on travel outside Luang Prabang imposed after the Hmong rebellion earlier in the year had been eased, and that afternoon we set out in a four-wheel-drive, Clive at the wheel.

Henri Mouhot's travels revealed to the west the glories of Angkor Wat, the complex of temples in neighbouring Cambodia, but he perished alone, far from home. His guides, whom he honoured for their abilities but did not understand or love, were unable to help him. But they buried the *felang* and delivered his journals to Bangkok.   CAUCASIAN

If I ever find myself in similar strife, Clive Rankin is the sort of reliable person I'd want to have around. Sinewy and bearded, he scanned the streets intently, as if checking that everything was in its place.

'People have this idea, especially some journalists in Bangkok, that since they've allowed foreign investment suddenly everything has changed', he said. 'But it hasn't. They say, "Oh Luang Prabang is like Chiang Mai twenty years ago. It's finished!" But remember, Chiang Mai is in the middle of a large plain with a very big surrounding population, many of whom moved into the town. This is a very sparsely populated area, and so far there's been limited immigration. If we can have rural development parallel to town development, we might avoid the worst.'

Luang Prabang, with 25 000 people, several hundred monks and several dozen wats, is a shadow of the thriving town it was early in the Indochina War, when a steady stream of immigrants fleeing the fighting in the countryside inflated its population to almost 50 000, and a French military mission provided education in the town, red-bereted guards stood watch outside the royal palace, and annual festivals, both pagan and religious, were energetically observed.

It was just after lunch as Clive and I headed out of town through streets deserted by siesta, which eventually surrendered their neat grid and smooth tarmac to ravines and scree. The road took us past the weavers' village of Ban Pha Nom, through a swamp where buffalo grazed and a man ring-barked one of the teak trees which lined our route. The air was thick with the heady perfume of frangipani, known as *dok champa*, the flower of tears, sadness and love.

'Foreigners complain that this is the land of "*Baw pen nyang*" ' Clive said. 'You know, "Never mind, we don't have it, we can't help you"—but I say this is the land of "*Baw mee ban haa*", which means "We don't have what you want, but it's no problem. We'll do without, or we'll find another way." And when they say that, they'll smile. But it doesn't mean they're happy they've frustrated you. It means "I'm terribly sorry, so why don't we sit down and think of a way to get around this problem." '

Henri Mouhot had been advised differently, by a Chinese mandarin he consulted before setting out.

'Buy a *tam-tam* (horn), and wherever you halt, sound it,' the mandarin advised. 'They will say, "Here is an officer of the king," robbers will keep aloof, and the authorities will respect you. If this does not answer, the only plan to get rid of all the difficulties which the Laotian officials will be sure to throw in your way is to have a good stick, the longer the better. Try it on the back of any mandarin who makes the least resistance and will not do what you wish. Put all delicacy aside. Laos is not a country of the whites. Follow my advice, and you will find it good.' When I had read the passage from Mouhot's notebook aloud, I looked for Clive's reaction. He was boiling.

'That's horseshit!' he said. 'Never lay hands on a Lao. Appreciate the fact that people will almost always treat you very well, and try to behave as well as they do. Unfortunately, there are a lot of foreigners who don't always do that, and it causes shock in a place where they haven't had contact with Westerners for a long time. The Lao just can't believe that anyone can treat others rudely and aggressively.'

It reminded me of a story told by a Vietnamese friend whose father had done many years of 'fraternal duty' in Laos. 'Never shout at a Lao,' he'd told her. 'For if you do, he will look at his shoes. And when you have finished shouting, he will go home. And early the next morning, he will swim to Thailand!'

Our indefatigable little truck climbed in and out of potholes and fearlessly forded expanses of muddy water. After some time, a substantial stream could be seen through the forest, running wide and shallow. It was the Nam Khan. A roughly fashioned bench in the middle of nowhere signalled our stopping point, where a dirt track fell steeply to the river. As I put on mosquito repellent, Clive showed the way.

The cause of Mouhot's death has never been established, but in his final days he complained of fever, probably malarial. After he became ill, his servants repeatedly suggested that he write a letter to his kin. That spooked him. 'Wait, wait. Are you afraid?' was his invariable reply.

His diary entries for October 1860 dwindled in frequency and length.

'16th. . . .
17th. . . .
18th. Halted at H . . .

19th. Attacked by fever.

29th. Have pity on me, oh my God . . . !

His famous concentration and attention to detail were failing and his energy was low. He died on 10 November 1861 after an ordeal lasting more than three weeks. According to his brother, Charles, the servants reported that he had been insensible for three days, before which time he had complained of 'great pains in his head'.

As we approached the river, its roar grew and roots twisted across the path, making steps. Clive was waxing lyrical about the countryside, his big mountain boots making light work of the rugged path. He spoke of the ravines up country, and bizarre limestone hills similar to China's Three Gorges, heavily forested and cut through by fast-flowing rivers.

'We used to take our boat up the Mekong and its tributaries every Sunday for picnics and things like that,' he said. 'We'd climb up to the top of the mountains to the plateau where the Hmong live, and that's a different world again. There's a whole series of worlds—the valley world, and the mountain world, and the in-between world. But we don't go any more. We sold the boat. A river family lost theirs—it sank—and since it was their only means of support we sold them ours. After their accident, my wife's not too keen on taking the family up river anyway.'

We emerged onto the mud flats which only weeks earlier had been under water. Flotsam was still hanging from the bushes all around us. Butterflies—yellow, black, blue, brown and white—fluttered in the cool shadows of the high river-bank. The river was still flowing fast, eddying across rapids in its path, by turns smooth, then ruffled. There were white caps in the middle, and the green hills rose up steeply on both sides. We walked a few hundred metres along the flat, Clive occasionally looking back over his shoulder past me, which was a little unsettling. Eventually, to our right, the dry bed of a dead tributary opened up, meeting the Nam Khan beneath an enormous banyan tree. Trudging into this ravine, over ants, creepers and worms, we came to a white concrete monument in the shape of a casket. At one end was an inscription: 'La ville de Montbéliard fière de son enfant 1990'. The people of Mouhot's home town had made the trek here to restore his grave. In their condolences to Charles Mouhot upon the death of his brother, members of the Société d'Emulation of Montbéliard wrote of Henri: 'His work remained unfinished, but it was gloriously commenced, and his name will not perish.'

Dark clouds had begun gathering and the sky was full of dragonflies. We decided to return to Luang Prabang, a city Mouhot had feted in his better days. 'The situation is very pleasant,' he had written, '. . . if the mid-day heat were tempered by a gentle breeze, the place would be a little paradise.'

Driving back through Ban Pha Nom, Clive swerved to avoid a chicken crossing the road, but managed instead to decapitate the poor bird. He stopped, reversed, switched off the engine, and waited. The body of the bird was still quivering, its black blood forming a pool on the road. A little boy ran out from the village to pick it up, head in one hand, body in the other. Hoisting the gory remains above his head he called to friends and family, 'Our bird! They've killed our bird!'

A crone soon joined him, laughing at the display, or perhaps the unusual neatness of the job. She was followed at length by an elderly man with an impassive expression. He took the body and then the head, examining them minutely, saying nothing and looking displeased. The crowd had built up to about 50 people. Many chickens had died crossing this road, but none had been beheaded so precisely. Was it a sign? The owner of the chicken paced back and forth, checking and re-checking the body of the bird and its severed head, weighing them in his hands. We braced for compensation, silently marshalling our arguments against his demands, even before hearing them.

But the old man's problem was that the bird was undamaged, apart from the fact that it was dead. The whole of his family could barely conceal their glee at the thought of that evening's chicken dinner. In the end the old man walked away, saying nothing. Clive recalled the story of a friend who, encountering similar misfortune, negotiated a payout of 1500 *kip*. From that day forth, instead of haggling, he would simply tuck the same sum under the warm body of every chicken he ran over.

'You should be more careful, my friend, driving on this busy i-way,' said a voice, apparently from nowhere.

A man stood beside the car, but I was blinded by the sun behind him and couldn't make him out.

'Lucky for you, there is no I-way patrol in this area!'

'Allow me to introduce myself,' said the speaker, who was dressed in white and sucking on a pipe. 'I am Monsieur Perrot, and I am en route to see the friend of my friend. Would you like to join me?'

Clive knew this fellow, but didn't seem to like him much. He decided to head off to the weavers' stalls nearby, leaving me at the mercy of the silver-haired Frenchman.

Perrot led the way through the neatly laid-out dirt streets of bamboo and thatch houses, raised on stilts with the children playing and animals eating underneath.

'Today you are lucky,' he assured me. 'We will meet a famous dancer. Madame Peng Dee! She is looking after my friend's children.' This was a Lao female friend who'd been jailed for four months 'because she loved a *felang*,' as he put it. 'It's forbidden!' he said, looking shocked. 'More than 100 local women are in prison for similar offences.'

As we walked, Perrot told me about himself. His father had come to Luang Prabang on horseback from Haiphong in 1924, staying in the country until just before the outbreak of the Second World War. He himself had spent 40 years in the hotel business, in France, Africa, the Middle East and Polynesia, but this was his first time in Asia. Like Santi Inthavong, he had been forced to change the name of his establishment by the Ministry of Information and Culture. He had revived a villa, once the home of the former neutralist prime minister under the old regime, Prince Souvanna Phouma, a cousin of the king. Originally, the hotel had been named after the prince, but had dropped the final 'a', much as a gecko will drop its tail to survive, and was now called the Hotel Souvanna Phoum.

'You know who built this village?' asked Perrot as we walked, while children danced around us and used used long bamboo staves to pluck *markam*, green tamarind, from the trees.

'No. Who?'

'The king!'

'Really? Why?'

'For his concubine!'

Ban Pha Nom was, it turned out, a resettled village, populated by Lu people, paddy farmers of the plains, not quite Lao Loum, but closely related. They'd been brought to Luang Prabang province from the northern town of Luang Namtha by Sisavangvong, to satisfy his need for fine cloth and entertainment. It was a village of weavers and dancers, insiders due to their proximity to the court, outsiders since they'd migrated to the area and taken up a large tract of land. Before the revolution they'd been envied, after it despised, and now, with the tourists returning, their star was once more ascending.

We found the dancer at her spinning wheel beneath her house. Both she and it were seated on a wooden bed base covered in a straw mat and raised above the beaten earth floor. Peng Dee was a statuesque, middle-aged woman with clever eyes and a determined jaw. She sat with her legs tucked beneath her to one side, a distrustful glance fixed on the spinning wheel, which had been fashioned from a bicycle rim, as if it might at any moment roll away. She was winding thread onto spools for use by the weavers whose stalls Clive had gone to inspect in the central square. Perrot greeted her with a double handshake, introducing me as a British journalist who had come to write a story about her. Before I could set her straight, the spinning wheel had lost momentum and the air was filled with a melodious cackle. 'Everybody knows Peng Dee,' she said, adding darkly, 'but this is a jealous village.'

She was the sort of woman you passed in hundreds of villages, her hair in a modest bun, and wearing a colourful blouse over tanned shoulders and arms. But there was something different about Peng Dee, a certain theatrical animation which transformed her features from moment to moment. She appeared at turns wise and sly, bawdy and matriarchal, warm and tough. I suppose she had been beautiful, the village *belle* in her time. Now she was a widow, with eight children.

Born in 1942, Peng Dee had begun learning the ancient movements of the *nan keo*, the Lao classical dance version of the Ramayana, when she was eight, and was later chosen to perform for Sisavangvong, who had created a full-time dancing troupe in the early 1950s. She belonged to a troupe of fifteen dancers, mostly girls in their teens, trained in the ancient rhythms of the court by a retired dancer. Her family lived free of rent and taxes close to the palace for the six years her career lasted.

When the girls were not dancing they were weaving, a skill that proved useful in later years, when war and revolution swept away the monarchy and the favoured class of artists and artisans. It now earned her 2000 *kip*, about $2 a day. She was also teaching her daughters to dance, as the profession was enjoying a revival with the return of the tourists. As we sat beneath the stilt house, two of the girls leapt spontaneously into the open air and began to dance, precocious arms weaving a spell their mother had taught them. Peng Dee was beaming with pride, crowing like a rediscovered village diva. Some of the children at the house, of course, belonged to Perrot's Lao female friend. He had come to deliver some money, his contribution to supporting them.

Peng Dee spoke in an amalgam of Lao and French to Perrot, who then spoke to me in French and English. It was a confusing conversation, broken at one point when Perrot used the words *mia noi*, Lao for 'minor wife', and Peng Dee—thinking it referred to her position in the court of Sisavangvong—almost slapped him.

'Never!' she cried. 'He asked me. But I refused!

'Those were the happiest days of my life,' she went on, lifting her eyes momentarily from the wheel. 'In the evenings there would be great feasts, followed by the dancing. The palace was full of light, and the nights there were very colourful and exciting.'

But the king did not dance.

Her children laughed self-consciously at Peng Dee, who was no shrinking violet and had strong opinions on most things, including the decline in the performing arts since the revolution. 'The dance they teach them nowadays is not the real dance,' she scoffed. 'They teach them in four months. It should take years.' To prove her point she twisted her arm, supple, graceful and alluring. She still had it. The king would have been pleased. In the 1960s, Laotian classical dancers were still performing *danse sourya*, the sun dance. It described the landscape at sunset along the river which underpins Lao Loum culture just as the Nile does for the Egyptians. 'The sun at its setting falls slowly, spreading its rays,' the dancers would sing. 'The red clouds watch the forest, where the colours of the trees mix with those of the sun.' Lao poetry conjured up the spirit world of the *kinara*, a strange creature with the head of a man and the body of a bird which lived on mountains and in caves. *Kinari* are the women of the *kinara*, and traditionally they are dancers. For 600 years, the arts and religion and monarchy of Laos had formed a seamless whole, anachronistic perhaps, but indigenous. The whole structure had collapsed like a house of cards with the abdication of the last king.

I asked Peng Dee for photos of her glory days, but she didn't have any. She said she hoped if she talked to me, a dance school in America would hear about her and invite her to teach the secrets of the Lao dance. I told her I was hoping to visit Cambodia soon, for a performance of the Ramayana to be danced before King Sihanouk in the ruins of Angkor. Just across the border, a shaky monarchy had resumed its role as the ark of a nation's culture.

We said goodbye to Peng Dee, found Clive, and headed

back to Luang Prabang. On the way Perrot told me that many other survivors of the *ancien régime*'s art and culture were still living and working in Luang Prabang. The next day I went in search of some.

Bicycling along the Royal Mile linking the palace with Wat Xieng Thong, I passed long lines of mottled sausages drying in the sun. The humble tinkling of hammers on anvils accompanied me down a narrow street to a two-storey building which was the home and workshop of Thitpeng Maniphone, whose family had for generations been patronised by Lao kings. A genteel man in his 60s, Thitpeng was sitting in his parlour with his wife, Chan, when I arrived unannounced. An open shed at the rear was occupied by several men earnestly hammering detail into silver scabbards and bowls. Sheet silver had been bent around moulds of a sticky brown resin called *kisee*, which gave it shape. After the item had been decorated, the resin would be heated and detach itself from the beaten silver. Thitpeng's methods had remained unchanged in his 43 years as a smith. The silver ingots were still softened over charcoal before being hammered into shape.

'The king never came here,' he told me, his eyes creasing with a smile as Chan poured tea. 'The royal family would usually send a secretary or the protocol officers to order for them.' Royal haughtiness aside, in a society where silver defined status, the craftsmen of the court formed their own aristocracy, often inter-marrying like the royal family did. Chan was a kind of precious metals princess, the grand-daughter of Saene Makoune, a royal goldsmith, whose work graced the ears of the king's wives. The silverware produced by her husband and the works of the goldsmith Phia Thong had filled the palace and were often presented to visiting dignitaries.

In 1972, at the age of 42, Thitpeng had been called to the palace during *pimai*, to be presented with a royal award. 'When I went to the palace I joined a long line of people receiving medals,' he recalled. 'We were standing with our heads bowed. I didn't look at the king, and he didn't say anything to me. Later, in the evening, we went to a big feast inside the palace, with music and dancing. But again the king sat in a separate room, and we didn't see him.'

The following year he was called back to the palace, this time to receive a certificate of nobility. The monarchy produced awards and decorations the way a catherine wheel throws off sparks. One could be made Commander of the Million Elephants and the White Parasol, Knight of Civil Merit, or Officer of the Silver Reign of Laos. I once met a man who was all three. A medal featuring a portrait of Savang Vatthana had held pride of place in Thitpeng's home until 1975, when it was melted down for fear of punishment from the communists and hammered into a silver bowl.

'After the king abdicated it was dangerous to have such things around,' he said. 'If you kept them, people might think you were against the new regime, and life could become difficult for you and your family.'

Life became difficult anyway. With the king and queen forced out of the palace and deprived of an income, and those closest to them being sent into internal exile, Thitpeng considered himself lucky to stay in Luang Prabang. But his efforts to continue working were bedevilled by the government's view of the petite bourgeoisie as exploiters of labour, the economic downturn and the lack of royal patronage. In 1977, like most other smiths and small businessmen, Thitpeng closed shop and dismissed his craftsmen. Soon the clink of hammers was no longer heard in the town. Nine years later, the government announced its New Economic Mechanism, and Thitpeng decided the times might be right to re-open his business. His workers were recalled, and resumed hammering away in Kop Keah, 'the street of rose-apple trees'. At last count he was employing eighteen people, including two sons who were expected to inherit the business when he retired.

'Silver-smithing is a good business,' Thitpeng replied diplomatically, when I asked what sort of money he made. His wares were sold by the kilogram, and his customers included the Thai royal family—who, unlike the kings of Lan Xang, had visited his workshop—and Lao government leaders such as President Nouhak Phoumsavanh, who took one of Thitpeng's silver bowls as a gift for Sihanouk when he visited Phnom Penh in 1995.

I asked Thitpeng if he or his wife could confirm a fragment of folklore I'd picked up on the Internet. The story went that in 1910, the French government had sent a curator from the Louvre to choose pieces from the priceless collection which formed the crown jewels of Lan Xang. The jewels were to be part of a grand exposition in Paris, at which the French public would be acquainted with the magnificence of the protectorate of Luang Prabang. Reluctantly, the young Sisavangvong had agreed and the selected Buddha images, precious stones, gold and silver were loaded aboard the gunboat *La Grandière*. But the boat sank, taking the treasure to a muddy grave on the bottom of the Mekong. Chan's grandfather had probably made the jewellery, and she told me the story was true. 'I think the boat went down about 30 km north of Thadeua, where the ferry crosses the Mekong.'

The Website said that in 1964, the British government made plans to salvage the gunboat, and hopefully the treasure. The British embassy in Bangkok had been unable to confirm this part of the story, however. 'Although there were plans during the 1960s for the wreck to be raised these were abandoned on cost grounds,' they informed me by fax. 'It would seem that no preliminary survey was done, and so it is still not clear what, if any, artefacts remain.' I'd heard renewed recovery efforts were afoot.

That morning, accompanied by Boun Kham, I had witnessed one of Luang Prabang's timeless rituals—the morning alms-giving to the monks. Their day began at 6 a.m. on Rue Sakarine, with the monks filing barefoot out of Wat Xieng Thong and the other temples to beg for their food. They followed the streets of the old quarter, where a member of each household, usually a woman, knelt holding a bowl of cooked sticky rice. As each monk passed, she would place a handful of rice in his bowl. Gratitude was neither expressed by the recipients nor expected by the donors, whose reward was *boun,* or merit. It had been happening like this for perhaps 500 years, so long that the ritual had been stripped of superfluous ceremony. All that remained was the reality that the monks relied upon the people for their food. At the end of their rounds, we followed the monks into Wat Xieng Thong, the Temple of the Golden City, admiring its sweeping towers, ornate chapels and elaborate finials whilst they ate the collected rice.

The *wat* was built in the sixteenth century, in the reign of King Setthathirath, whose father had died after falling from an elephant, one of 2000 he owned, during a demonstration of elephant-roping staged for an audience of foreign ambassadors in 1550. Ten years later Wat Xieng Thong rose on the banks of the Mekong, one of the high points of Lao classical architecture, and continued under royal patronage until 1975. The last king, Savang Vatthana, spent much of his time maintaining and embellishing the royal *wat*—too much time perhaps, for he was now no longer king.

A holy racing pirogue was parked in a boat house behind a *sim.* In another, dozens of Buddhas were stored, including a famous reclining figure which had been taken to Paris in 1932 for an exposition and only came home in 1964, after a period in Vientiane. Outside the chapel, a group of novices, having finished their breakfast, were practising martial arts. These fighting monks of northern Laos were not mentioned in any guide book.

Boun Kham clicked his tongue disapprovingly. 'Oh, they are very naughty,' he said.

'They're just getting some exercise, Boun. What's wrong with that?'

'That's OK. That's OK. But sometimes they're smoking.'

Are they not allowed to smoke?'

'No. They can smoke. But they cannot drink alcohol . . . or talk to women. Oh! It's very naughty!'

Boun Kham's face had adopted a permanently worried expression which I put down to an impending solar eclipse. Laos is a country of amateur astrologers permanently on the look-out for bad omens, and Luang Prabang people are said to be the most superstitious of all. When Sisavangvong died in 1959, for example, preparations began for his funeral and the new king's coronation. When a sudden storm struck the town, tearing the roofs from many houses and demolishing the funeral arches, anxious tongues spoke of an ill omen. A soothsayer prophesied that Savang Vatthana would never be crowned, and the people of Luang Prabang, even the new king himself, were prepared to believe it.

Throughout the 1960s, Savang Vatthana delayed his coronation. He reasoned it was inappropriate whilst parts of his country—the Ho Chi Minh trail and the provinces of Houaphan and Phonsaly—were under the control of North Vietnamese and Chinese forces. The king was under constant pressure to play a more active and direct role in politics, pressure he almost always resisted. He was not a swashbuckling ruler, like his father or Sihanouk, endlessly intriguing and always surviving. He wanted to remain above the fray, a position which satisfied nobody. The Right complained that by refusing to be crowned, he was failing to express his confidence in a democratic, constitutional system of government. The Pathet Lao argued that he had already abdicated his responsibilities by allowing the Americans to conduct their secret bombing campaigns in Laos.

Savang Vatthana was commander-in-chief of one of the world's most comical fighting forces, the Royal Lao Army, who were happy to leave most of the fighting to the Vietnamese, the American bombers, the Hmong irregulars and the Pathet Lao. Among the latter's armoury of psychological weapons was the 'tricky pebble'. In the dead of night, communist troops would crawl close to royalist camps and toss pebbles onto their roofs, their way of saying, 'We could have thrown a grenade, but we like you'. For good measure they'd include a note inviting their Lao brothers to pull back another 10–12 km, just for the sake of peace and harmony. Those demoralising pebbles seem to have played a key role in the Pathet Lao's gradual victory.

Somdet Pra-Chao Lan Xang Hom Khao Luang Prabang, the Lord of the Kingdom of the Million Elephants and the White Parasol of Luang Prabang—could trace his ancestry back to Khoun Borom, the first Lao king, who, according to legend, descended from heaven to rule an earthly kingdom near Meuang Thèn, or the place of heavenly spirits, somewhere in southern China. Khoun Borom's eldest son, Khun Lo, moved with his people towards the Mekong, settling at a place they called Muong Swa, south of the junction of the Nam Khan and Mekong rivers, on the site of present-day Luang Prabang. Unlike the literate Chinese, he and his successors had no scribes to chronicle their doings. Twenty-one kings followed Khun Lo, but it was not until the fourteenth century that history noticed one of them. Fa Ngum had been exiled when still young, and he and his father were given shelter by the Khmer court at Angkor, where he married a Khmer princess and became a Buddhist. Furnished with an army by his Cambodian father-in-law, he fought his way back to Muong Swa, seized the throne and declared Buddhism the state religion of what was to become the Kingdom of Lan Xang. Pleased with the success of their protégé, the court at Angkor dispatched a delegation of priests carrying a 500-year-old solid gold statue of the Buddha from Sri Lanka, the *pra bang*, which they installed in the Muong Swa stockade.

In the late seventeenth century, the commercial agent Gerrit Van Wuysthoff, of the Dutch East India Company, found a grand kingdom on the Mekong where flourished literature written on palm-leaf paper, and music played on wooden xylophones, gongs and drums; where teak and gold decorated ornate temples and palaces, and where the people were clothed in fine fabrics woven on the kingdom's many looms. In 1700, when a king died without leaving a mature heir, Sai Ong Hue took the throne with the help of the Vietnamese. His gambit split Lan Xang in three, with separate kingdoms proclaiming independence at Luang Prabang and Champassak in the south. Soon the new kingdoms were warring among themselves, as always with foreign assistance. Burmese troops helped Vientiane conquer Luang Prabang, whereupon Luang Prabang conspired with Siam to topple Vientiane. In the end, Siam replaced Burma as suzerain. In 1828, king Chao Anou tried to reassert Lao independence, but in return a Siamese army burnt Vientiane to the ground, depopulating the city. By the end of the century, Vientiane's population was still only a quarter of what it had been at the time of the war, and so weakened was the kingdom that when French colonists arrived there was little to oppose them. The French moved gradually, persuading the Siamese to allow a French vice-consul, Auguste Pavie, to be based at Luang Prabang. When Pavie personally rescued King Oun Kham during fighting between Siamese troops and Chinese bandits, the king asked for the protection of France. It was the start of a marriage of convenience between Paris and Luang Prabang. Oun Kham remained on the throne, but his counterpart in Champassak was reduced to the role of a local official in the French administration.

The Chinese philosopher Meng Tsu wrote in *The Politics of the Royal Way* that if a king did not rule well, the people had the right to overthrow him, and some argued that this even justified regicide. To Meng Tsu, the people came first, the country second, and the king third. But the Lao monarchy, in the eyes of some, had come to represent the rule of one family. Birth counted for more than intelligence or ability, and ambassadorial posts and other senior positions were virtually inherited. Succession followed the male line, unlike in Cambodia, where election of the king by the royal council allowed for a measure of choice based on candidates' ability. Critics of the monarchy maintained that by the time Savang Vatthana came to the throne, the royal gene pool was well and truly depleted. But the revolution robbed the people of Luang Prabang of an institution which for centuries had been the focal point of their lives. The artisans and performers lost everything.

Among them were the former royal puppeteers. I had heard of their plight from my friend Roberta Borg, a Canadian woman who'd been a media consultant with UNICEF. She was a fan of traditional puppetry and wanted to use it to spread community health messages. Asking around Vientiane, she learned that the ancient art of puppetry in Laos had died out. The only known troupe had been trained in fraternal Bulgaria, which sounded none too promising. The traditional Lao puppet troupe based at Luang Prabang, and funded by the former king, had ceased to exist in 1975.

In the old royal capital, people told Roberta there had indeed been a full-time troupe of fifteen puppeteers, who had performed with fine hand-made puppets until the revolution. Most of them, now in their 70s and 80s, lived at Wat Xieng Thong. In their days as dependants of the royal family, they had lived in houses attached to the royal *wat*, where they were fed by the monks. During the civil war, in the late 1960s and early 1970s, their performances became less and less frequent. When the Pathet Lao came to power and cancelled the stipend which had supported the royal family, the troupe was done for. Of the original fifteen members, eight were still alive in 1991, including Souvanh, the keeper of the puppets, a stick figure with shaved silver hair who still wore the trademark white jacket of the court. Souvanh told Roberta the king himself had helped make the puppets the troupe used. He dated the surviving ones to the 1950s, but said they were modelled on their predecessors 'like son on father', and that this passing-on process had been going on since antiquity. Every stage of the puppets' construction was accompanied by quasi-religious ceremonies, beginning with the blessing of the balsa-like tree from which they were made. Roberta asked if she could see the puppets. Souvanh said the box had been closed for fifteen years. Evidently, the puppets were kept in the grand garage housing the funeral carriage of Sisavangvong, also within the Wat Xieng Thong complex. Aged in his 70s, Souvanh was the only one who could open it because he alone knew the correct prayers for such an occasion. The prayers were in Pali, the language of the monks.

The Lao government agreed to Roberta's request through UNICEF to stage a performance by the royal puppet theatre. She had travelled back to Luang Prabang, accompanied by the Bulgarian-trained director of the national puppet theatre in Vientiane. After much cajoling, and promises to pay for the expensive ceremony involved, a reluctant Souvanh agreed to revive the sleeping marionettes. The director of the national puppet theatre had never seen the puppets, such was the self-induced cultural amnesia of the Lao revolution, and the opening of the box at Wat Xieng Thong seems to have been a profound experience for all involved. Roberta says it broke her heart.

'When they opened the box, there were various ceremonies they had to go through, these old guys and ladies. Even the act of touching the dolls required the permission of their keeper. It was a miracle the dolls hadn't been devoured by termites or something. And when they picked up these beautiful figurines that they had worked so intimately with for so many years and then been parted from for decades, it provoked a complete physical transformation. Souvanh was like a sixteen-year-old. For him, they were not wooden dolls. They were real, and the puppets themselves are of such a fine design and have such strong faces that you could easily believe they were real too. Once that box was opened, all this love started flowing.'

Hundreds of people were gathered in the grounds of the *wat* for the opening ceremony. The hushed members of the crowd were aware of magic in their midst. A pig had been slaughtered and its grinning head was prominently displayed, surrounded by coconuts, bananas, buffalo liver, blood jelly and cans of 7 Up. All those items, not forgetting the *lao lao*, or rice wine, costing what a Lao family might spend on a wedding, waited to be offered to the *tookatah*, or puppets, in a *baci*, the ceremony held to mark weddings, departures, or indeed any significant event in Lao life.*

---

* In Lao tradition the body houses 32 *khouan*, or souls, one for each bodily function and faculty. The *khouan* have a tendency to wander and when they do, sickness or disability results. In a *baci*, strings hanging from a flower arrangement are tied to the wrists to prevent the escape of the *khouan*. A feast of chicken, eggs, sweets and *lao lao* always follows.

Souvanh untied the knot which restrained the spirits and, cradling them in his hands, lifted one, then another, then another of the dolls from their sleep. There were about 40 of them, their wooden faces polished to resemble porcelain, painted with flowing costumes in red, green and gold. The old man looked stiff and emotional. When the dolls had been taken from the box, Souvanh dragged deeply on a cigarette and began to blow smoke across their faces, then took a mouthful of *lao lao* and sprayed it over them. He lit another cigarette with one of the tapers in his hands and placed it on the lip of one of the puppets.

Buddhist novices, heads shaved, listened intently as Souvanh spoke in long sentences, his voice rising and falling in waves of emotion, a voice in which to announce great things.

'Oh, after 25 years, we see you!' Wooden xylophones chimed in, cascading scales and cymbals, as the ensemble gained momentum, puffing and wheezing like a steam engine. Suddenly the old man began to weep, his conversation with the puppets breaking up into wretched, constricted phrases. But they were tears of relief, for the puppets had partaken of the *lao lao* and their *phi*, or spirit, was now good. They would play well, and behave—important to know, for wayward puppets had a tendency to mischief and were feared as poltergeists. Souvanh kept putting a lighted candle in his mouth, extinguishing it, and blowing the smoke over the puppets. Others passed the bottle of rice wine around.

'Remember the old movies where the ventriloquist's dummy takes over the ventriloquist?' said Roberta. 'Well, here it's for real. Puppets have a spirit, and you have to appease it before a performance, otherwise they can misbehave.'

No-one in the gathering was more awestruck than the young trainees from the National Puppet Theatre, who'd accompanied their director to Luang Prabang. The puppets they'd seen in Bulgaria, and which they had copied upon their return home, were crude figures. The royal Lao puppets were smaller, dressed in wildly coloured frocks with tikka

marks on their foreheads. Some were quizzical, others enigmatic. Their graceful hands were bent back 45 degrees at the
wrist. The prince of the puppets was pearl-faced with fine
features and a winged golden helmet. A demon puppet, with
a green face and white fangs protruding from blood-red lips,
wielded a sword. The smoking puppet ballooned his cheeks,
a weedy fag on his lip—an internal tube allowed the puppeteer to smoke for him.

By evening the crowd at Wat Xieng Tong had grown to
almost a thousand, and after hours of unwrapping,
wonderstruck fondling and renewing of vows, the old troupers
were ready for their comeback. Their play told the story of
a young and wayward prince sent out by his family to make
his own way. He marries, but his young bride is abducted.
Three wives later he finds her again. Eventually Roberta
realised she was watching one of the countless interpretations
of the Hindu epic of Rama, Sita and Ravana. The puppeteers,
who also provided the narration and the voices, stood behind
a thin bamboo screen on which scenery was painted. They
supported the head of their puppets with a central rod made
of bamboo and controlled the hands with two very narrow
rods. Souvanh said his father had trained him in manipulating
the rods by giving him a pair of chopsticks and telling him
to play with them. Only after six months was he allowed to
touch a puppet. 'But the puppet knows his own mind,' he
said. 'The puppeteer is just a medium.'

There was no written script, and one old woman couldn't
remember all the words she'd learnt from her parents. Peering
through the blind, the puppeteers began improvising jokes
about individuals seated in the crowd, to the delight of their
rapturous audience. When the time came to put the puppets
to sleep, Souvanh was in tears, apologising to his wooden
partner and wiping his eyes. He lapsed into Pali again. 'We
brought all these things for you,' he told the puppets. 'We
have head of pig, chicken. We will never see you again.'

'You silly old man,' called one of the others. 'Don't get so
emotional.'

Souvanh picked up a plastic cup of rice wine, doused the tapers in his mouth and blew the smoke into the *lao lao*. He then took mouthfuls of the wine and sprayed it again into the puppets' faces. 'That's enough *lao lao* for you!' he said, thanking each one by name and stacking them back in their wooden chest. Finally, coconuts were placed on top of the box, and a saffron cloth tied the puppets' spirits in.

When the new regime took power in 1975, local officials of the Ministry for Information and Culture decreed that the puppets of Wat Xieng Thong address each other as 'comrade'. The puppets refused. Now, in their own modest way, the puppeteers of Wat Xieng Thong had cheated history. Lao puppetry had been born again. The one-off performance at Wat Xieng Thong inspired the Bulgarian-trained young generation to set to work and reclaim their heritage. In the ensuing days they brainstormed with the elders, recording the stories and songs and taking photographs and measurements of the old, frail puppets. Back in Vientiane they began making replicas, larger than the originals so they could be seen at less intimate venues. The music, performed live in royal days, was taped. When they were done, they loaded the new puppets into a truck and drove them to Luang Prabang. Their first performance was before the surviving members of the royal puppet troupe, who pitched in enthusiastically with advice and with fragments of the story recalled since their own performance. Suitably fine-tuned, and lasting 90 minutes, the show was then taken on the road through the province's villages. Roberta set to work raising money to buy a glass case in which to exhibit the old puppets in the former palace. But, like the monsoon, the rain of enthusiasm had somehow passed, and the fragile figurines still languished in a box somewhere in Wat Xieng Thong.

Boun Kham and I crossed the courtyard to enter a vast wooden building, decorated with the usual red and gold-leaf panels detailing episodes from the Ramayana. It was the garage of the funerary carriage of the last Lao monarch to be given a ceremonial cremation, Sisavangvong. This was where Roberta had said the royal puppets resided. I poked about among the boxes there but saw none tied with saffron ribbon. Most of the space in any case was taken up by the grand carriage, built to resemble a pirogue. On its 'deck' stood three wooden urns which, according to Boun Kham, had held the ashes of the king, the queen and one of their children. There was also a large metal urn which had held the embalmed body of the king. This had stood in the throne room of the palace for almost a year before being loaded onto the carriage on 7 August 1960 and taken to the sports ground below Wat That Luang at the other end of town, where the body was taken out and burned. Sihanouk was among the mourners. After the cremation, Sisavangvong's ashes were entombed in the stupa at Wat That Luang and the civil war resumed. A few days later, in Vientiane, a neutralist general, Kong Le, staged a coup against the government of Prince Somsanith while most of the cabinet was still in Luang Prabang conferring with the new king.

The carriage was covered in magnificent carvings, including the triple-headed elephant beneath the parasol that symbolises the three kingdoms under one nation—Vientiane, Champassak and Luang Prabang. The whole structure seemed to float on dragon-headed serpents, whose fiery tongues burnt a path through evil for the deceased ruler. We returned to our bicycles, passing along streets whose names were lost in a tangle of politics and history. Since 1975, attempts to rename them had foundered on habitual Lao reverence for the past. Since colonial times, the streets had borne the names of kings, but on the 1994 city map produced by the Service Geographique National, Rue Sakarine became Xieng Thong, Rue Sisavangvong was Navang, and Phothisarath was Phalanxay. Yet fly-spotted maps plastering government offices around town obstinately stuck with the old names: Sakarine, running from Wat Xieng Thong to the École Primaire, Sisavangvong continuing to the Post Office. Even the name of the royal capital itself had been lost in a haze of trans-literation. Was it Louang Prabang, as shown on the maps drawn by Henri Mouhot, or Luang Prabang, as in the country's only English-language newspaper, *The Vientiane Times*? The Service Geographique National was hedging its bets, with its maps favouring both Louang Prabang and Louangphabang. My favourite—Loowung Phwabung—had little chance of adoption because, like most accurate Anglicisations, it was simply too ugly. The very word Laos is unacceptable to some, who believe the correct name of the nation should be Lao. Breviloquent government officials incessantly referred to their homeland as the Lao P.D.R.

In the shop houses lining Rue Sisavangvong, people were gathered around televisions watching Thai stations which had suspended normal programs to cover the solar eclipse. For weeks, newspapers and magazines throughout South-East Asia, except in Laos, had been devoting column metres to the event. In Thailand—where, on 18 August 1868, King Rama IV, known as the father of Thai science, had accurately predicted a similar blackout—interest was intense. The eclipse we were about to witness coincided with the Golden Jubilee of Thai King Bhumibol Adulyadej's rule, so it was seen to have mystical significance. Hotels in the narrow strip of total darkness—no more than 255 km wide, crossing India, Thailand, Cambodia and southern Vietnam—had been booked out for months by scientists from many nations. The temples of Angkor Wat, also in that strip, were a prime observation site, but a partial eclipse would still be seen up to 5000 km away.

Boun Kham said the best place for viewing this miracle would be from the highest point in Luang Prabang, Mount Phousi. The hill was about 150 m high, and climbing the 329 red-brick steps to its summit left me puffing and wheezing. In the streets below, people were peering at the sun through pieces of photographic film. The moon, like a great 'Pacman', was already beginning to devour the solar orb. According to legend, Mount Phousi had once been home to two hermit brothers, the first residents of Luang Prabang. Later it played host to several monasteries, including That Chom Si, built in

1804, a fat finger of dull gold emerging from bare rock. Boun Kham pointed out Route 13, stretching southwards towards Vientiane, noting with disgust that Vietnamese road gangs were still working to upgrade the road. The importation of cheaper Vietnamese labour was resented by many Lao, still bitter about the basing of Vietnamese troops in their country during the war years. Two decades on, the government had yet to secure the highway, and travellers risked being robbed or murdered by bandits or anti-government Hmong groups. Most people felt safer moving along the road at night, when ambushers were reluctant to attack because it was harder to see whether their victims were armed or not.

Thirty minutes before totality, sunlight flashed off the golden spire surmounting the Royal Palace. Beyond, the Mekong flowed like molten chocolate, its high banks exposed and a few isolated dwellings nestling in dense jungle on its western bank. By now the temperature had begun falling and shadows had become blurred. Roosters crowed, and the palace spire abruptly lost its lustre. Within the precincts of Wat Aphay, Buddhist novices gathered around a *stupa*, staring skyward through their bits of film. Borrowing a strip of film from a French tourist, I saw that the moon had almost entirely covered the sun. The air was utterly still, and slightly chilly. The novices at Wat Mai, adjacent to the palace, leapt in and out of the *sim*, excited by their strange shadows, whilst others pounded the temple drum. The eclipse had captured the imagination of the entire population except one earnest, unseen fellow whose bandsaw continued buzzing throughout the spectacle. It wasn't long before betel-chewing women were again using their umbrellas to shield themselves from the midday sun.

Back in the cool comfort of Villa Santi, I spent the afternoon reading books and news reports about Laos. 'There are many tales about the fate of the members of the royal family, who disappeared after the Communist revolution in 1975,' said a story clipped from the *International Herald Tribune* of June 1995. 'Some say they are still alive in a re-education camp . . . others say they perished in the limestone caves of Sam Neua, in north-eastern Laos, where they were being held by Pathet Lao officers . . . Others say they died of malaria in their garden in Luang Prabang, as there was no medicine available, certainly a plausible version since the Lao Revolutionary Museum in Vientiane proudly displays quinine tablets as part of the benefits of the 1975 revolution.' The story did not mention that the revolutionary leader Kaysone Phomvihan had declared the king to be dead at a news conference in Paris in 1989. Keesing's Contemporary Archives quoted a government spokesman as confirming that in 1977 there had been an unsuccessful attempt to rescue the ex-king by rebel elements, and that as a result he was well-guarded 'far from the Mekong'. The most common interpretation of this was that the king and his family had been taken to the communist re-education camps in the remote north-eastern province of Houaphan, bordering Vietnam. Their departure date, at least, was known: 11 March 1977.

'It is as if, in British terms, Queen Elizabeth, Prince Philip and Prince Charles were taken from Buckingham Palace in 1977 and removed to the north—not to Balmoral, but to some workcamp in the Scottish highlands—never to be heard from again,' thundered the journalist James Pringle after a visit to Luang Prabang in 1989.

As I read, the sound of children in the playground of the *école* opposite filled my room with a kind of light, and now and then the young receptionist, nicknamed 'Joy', or slim, came in with coffee. Once he asked what I was doing. The question seemed to unlock an idea that had been maturing in some anonymous cellar of my mind, and which only then became known to me.

2

The empty palace

In Luang Prabang, the *felang*, or foreigner, has another name coined by Lao youth—*felang ki nok*—derived from the ancient truth that when a bird shits, the person with the biggest nose is most likely to catch some. How would the government react, I wondered, to a foreigner poking his big nose into the events of 20 years ago? The fate of the royal family was a state secret. Was it not up to the Lao to write their own history? And if they chose to omit certain passages, to forget the fate of kings, for example, why should that bother me?

According to various accounts, the king had died 'in 1981', 'in 1978', 'in or about 1979', 'in 1984 of malaria', or 'of a broken heart'. Yet others maintained 'He lives normally (in a villa in Viengsai), has a few servants and a garden he can tend.' Officials explained their reluctance to comment: 'Since 1975, the king has been an ordinary person, so if he died tomorrow, we would not print an obituary.'

Santi Inthavong was expecting me for drinks that evening, and I resolved to begin my inquiries with him. With a few hours to kill, I took a travel-weathered copy of the *Sydney Morning Herald* upstairs to the terrace. There, overlooking

Sakarine Street, I read a story headlined 'Tsar's identity finally proved'. It reported the positive identification of the bones of Russia's Nicholas II, executed with his family by the Bolsheviks on 17 July 1918. Researchers had extracted DNA from a skeleton excavated at Yekaterinburg and compared it with DNA from the remains of the Tsar's younger brother, who died in 1899. The samples matched. 'This is a murder mystery, and we have resolved it with greatest certainty,' said Mr Pavel Ivanov, one of the researchers.

Santi arrived and ordered himself a whisky and a vodka tonic for me.

'Is your wife joining us?' I asked.

'She sends her apologies. But she has some family business to attend to.'

The disappointment must have shown in my face.

'Are you married?' Santi asked.

'Me? Oh, yes. My wife is from India.'

'Indian women are very beautiful. She did not come with you?'

'She's in Delhi. I'll join her there, but I'm taking time to see Laos.'

'You've come to the right place. For me Luang Prabang is the real Laos. People are different here from elsewhere in the country. Religion is still respected, and once you're here you feel quite close to nature. It's something I can't find in Vientiane or other provinces. In all of South-East Asia, there are not so many places like Luang Prabang!'

It was such a pleasant afternoon that I soon forgot my intention of cross-examining him about the dead king. His own nostalgia seemed more appropriate.

'When I came here first,' he said, 'they had a very small dam. It looked like a paddy field! During the rainy season we had power. In the dry season, three days with, three days without. It was like that until, I would say, the middle of 1992. When we opened I told the guests, "We have power from 6 p.m. until 6 a.m. So wake up early if you have an electric razor!" It took ten months to renovate because there was no electricity. It was quite an adventure.'

The sun had dissolved and a candle lamp lit by one of the girls took up the task of lighting Santi's face. The shadow of the flame flickered on the white-washed arches that sequestered the balcony from the night.

'When I first saw this house, it was in quite bad condition. From outside it looks big. But once you open the door, you realise it's quite small. It was more difficult to renovate this house than to build a new one. In the French time, they built with sand, big bricks and plaster—no cement at all. So when I wanted to put in a new door, and I was obliged to break down the wall, I was really afraid the whole thing would collapse.'

It seemed a reasonable neurosis. So much else had.

Santi's recollections coiled around their central theme—Luang Prabang—like copper wire wrapped around a guitar string, and as his memory plucked, they resonated.

'You know, this building used to belong to Queen Khammouane, the wife of Sisavangvong. When the king died in 1959, she gave it to the Crown Prince and Princess Mahneelai—that's my wife's mother. After 1975 Mahneelai lent it to the administration, and they used it as a warehouse. Then a couple of caretakers lived here. Today they still work for my mother-in-law.'

Santi's mention of his mother-in-law could not be ignored. Princess Mahneelai was the senior member of the royal family still living in Laos, the wife of the last Crown Prince, and a grand-daughter of King Sisavangvong. Like everything in the country, the details of her life were hazy. I asked if I could meet her.

'Unfortunately,' replied Santi, 'she is not in Luang Prabang. She is in Vientiane, awaiting a visa to Australia.'

'What?'

'*Oui.* Her daughter lives there.'

Of the Crown Prince's six children, two had settled in Australia, two in the US, and one in France. Only one, Santi's wife, Tin, had stayed in Laos. Her full name, Sawee Nahlee, meant 'Splendid Lady'. I was to glimpse her many times over the coming days but never spoke more than a few words to her. For someone who did 'nothing', Tin seemed rather active, always on the move between the hotel, her home, a small souvenir shop she ran and, of course, the *wat*. One day I ran into her in the hotel lobby and she seemed nervous, but agreed to meet me for coffee the following afternoon. Joy agreed to act as interpreter. At the appointed time, armed with a photocopy of the royal family tree from a book Perrot had loaned me, I positioned myself in the hotel lobby, only to be approached by a smiling receptionist. 'You are here for the meeting with Sawee Nahlee,' he said. 'But I'm sorry, sir. She cannot come today. She wants to wait for her husband, Mr Santi, to come tomorrow. Then you can give an indication of what questions you will be asking.'

I unfolded my genealogical chart and showed it to him, pointing to the empty boxes I'd drawn in where the princess and her children should be. I was having less luck than Henri Mouhot, who crowed in his journal: 'After a few minutes more conversation, the king held out to me his hand, which I kissed, and then I retired, but had not proceeded far when several officials ran after me, exclaiming, "The king is enchanted with you; he wants to see you often."'

That night after dinner, I took my usual constitutional down to the confluence of the two rivers. A full moon cast diamonds on the water as it flowed free and wide, heavy with the silt of China, toward Vientiane, Phnom Penh and the South China Sea. The sky was a lavish navy blue lightened with clouds of luminescent white, and the hills were thickly thatched and dark. There were cars on the miniature colonial streets, but not many, and restoration was proceeding on a few of the old buildings, but not much. People stretched themselves on the pavements outside their shop stalls, yawning and playing with their children.

I wandered in the moonlight into the deserted courtyard of Wat Xieng Thong. It was here in the 1960s that a tourist had asked an elderly Lao man to explain some aspect of the Buddhist religion. The softly spoken gent obliged, impressing the visitor with his encyclopaedic knowledge. Later, whilst handling some of the local money, the tourist recognised the man from his portrait on the *kip* notes—his guide had been the king of Laos.

Santi was right; Luang Prabang was different from anywhere else in Laos. At first, I thought this could be explained by its status as a centre for religious instruction, but Vientiane was equally devout. If there was a parallel, it was in the former Vietnamese imperial capital, Hue, which had a similar grace and calm despite the devastation of the war. The rest of Vietnam was a cacophony of car and motorcycle horns, karaoke bars and shrill loudspeakers. In Hue, it was quiet. The ruins of the Forbidden Purple City, home to the Vietnamese kings until 1945, were like a graveyard, and the Perfume River stole through the town in a hush.

In Luang Prabang too, history spoke in whispers, and following them took you to an oversized bungalow on Sisavangvong Street. At *ho kham*, the Golden Palace, a pair of impotent canons stood guard at the end of a gravel drive. Before the French came, the Lao kings had lived in bamboo houses, but the offer of a brick house by the colonial power was too good to refuse, and in 1909 the palace opened. Soon, Lao royalty were wearing gold-braided uniforms, reading Proust at French academies and holding formal parties.

My guide from the local tourist office was a petite young woman called Somsanith, who told me that, as a schoolgirl she had danced the Ban Keo for the king and his family at *pimai*. 'We would come here every day after school for a year,' she said, pointing to the expansive lawns surrounding the palace, upon which chickens now roamed. 'We performed only once, on *pimai*, in the open air. The king would often walk past while we were practising. He seemed a very kind man, always talking to the palace staff and enjoying walks in the grounds.'

As he strolled in the palace grounds in early 1975, dressed

in a plain business shirt worn over *sampot* and watching the
dancers practise, 67-year-old Savang Vatthana did not have too
many pleasant strolls ahead of him. As a young man he had
been politically active, leading resistance to the Japanese
occupation and being exiled to Saigon for his trouble. But
upon becoming king he confined himself to fulfilling largely
ceremonial state and religious tasks. He had suffered from
comparisons with his father, Sisavangvong, he of the mane of
wild black hair, prosperous waistline, and twelve—some say
eighteen—wives, and at least 24 children. Undemonstrative
and self-effacing, Savang Vatthana had one wife and five
children—enough for a suburban solicitor perhaps, but not for
a king. He was a tall man, with a tendency to talk in riddles,
deeply religious and irretrievably superstitious, increasingly so
as he got older. He had once lamented to his Cambodian
counterpart, Norodom Sihanouk, 'Alas, I am doomed to be
the last king of Laos.'

The well-groomed Somsanith guided daily tours around the
palace, a job which paid better than her work as an account-
ant. Weaving a path through a just-arrived tourist group, we
made our way to the gallery housing the sacred gold Buddha,
the *pra bang*. There was a commotion behind us as an elderly
man in shorts tumbled backwards onto the ground as he
photographed his wife. At first I thought he was a Lao, but
soon realised that all the Asians there, apart from the guides,
were Singaporeans, Japanese or Thais. For the locals, it was
not advisable to show too much interest in the old days.

The golden *pra bang* stood in a room which opened onto
the terrace, presenting the palms of its hands, which appeared
dull and painted. Weighing more than 50 kg, it was kept
behind bars which looked hardly robust enough to protect
what the museum's printed guide called 'a chief source of
spiritual protection for Laos since it was brought from Cambodia in the fourteenth century'. Members of the former royal
family claimed that after the revolution, the *pra bang* had
been given to the Vietnamese by Kaysone Phomvihan to repay
them for helping him gain absolute power, and had somehow

ended up in Moscow. Others claimed it was kept in the vault of the Central Bank in Vientiane. The genuine article was supposed to have gold leaf shielding its eyes and a hole drilled in one ankle. Somsanith blushed and smiled into her hand when I asked her whether the statue on display was the real thing.

'Nobody know,' she giggled.

'But it says here that it is,' I cajoled.

'Maybe. Maybe. I don't know.'

In the reception hall of the palace was a carved gilt throne which belonged not to the king but to the *pra sangkharath* of the Buddhist church in Laos. Since the communist takeover, the patriarch's job had been taken over by a committee. The last *sangkharath*, Boun Than, had fled to Thailand, where he'd become ill and died.

In the 1930s, King Sisavangvong—whose statue still stands in the grounds—commissioned a French artist, Alix de Fautereau, to help imbue the palace with the life of the country around it. De Fautereau's murals cover the walls of the king's audience room, where ambassadors would present their credentials. It was customary on such occasions for all guests and officials to wear white. A former Australian ambassador to Laos once told me of his visit to Luang Prabang. He was accompanied by his Russian counterpart, who'd arrived the same month, and they flew together to the northern capital. The bridge over the Nam Khan had been washed away by floods, so they had to cross on a pontoon, then scale the steep, muddy bank. The two ambassadors sank knee deep in silt, and arrived at the palace looking more like Dalmatians than diplomats.

The frescoes depicted the village life of the Lao Loum, the chosen people of the lowlands, as well as the country's many festivals. Dressed elephants lumbered across one panel, whilst another showed a bamboo bridge across the Nam Khan, since replaced by iron girders. In a corner of the audience hall stood the bronze busts of three kings—Oun Kham, Sisavangvong, and Kham Souk, or Sakarine as he was also known. The sculptor must have been a lover of continuity, for the reign dates he had chiselled in the bases ignored at least three interregnums.

Entering the throne room, Somsanith turned apologist for the regime. 'This is the throne,' she announced, pointing to the only chair with a back on it. 'The last king never sat there.'

The central problem for the revolutionary historian is how to give the destruction of national institutions the appearance of a calm, ordered and inevitable verdict of history. In the case of Laos, they asserted that the last king wasn't really a king. 'King Sisavangvong died in 1959,' said the museum brochure. 'He was succeeded by his son, Sri Savang Vatthana. For the coronation ceremony, the crown prince enlarged the throne room by adding two equal-sized rooms, one on each side. The establishment of the Lao People's Democratic Republic on 2 December 1975 prevented the coronation from taking place. The king abdicated from the throne and was appointed Supreme Advisor to the President.'

Until the final week of November 1975, the Pathet Lao's intentions towards the monarchy were kept deliberately vague. The National Political Consultative Council, headed by the 'Red Prince', Souphanouvong, and based in the royal capital, had endorsed constitutional monarchy as the appropriate form of government for Laos. The new regime had even installed a statue of the penultimate king, Sisavangvong in the palace at Luang Prabang in October. But it had also declared 12 October—the anniversary of the 1945 uprising when Lao Issara nationalists temporarily deposed Sisavangvong—as the national day. On the eve of the anniversary, less than two months before his abdication, Savang Vatthana summoned all able-bodied male members of the royal family in Luang Prabang and issued them with weapons from the palace armoury, ordering them to stand guard throughout the celebrations of the new national day—in which he pointedly took no part. The king had been due to depart on a tour of Paris, Moscow, Beijing and Hanoi. In diplomatic circles there were rumours of exile, but in the event, the government—now dominated by the Lao People's Revolutionary Party—informed the king that the timing of his proposed trip was inappropriate.

The new national day was celebrated in Vientiane with a performance by Russian acrobats. But in the remote north-east town of Viengsai, near the border with Vietnam, a more exclusive and important gathering took place. Senior leaders of Indochina's three communist parties, representing Vietnam, Cambodia and Laos, met for the first time since coming to power. Representing Cambodia was Ieng Sary of the Khmer Rouge, who had arrived from a Phnom Penh already cleansed of people at the start of 'Year Zero' and who remained at Pol Pot's side until 1996. Twenty Vietnamese advisors were awarded medals for their contributions to the Lao revolution. Party leader Kaysone Phomvihan said the revolution would 'speed up'.

At Kaysone's right hand was the king's cousin, Prince Souphanouvong, a blue-blood with a royal-sized chip on his shoulder. He was born in 1909 into the lower branch of the royal family, the son of a commoner concubine. He picked up his socialism whilst studying in France and consummated it with his marriage to a Vietnamese fellow traveller. In 1945, he eagerly participated in a rebellion which temporarily deposed King Sisavangvong, then fell out with his nationalist colleagues after they agreed to restore his uncle to the throne. Expelled from the nationalist Lao Issara in 1949 for his extreme views, he helped form the Pathet Lao the following year. Souphanouvong saw himself as the Lao version of the great socialist leaders of the time, and moved around with a 23-member Vietnamese bodyguard. He was wounded in the anti-French struggle, escaped from prison (or was released after the intercession of his powerful relatives, depending on whom you believe) and led a little 'Long March' overland to the safety of the Vietnamese border areas, where he spent a decade living in a cave during the American bombing. It was quite a legend, but it came at a cost. The Lao people admired Souphanouvong's willingness to forsake his royal birthright but were uneasy about his Vietnamese friends—and rightly so. In return for Vietnam's backing, Ho Chi Minh demanded a decisive say in Lao affairs, subsuming the country within a Hanoi-dominated Indochinese 'federation'.

Savang Vatthana found events moving too fast for his liking. He told a western diplomat that Souphanouvong had shown a lack of appreciation of Lao traditions, and suggested the country's future could be in the hands of a foreign power. By 4 November, when another ambassador presented his credentials, even the king was no longer free to speak openly.

'The king was jovial,' recalled the ambassador, 'but he spoke of the need to adjust to the new situation, given the fact that there had been a complete change in Laos. He then remarked that he was by no means convinced that the monarchy was the best system for Laos, looking pointedly in the direction of the cabinet minister attending the ceremony, the Pathet Lao minister for religious affairs.'

On 25 and 26 November, the National Political Consultative Council convened at Viengsai and decided to abolish the monarchy and declare the People's Democratic Republic. The next day, a rally in Vientiane denounced the monarchy and called for a popular and democratic regime. Prince Souphanouvong, who had been in Viengsai for the NPCC meeting, flew to Luang Prabang to propose to Savang Vatthana that he abdicate, and advise him on the appropriate form of words. Shaken by the demonstrations against him, the king had earlier told the British ambassador he intended retiring to his farm at Pak Xuang.

On 30 November, Crown Prince Vong Savang carried the king's letter of abdication to Vientiane. Many members of the Lao royal family who now live in exile in Paris claim the king rejected a prepared letter of abdication handed to him by Souphanouvong, and wrote his own. The venue for the secret congress of people's representatives, an American compound the Pathet Lao had besieged in May 1975, still had the feel of enemy territory, with its modern amenities and bungalows dotted amid gardens. The leaders of the new government, including party chief Kaysone Phomvihan, had already requisitioned some of the bungalows for their personal use, a gesture symbolic of their total victory.

The Crown Prince had represented the king faithfully throughout his apprenticeship. Because of his comparative youth, he had been able to travel to remote and difficult parts of the country, including those few small areas where the Royal Lao Army had enjoyed military successes. Vong Savang was impatient in matters of state, always questioning why the government was not doing more to defeat the Pathet Lao, but to him fell the bitter duty of announcing the end of the 600-year-old monarchy.

Wearing a dark pin-striped suit with a small Buddhist medallion pinned to the lapel, a striped tie and spectacles, he read his father's letter of abdication with a dour face, unmoved by rousing applause. The only consolation was the careful wording of the letter which, as reported by the party newspaper *Sieng Pasason*, handed power not to the Pathet Lao administration but to the Lao people.

'Confronted with the new political situation in Laos,' it read, 'the co-existence of a monarchist regime, defined in the constitution, and the popular sovereign power is impractical and could be an obstacle towards the country's progress. In order to ease the path towards progress and to consolidate national unity, I solemnly renounce the throne from today, meaning I sincerely and completely renounce all goods willingly. I entrust the destiny of the country to the Lao people. Once more, this confirms the sovereignty of the population in all the territory of Laos. As a simple Laotian citizen, I sincerely address my best wishes for unity, independence, welfare and prosperity of the beloved Lao people.'

The document was signed and dated 'Luang Prabang 29th November 1975, the eleventh day of the decreasing moon, of the 12th month of the year 2518'.

Vientiane Radio, by then under the control of the communist propagandist Sisana Sisane, broadcast an eight-minute report apparently based on the letter of abdication prepared by the government, but not signed by the king. It said: 'I agree to abdicate the throne, and from now on I dedicate my royal properties to the nation with a clear conscience. I agree to totally accept the new administration and put my faith in it. I ask the Laotian people to guide the future of the country, and to seek unity and a better life.'

Prince Souphanouvong's crowning victory was at hand. Since embarking on his long quest to shake Laos from its complacency, he had cultivated a ruddy, egalitarian manner, and was careful not to behave as a high-handed noble. To many he was a genuine patriot. But a western diplomat who had contact with him saw 'a vain, ambitious snob. Emotional, with a savage streak, who commands respect because people are afraid of him.'

'He never really listened to you,' a member of the former National Assembly who'd spoken to the Red Prince in the dying days of the *ancien régime* told me. 'He had a pat answer for everything. It was impossible to have a normal conversation with him. It was always a cat and mouse game. And you felt like you were the mouse.'

In his usual robust and clear voice, Souphanouvong addressed the congress. 'I am extremely happy in joining you here to celebrate the victory against imperialism and the destruction of the old and corrupt administration,' he told delegates. 'I am confident under the new regime which will be adopted by this meeting, that our beloved country will have its independence, its unity and its prosperity, and that the Lao people will have a better life and greater liberties.'

He then proposed that the king become his 'supreme advisor' and former Prime Minister Souvanna Phouma became advisor to the government. A resolution to that effect was passed unanimously.

On 3 December, Pathet Lao radio reported that the former king was living in an orange plantation—probably a reference to the orchard at Pak Xuang.

'The communist Pathet Lao put an end to the last pretences of coalition government in Laos on Wednesday,' reported *The*

Economist on 6 December 1975, 'when it forced the powerless but respected figure of King Savang Vatthana to abdicate and dissolved the cabinet of his cousin, the neutralist Prime Minister, Prince Souvanna Phouma. Like most of the milestones since its military victory in May, this latest move served mainly to formalise existing political realities . . . Well-organised demonstrations against the monarchy during the past week were a clear signal that its end was nigh . . . the dream of a national reconciliation is clearly dead.'

Others saw the hand of the Vietnamese behind the abdication. The historian Arthur J. Dommen, writing in his book *Laos: Keystone of Indochina*, said: 'The Vietnamese stage managers of this transfer of sovereignty were doing no more than following the pattern set in 1945, when the Emperor Bao Dai abdicated in favour of Ho Chi Minh's government in Hanoi. The Vietnamese Communists basically are firm believers in tradition.'

Touches of grandeur survived in the king's private quarters behind the throne room, where four gigantic lamps stood at each corner of the royal beds, and a palanquin was parked outside the king's bedroom door. But some of the furniture, notably Queen Khamphoui's bed, resembled rejects from a garage sale. On the king's king-size bed, ornately carved in teak with the initials 'SV' on the head, one of the ivory tusks was missing from the triple-elephant crest at the foot. The wooden frames for the mosquito nets were no more elaborate than the ones you could buy in Hanoi for a few dollars, and the dressing tables and chests of drawers resembled filing cabinets. Another feature of the bedrooms was the enormous number of doors. No fewer than nine led to the king's suite, almost all of them windowed. Were bed-hopping and peeping all the rage at the court? The amorous air of the bedroom was heightened by the strategic placement of an old HMV Victrola gramophone outside the king's boudoir, primed to go at 78 r.p.m.

Glass cabinets lining the walls displayed royal orders from the emperors of France, China and Russia, none of them still in power—bad omens heaped one upon the other. The royal rubber stamps, without which little could happen, were also on show, bearing the words '*Pra Chao Lan Xang*'.

Turning a corner into what was once the ladies' sitting room, we came face to face with Savang Vatthana, or at least his larger-than-life image in oils. In 1967, the Russian artist Ilya Gazurov had seen no trace of doubt about their future in the faces of the king, his queen and his heir. Their portraits exuded confidence and strength. Savang Vatthana wore an emerald silk tunic, an enormous belt with the triple elephant crest, and baggy *sampot*. He carried a gold sabre and over his shoulder loomed the Buddha. In a glass case beside the portrait was a red-and-gold silk tapestry sent to the king as a gift by Ho Chi Minh. Addressed to the Roi du Laos, and written in French and Vietnamese in 1962, the accompanying letter read:

> Your Majesty,
>
> I would like to express my sincere gratitude to you for informing me of the appointment of Prince Vong Savang as heir to the throne.
>
> On behalf of the government of the Democratic Republic of Vietnam and myself, I would like to take this opportunity to extend our congratulations to you and Prince Vong Savang. I believe under your wise leadership, the Lao people will embark on the path of peace, neutrality, independence and prosperity. May the friendship between the nations of Vietnam and Laos continue to grow.
>
> My sincerest regards to you and Prince Vong Savang.
> Ho Chi Minh

Ho was perhaps being less than sincere. It was well known that the king had initially regarded Vong Savang as an unsuitable heir. The Crown Prince had not obtained degrees or diplomas from his studies in France, and he spoke French with a heavy accent, owing partly to his malformed front teeth.

Ho's pennant wasn't the only gift from across enemy lines. Prominently displayed in another glass case was the comb-

and-mirror set given to Savang Vatthana's wife, Khamphoui, in April 1958 by Madame Vieng Kham Souphanouvong, the Vietnamese wife of the 'Red Prince'.

Some say that in terms of the 'Red Terror', when Cambodia got pneumonia, Laos caught a cold. But like the Khmer Rouge, the Lao communists sought to transform society. They too imbued toil on the land with a mystical significance, and removed ancient symbols like the triple-headed elephant from the flag. Since the revolution, the palace at Luang Prabang, like the Winter Palace in St Petersburg, had functioned as a museum rather than being occupied by the new regime. The royal capital had long since ceased to be the national capital, and there were plenty of suitable buildings in Vientiane to accommodate the new rulers. Yet the failure to fully occupy the site seemed to suggest a lack of self-confidence on the part of the regime. The empty palace spoke of a vacuum in the national soul caused when 600 years of history came to a dead end.

What was the point of this bizarre exhibition, I wondered? Were the gifts and expressions of regard of the communist leaders supposed to show what good fellows they were? Or was there something noble about rat cunning that I had missed? Were we supposed to wander awestruck amid the evil wealth of the former king, which actually appeared to be rather modest? Or should we admire the Lao government for carefully preserving an important part of the nation's history, and encouraging foreigners, if not Lao citizens, to inspect it? The Lao revolution craved continuity.

Somsanith drew close to me as I gazed up at the king's portrait. 'Now he is in the north of Laos,' she said, blushing.

'He stays there? Or . . . ?'

'I don't know.'

Shaking her head, she led me into the next room, formerly the royal dining room, where gifts to the king from foreign leaders were now kept. These ranged from the kitsch—moon rocks brought back by the Apollo astronauts and presented by US President Richard Nixon—to some rather nice carpets from Iran, and fine Cambodian silver. The Lao flag carried to the moon and back by the astronauts bore the red and white triple-headed elephant symbol of the royal government. In hindsight, they might as well have left it there. There was also a boomerang presented by Australian Prime Minister Harold Holt in 1967. Nixon's fate was well-known and Prime Minister Holt was missing presumed drowned.

'Have you ever been to China?' Somsanith asked me as we stood before a case containing gifts from Laos's huge neighbour. No, I said.

'Still, you are lucky,' she continued. 'You can travel around the world. I never go.'

'Well, maybe in a few years.'

'I hope so. I like to travel. But I can't do that.'

My companion's name had been bothering me. Was she perhaps related to Prince Somsanith, a former member of the King's Council, who had stepped down in 1975 and remained in Laos until his death? Yes, she said, her father had been in the government before the revolution. But when I sat on one of the upholstered benches, she told me curtly to get up, as it was not permitted.

Before leaving, we paused at the visitor's book positioned just inside the entrance. It was filled for the most part with gushing tributes to the preservation of Lao culture. One couple complained about being unable to take photographs and desired a more detailed brochure. An American had written: 'Dining room table. Position of chairs incorrect. Larger chairs go at the end of the table.' Somsanith, whose mood had suddenly become icy, ordered me to make an entry. As she chatted with her friends at the museum shop, I scrawled something about 'stalking the halls of the Elephant Kings'.

On Rue Fa Ngum, the Phukdee 'Friendship' store offered a collection of old costumes from the palace for sale, including one midget-sized uniform covered in gold braid, which the one-eyed shopkeeper said had belonged to his grandmother. A glass case contained several small statues of the Buddha, which he called *pak ou*—the name of a settlement upriver where the Mekong is met by the Nam Ou. The town was opposite the Tam Ting caves, a placid sanctuary containing thousands of Buddha figurines, standing with arms at their sides, the Luang Prabang posture calling for rain. The shopkeeper selected one of the statuettes, about the size of my index finger, its exquisite features carved from wood and mottled in gold dust and soot.

'Maybe it from old temple,' he said.

It cost $6 and I bought it without bargaining, placing it in the parcel rack of my bicycle. As I rode back towards the hotel, the Buddha statue, wrapped in brown paper and string, bounced lightly in the tray. Suddenly, an irresistible force seized the handlebars, turning the bike off the road and sending me crashing through a fence.

'What happened?' cried the man who extracted me from the wreckage

'I don't know. The bike had a mind of its own. I couldn't stop it!'

Inspecting the bicycle, the man pointed out that its lock was situated on the front forks. The key must have been turned by the bicycle's vibration, closing the lock and disabling the steering. When the forks had been straightened and the bamboo fence pieced together again, I re-mounted and rode uncertainly back to the hotel.

Later that evening, Joy came to my door. He was holding the brown paper package containing the Buddha figurine, which someone had just dropped off at the hotel. In the shock of the strange accident, I'd left it behind. I unwrapped the statue and looked at it again. I thought I saw a mischievous expression on its face.

Outside in the lobby, Santi was slumped on a lounge drinking coffee. He greeted me warmly. 'Having a nice time?' he asked me, beaming as if there could only be one answer. 'Did you go to the Tam Ting caves?'

'No. Why do you ask?'

'No reason. I first went to the caves in 1989,' he went on. 'I was very impressed by the number of Buddhas there. They told me there were approximately 8000 Buddhas in the caves. Do you know how many there are today?'

I had no idea.

'Two thousand, maybe 3000 maximum. Now, all those Buddhas, of course, are not stolen by Lao people. For them, it's a sin. They're afraid to touch a Buddha like that. But for tourists, it's something else. It's a souvenir, or a decoration for their desk. If we select the good type of tourists, we can avoid this. But if we get mass tourism or backpackers in Luang Prabang, that will damage the town.'

I excused myself and went to my room, opened my suitcase and found the figurine. The old Buddha smiled back at me. I returned to the lobby and handed it to Santi.

'I'm almost certain it's from Tam Ting,' he said, appraising the statuette. 'Even if it isn't, it is surely very old. Certainly an antique, and from a temple at least, but probably from the caves.'

I felt about as small as my tiny Buddha. The craving for old things must be one of life's more banal addictions. I had seen for myself the pillage of Angkor Wat, and knew diplomats whose personal effects included whole periods of their host country's archaeology.

'Please, Santi, do me a favour,' I said.

'Sure. Anything.'

'How often do you go to Tam Ting?'

'Maybe once a month.'

'Next time you go, take this.'

I handed him the statue.

'Take it? Why?'

I told him about the strange force that had possessed the bicycle. Santi chuckled.

'Small but powerful, eh?' he said. 'OK, if you wish, I'll take it back to the caves.'

'*Kop chai lai lai,*' I said. 'Thanks very much.'

It was my last night in Luang Prabang, and still I hadn't been able to talk to Santi's wife, Tin. Even better would be a chat with her mother, Princess Mahneelai, back in Vientiane.

In Laos to directly ask for something from a mere acquaintance verges on violence. Yet it is in the Western nature to force issues.

'Santi,' I said. 'I need to meet your mother-in-law before she goes to Australia.' I muttered something about doing a report on her in time for her visit there.

'Well, I'd have to ask her first,' he said. 'Many have asked for an interview, but the Ministry of Information and Culture has refused permission. You know, officially, you are supposed to give them a list of the questions. And then they probably won't allow it anyway.'

'Which is why I'm not asking for an interview. I can just meet her,' I said, a sinking ship.

'You know it can create difficulties for us,' Santi continued. 'We don't want to make trouble.'

'But what about your business? You need publicity so tourists will know about the hotel and come here, don't you?'

'Sure, sure.'

The silence rang with hopelessness.

'Look,' he said. 'Why don't you try to meet her when she's in Australia?'

'Santi . . .'

'Well . . . well, all right. I'll talk to her. But remember there is one French journalist from *Le Figaro* who will never be allowed to come back to Laos. He was supposed to write about the Mekong, but he wrote about the anti-communists.'

'I know.'

'Maybe I can ask her if she would like to meet you. But you must not ask her political questions, or questions about her personal feelings.'

'Of course not!'

'She is a hidden person. She has many painful memories. You shouldn't disturb them.'

The next morning I awoke early to attend a religious ceremony at Wat That Luang. The scheduled time was vague, so I quickly showered and changed and packed my bags, ready for a speedy departure for the airport when I returned. On Rue Sakarine I hailed a *tuk-tuk* and headed for the temple.

The precinct of one of Laos's most important *wats* is one of the few places in the country that ever fell victim to bombastic Soviet ideals of town planning. After 1975, the authorities planned to build a heroic stadium with the bleachers backing onto That Luang. The project was linked to 1990's fifteenth anniversary of the founding of the People's Democratic Republic. Five years on, a triumphal arch stood isolated in a wasteland, a painted hammer and sickle—since removed from the national crest—rusting ignominiously. Clouds of grasshoppers rose before my feet as I picked my way across the abandoned open ground between buffalo pats and marshy patches. The temple sat on a ridge, mist-encircled peaks rising behind it and a chorus of wooden xylophones and bells issuing from within. Beyond a steep staircase stood a large *sim* and two *stupas*, one listing at a menacing angle. The collapse of old *stupas* provides a regular source of treasure for the nation's museums, for the shrines are repositories of votive statues of the Buddha, rings and other valuables.

In the grounds of the *wat*, early arrivals—mainly elderly women—had begun burning incense and draping marigolds over the bases of the *stupas* while novices in brown and orange lounged under the mango trees. It was the strength of women like these that had bolstered the faith through the difficult years after 1975, when the government interfered heavily in Buddhist affairs. Whilst the men of the Politburo banned alms-giving, their wives never ceased going to the temple. The new religious policy was quickly recognised as culturally unacceptable and abandoned. Lao women had stayed true to Buddhism all through their menfolk's fling with Marxism.

Inside the temple the devotees were segregated, with the men seated on the floor at the front. Their feet, which must not point at the altar, were tucked beneath and beside them, and under a large statue of Buddha painted in gold were collected dozens of cellophane bags containing washing

powder, school exercise books, condensed milk, airmail enve-
lopes and toilet-paper rolls for the *kathin*, a once-yearly
presentation of robes and petty necessities to the monks. There
was a uniformity about the offerings which suggested they'd
been prepared en masse. Tape-recorded chants issued from a
battered public-address system.

Kathin was being performed all over the country at the
conclusion of the Buddhist Lent. The date for the ceremony
was not fixed, being left to the discretion of local communities.
But the ceremony at That Luang in Luang Prabang had another
purpose as well. It was the only place in Laos where, once
a year, the memory of a former king was honoured. It was
29 October, the anniversary of the death of Sisavangvong,
whose ashes were interred in the gold-tiled *stupa* at the
northern end of the *wat*. The ceremony had been banned
after 1975, but was revived in the early 1980s as revolutionary
fervour faded. Now it enjoyed official approval, and paper
flags featuring the national colours were interspersed with
Buddhist ones.

Churches have bells, but *wats* have drums, and the thun-
derous boom resounding from a tower outside heralded the
arrival of the main body of worshippers. They came in a
convoy of Japanese cars, *tuk-tuks*, a truck borrowed for the
day from the Water Supply and Environmental Sanitation
Department, and a bus provided by a local tour company,
which disgorged a squadron of monks. The lay worshippers
all wore white *pa peh*, sashes, and some of the women hived
off to a communal kitchen where they not only prepared food
but also worshipped. A US Army parachute slung between
Sisavangvong's *stupa* and the *sim* provided shade, billowing
like a vast mushroom as it filled with the breeze, then sagging
heavily under the sun.

Tin, the late king's great grand-daughter, had been up since
early that morning preparing food. She arrived in a white
pick-up truck and began unloading large pots of victuals
bound for the kitchen. She robustly carried some of the pots
herself, but with a deportment which matched her flawless

grooming. Her young son and daughter gambolled behind. When her contributions had been arranged, she donned a white *pa peh* and rounded up the children.

Seated outside the chapel I could easily hear the drone of the chants, but my view of proceedings was constantly hindered by crowds of inquisitive boys. Some of them were still using pieces of photographic film to stare at the sun, as if the eclipse of five days earlier might recur. The tallest of them indicated that he would like my pen—my 'Bic', he called it—and I gave it to him, causing much joy and envy. A few minutes later, I had to buy it back for ten times its value when I misplaced my other pen.

Under the parachute marquee, Tin was standing alone with her children, facing the *that* of King Sisavangvong. Her hands were clasped in prayer before her face. The children tried to replicate her devoted posture. She went down on her knees and lowered her head to the ground, and again they scrambled to follow. Then she began distributing garlands of marigolds, incense and wax tapers to the children. A man went over to help her light the candles, and a waxy fragrance spread across the courtyard. She helped the children press the tapers onto an iron grille which bordered the *stupa*, pausing regularly to bow in obeisance before the monument, incense sticks clasped between prayerful hands. The congregation inside the temple continued their invocations unawares, as did the women working in the kitchen. Tin's act of royal homage passed almost unnoticed. There was no reason why anyone should notice, I suppose. It was a simple act of remembrance by a young woman for her famous great grandfather. Yet in Laos, personal history was usually political.

Tin returned to the kitchen, dusting off her knees and dismissing the children. Dozens of helpers were soon carrying trays of food into the *sim*. There were mounds of sticky rice and bowls of meat floating in broth. They were passed inside from hand to hand. Tin shovelled ice into cups, which were then filled with soya milk and again transported to the congregation. With the arrival of the food, the atmosphere in the *wat* lightened. The old women got excited and the children turned feral, sparing no effort to steal favourite bits of lunch.

Buddha must have been smiling on me, for as I stood in the courtyard in the blazing sun, he sent a coy angel to feed me. She held up a tray of rice, pork and vegetables, and she seemed genuinely happy to see me. It was Tin.

Then from a window of the *sim* I heard somebody calling my name in a shout disguised as a whisper.

'Hey, guy?' it said. 'Come sit next to me.'

It was Boun Kham. Removing my shoes, I squeezed inside and crawled in his direction.

'No sweat,' he said. 'No sweat. You came, uh? That's good. Lots of ex-ministers, even current vice-ministers are here. You eat with me. Last Supper, eh? Before we go back to Vientiane, eh?'

As he beamed at me, his eyes darted self-consciously about the room. Sometimes he seemed to be flaunting our association to the assembled worshippers, but at other times I thought I caught the hunted glance of a former prison-camp inmate.

An elderly Buddhist nun, her head shaven, was seated in the midst of the assembly. She raised the new saffron robes and other donations in ceremonial recognition of the community's generosity. A bonze appeared, sporting his new kit, the creases in the robes still showing, and began to gather up the cellophane bags containing the groceries and carry them to the altar. Then the plate was passed and 1000-*kip* notes soon piled up on it. I threw in two, stirring a murmur of approval.

Then he launched into a post-repast diatribe which reminded me of my father's dinner-table homilies. 'They told us Marxism was good and communism was strong, and the US was the enemy. But now, see what's happened in the Soviet Union. So they were wrong. And Lao people know they were wrong.'

He sounded vindicated, but there was a ceiling to his satisfaction. The communists might have been proven wrong, but they were still in power. Instead of finishing them off, the west had rushed to prop them up. Why? he asked. My explanation—that Indochina was destined to be a brick in the new Great Wall against China—failed to satisfy him.

When I had eaten, I took my leave, agreeing to meet Boun at the airport, and walked along the dirt road which led from That Luang to Phothisarath Road. Luang Prabang was sunning itself in the clear air of altitude. I was thinking how much it reminded me of school holidays in Australia—hot, slow, and empty—when two barefoot boys rode past on a bicycle, tyres crackling the gravel, their voices joined in a gentle, melodic song.

Leaving Luang Prabang is always a melancholy experience. To cross the iron bridge over the Nam Khan is to cross the threshold between dream and reality, to break an ancient and mysterious spell. 'Such a pretty little mountain kingdom capital,' a well-travelled friend once told me, remembering those days before the revolution. 'Much like those in northern Burma or Thailand must have been. The small court, the craftsmen and dancers, and Their Majesties at the centre of all the ritual festivities and daily worship. All that semi-feudal apparatus that the Pathet Lao loathed. Such a pity they sent them away. In the normal course of events, a term of more than two years in a Lao prison was almost a death sentence.'

The brooding mountains reflected my mood as the hotel minibus bumped and jerked its way towards the airport. The other passengers were chatting around me, but I felt insulated, isolated by memories not my own, and by a sense that I was leaving Luang Prabang for the last time.

As I waited for the plane with Boun Kham on the open veranda of the terminal, I could see a portion of the runway at the bottom of the hill. A boy was riding a bicycle along the centre line. An elderly Lao woman sat watching us. She had maintained an aristocratic beauty, defying her age—delicate temples, high cheekbones and a fine, unlined forehead, long hair combed back and tied in a bun, a pair of simple gold earrings and a modest blouse tucked into a *sin* gathered by a silver chain belt. She displayed what were undoubtedly her entire worldly goods with dignity. Lao women often maintained great youthfulness and tranquillity into old age, earthy yet noble in flip-flops. I envied the secret of their calm, if not the standard of dentistry and addiction to betel nut, which had left this woman completely toothless.

As the afternoon dissolved, the Chinese Y-12 turbo-prop lifted off the runway over a shimmering river and a glittering city, the golden *stupa* atop Mount Phousi no bigger than the little Buddha I'd left behind. We followed the mountains' elephantine march down to Vientiane.

3

Vientiane

My initial impressions of Vientiane were of an enormous plainness. A few architectural extravagances told of a time when Lao leaders had aspired to and achieved greatness. But those aside, it was a low-slung, balmy town, cradled in a bend of the Mekong River, where the only tension was an intermittent struggle between the rising dust and the lowering dampness of the air. And the dust was winning, settling in small dunes along the roadsides, where it had been accumulating since the old days. The dunes encroached gradually on the narrowing roads, defying the efforts of grass to stabilise them, or of school children press-ganged on 'red' days of public service to sweep them away. On the city's main arteries, battalions of *tuk-tuks* and cars mimicked the Bangkok 'charge', careering between the handful of traffic signals.

The taxi crossed town and headed for Tha Deua road. I was going to the Sokpaluang temple area, where I would be staying with a friend. En route we passed many embassies, among them the Chinese, Swedish and Burmese. After the revolution, diplomats were prohibited from travelling more than 5 km outside the capital, and their homes were besieged by police and spies. Now things were considerably more relaxed, and my friend's home was an air-conditioned, bougainvillea-draped haven. Piu the gatekeeper met me with a gargantuan smile and Ket the housekeeper advised me to leave my shoes at the door.

Early next morning, I set out by *tuk-tuk* for a meeting with a Princess. Princess Mahneelai and her husband, Crown Prince Vong Savang, had been separated now for longer than they had been married. She came to the door of her suburban bungalow in bare feet, but wore nail polish and lipstick. Her hair was now grey, wild wisps of it refusing to stay in her bun, and she wore a simple brown *sin* which she constantly smoothed out over her knees. The sitting room was spanking new and bare of curtains and furnishings, except for a lounge suite and a square of carpet on the highly polished timber floor. A Lao weaving covered the coffee table. The bungalow was one of several in a compound which belonged to the Inthavong family, a sort of family guest house by the look of it.

The princess showed me her wedding photos: two young scions of the Lao elite, educated in Cambridge and Montpellier, France, transformed into avatars of an ancient culture. Her skin appeared as if washed in milk, hair bejewelled and tied back in a bun, clothes sumptuous. Her husband stood beside her, ornately dressed and grave. The bride was described in diplomatic cables as 'lively and intelligent . . . speaks fluent French and English and seems to have considerable influence over her husband'.

I had with me my chart of the royal family tree, which I showed to the princess in the sitting room. Gold-rimmed spectacles perched on her nose, she pored over the genealogy of her family, a maze of cousins and half-brothers, thanks mainly to the lusty King Sisavangvong. His first wife, Khammouane, had borne Savang Vatthana, the heir to the throne, but there were many other wives, including Mahneelai's grandmother Khamla, who had continued to bear princes, renewing the pool of high-born nobles, diplomats, secretaries and marriage material for the king and his heirs.

When, in March 1977, the government took the Crown Prince from Luang Prabang, they left his wife behind. Mahneelai raised her family of seven children alone in the white-washed villa in the former royal capital which is still her home. When I met her she was 54, and her children were spread across four continents.

As a student of English at Cambridge, she had met the Crown Prince in London during one of his trips to Britain, where he preferred to spend his vacations. He was at that time studying political science 'long and nonchalantly' in France, where he was seen as a loner. So although they had grown up in the same small town, the couple met on the other side of the world. Vong Savang had left Luang Prabang at age twelve to attend school in Hanoi when it was still under French rule.

'When we first met in London, it was as cousins meet,' said Mahneelai. 'He was intelligent and he never smiled. I didn't dare love him. He was my cousin, but intermarriage was still the way at that time. In fact, you were discouraged from marrying outside the royal family. When Vong Savang fell in love with me, he told his parents and they agreed to arrange our marriage. The new generation marry Europeans and people abroad, and they choose their own partners. I don't arrange. My daughter's husband, Santi, was not a member of the royal family, but they love each other. It's not like before.'

Before the wedding, Mahneelai said, she was carried in procession from her home—a villa near the Mekong—to the palace. She and her betrothed were dressed in golden tunics and shawls. The groom held a gold sceptre; the bride was laden with jewels. The palace chief of protocol, Prince Khamhing, fussed over the arrangements whilst attendants in white dress uniforms squatted with the ornaments of the *baci* ceremony in their hands, their faces grave lest the slightest hitch mar the occasion. The incantations of the shaman swelled and ebbed.

Vong Savang and Mahneelai did not have a honeymoon,

for the same reasons that Savang Vatthana was never crowned king. As the seers had foretold, his reign coincided with difficult years of war and political division, even within the royal family itself. 'For years we prepared for the coronation, but it never happened. We just prepared,' recalled Mahneelai. 'The crown was made by the goldsmith Phia Tong. But at that time there were two political parties within the royal family, and they were fighting. So they couldn't make the decision.'

The new king occupied himself with his projects, restoring Wat Xieng Thong, renovating the palace and developing a farm at Pak Xuang, 15 km upstream from Luang Prabang, which he used to introduce new varieties of oranges and avocados to Laos. Foreign leaders playing host to the king were sometimes surprised when he digressed from matters of state to inquire about the recommended local varieties of eggplant or grapefruit, and whether seeds were available. Vientiane-based ambassadors lucky enough to be invited to the palace would find themselves issued with wellington boots to go trudging through the manure at Pak Xuang with the king's son.

'The oranges were magnificent,' recalled Mahneelai. 'Once a year there was a ceremony for the threshing of the rice. Anyone who wanted to could attend, and many villagers would come.'

The garden at Pak Xuang should have impressed the Pathet Lao at least, but after his abdication in 1975, the king was no longer allowed to visit and the farm was allowed to go to seed. When the royal family were sent into exile in Houaphan province, many communist officials spoke of their fate as a kind of come-uppance. The man who once was king could now toil in the fields like the rest of the population. In fact, he'd been doing it for years, and it was one of his great loves.

During the fifteen months between his abdication and internal exile, the king continued to live in Luang Prabang, but was forced to leave the palace. He moved into a villa on the Mekong near Wat Xieng Thong and was not allowed visitors. In 1977, when the king, queen and crown prince were taken away in a Russian helicopter, Mahneelai was pregnant with her seventh child. She said she had soon become 'very depressed' and was helped by Anoulath, the head of the monks' school in Luang Prabang. 'He came to me and said, "It's not good for you to do like this." So the monk came and taught me every afternoon, about how the Buddha took 500 lifetimes to get over his troubles. And eventually I changed my mind, and accepted. I realised that if I allowed myself to succumb to my sadness, no-one would look after the children.

'I have never been informed if my husband is dead or alive,' she went on, fumbling with a gold bracelet. 'They just say he is studying at the concentration camp. When the party leader Kaysone Phomvihan said in Paris that Savang Vatthana had died, he didn't mention my husband.'

In the ancient and devout city of Luang Prabang, people have long memories. The royal family were no longer at the heart of government, but Mahneelai still had the respect of ordinary people, who would bow to her in the street. The mother of a Lao friend, upon hearing I had met the princess, said she would have crawled on the floor before her. But as far as Mahneelai was concerned, being 'common' had its advantages. 'Now I can go to the market, or anywhere I like. When I was a princess even shopping like an ordinary person was not possible, unless I was followed by security people, and that was unpleasant. I'm free now. I can go to the temple without a fuss.'

For most of her children, freedom of the mind was not enough. Four of the seven live abroad, some having risked their lives to get there. In August 1981, the heir to the throne, Prince Soulivong Savang, then eighteen years old, and seventeen-year-old Thayavong made a daring night crossing of the Mekong near Vientiane on a raft made of banana-palm trunks. The boys had taken their ageing governess with them, and a couple of young maids and guards. They ended up in Paris.

In 1991, Mahneelai petitioned the local authorities to return to her the small, run-down villa on Rue Sakarine which had been loaned to the government after 1975. Under the new economic policy adopted by the party, her request was granted. Work began to restore the building and open the Villa de la Princesse, which quickly built an international reputation, contributing greatly to the development of tourism. 'It's how I keep busy,' said Mahneelai. 'It's how I forget the past.'

I began to see the resemblance to her daughter—the impression of strength combined with reserve. There was a rock-like immovability about these Savangs. Fate had made them flexible, but also stubborn.

'I've adapted to the situation by going to the temple, and listening to the teachings of the Buddha. I don't think, like some others might, "Oh I'm very depressed." I learned from Buddhism that life goes in cycles, and Buddhist teachings are not a lie. You must accept the good and the bad, the high and the low, and learn from them.'

Suddenly she seemed to be speaking in one of the thousands of voices lost in the abyss of war and revolution, a voice of resilience and survival and faith. 'You can escape the sun. You can escape the rain. But you cannot escape the cycle of your own life.'

At one point in our meeting the telephone rang and she went out to answer it. When she returned, I asked about the disputed authenticity of the *pra bang*, the gold talisman of the nation displayed at the palace in Luang Prabang. Was the real one really in Moscow?

'Nobody dares say that,' she warned, 'because if you say it, and you're wrong, Buddhists believe you will die.' She laughed at my alarmed expression. 'Whether it's real or not depends on your heart,' she said. 'Even if not, we will still respect it, and that will make it real. At *pimai* last year, the people came to throw water at the Buddha image. And one person came from the village, and he said, "Oh, this is not the real Buddha. It doesn't shine!" But I told him, "You shouldn't say that. It's been kept inside the palace for a long time, so it hasn't been cleaned. It's just a bit dusty." And the people all around us said, "Yes, Mahneelai is reasonable! Mahneelai is wise!"'

I felt I had imposed on her time and hospitality enough, even though there were many questions I had still not asked. Santi had told me the princess preferred not to think about the past. So I ended with a question of philosophy. If kingship was bestowed by Buddha, was its destruction also a reflection of his will? Had the elephant kings lost the mandate of heaven? Her reply side-stepped the question of an almighty mantle. 'We've enjoyed good things in our past lives. Maybe our time has come to live differently. No-one knows into what incarnation they will be born. If they could choose their birth, everyone would be king. Even the women.'

She laughed joyously. But could the monarchy ever return to Laos, as it had in Cambodia? I asked.

'We are still the royal family,' she said. 'The royal spirit is in our blood. But now we live as ordinary people. It's difficult for commoners to enter the royal family and learn that style. But royalty can live as the common people. And we have. Yet we are still the royal family.'

An enigmatic answer to a political question, which I shouldn't have asked anyway, but repeated. 'It depends on the circumstances,' said Mahneelai. 'I don't think about it.'

'But you still have a place in society, whatever the government does or says. Do you still have responsibilities, moral if not political?'

'The power of the royal family is dead. Now it is history.' Mahneelai expelled the idea as if it were bad air. 'If it disappears, it will disappear forever. To be a king, you must enjoy the support of the people. Whether Laos has a king or not is up to the people's demand. If the people are not on your side, you can't rule.'

She smiled patiently, and with indulgence. 'Don't think too much,' she said. 'Every life is just birth and death. Birth and death, it's true.'

It was the end of the Buddhist Lent, and across the country, thousands of monks were filing out of their pagodas, and embarking on pilgrimages to far-flung places. They had confessed their evil thoughts and deeds to their superiors and accepted new mats, robes and begging bowls from devotees. Some went door to door, ousting *phi*, or spirits, believed to have taken shelter in homes during the rainy season. That night, the full moon drew my host Felicity and me down to the river for the Boats of Fire ceremony, *Lai Houey Fai*. The Japanese, who celebrate a similar festival, say the boats represent the footsteps of Lord Buddha on the Yamuna River in northern India, leading the souls of the dead back to heaven. The Lao festival is more straightforward. Its purpose is to dispose of bad luck by putting it in tiny boats carrying lighted candles and releasing them onto the river in their thousands, transforming the Mekong into a Milky Way.

In new, free-market Laos, one of the big industries is the party, and Vientiane itself became a brightly lit boat embarking on the sweaty, boozy river of night. Hawkers of lotus, incense and sticky rice in bamboo cylinders did good business along the Quai Fa Ngum, as huge crowds blocked the street that ran along it, crowding its temporary taverns and surrounding the many sound stages on which rock bands played. Soon we were swept up in the noisy human wave, rampant youths linking arms and jostling us as we held aloft our fragile *houey fai*, once made of dried banana leaves, now fashioned from fluorescent polystyrene. There were so many faces passing, and on every face was a different reaction to the sight of the two *felang* carrying the holy boats whilst the Lao partied.

At a small wharf, a handful of people were preparing to cast off their flame-bearing boats. Small boys glistened like otters in the water as they guided the lanterns away from the shore. My first problem was that I carried no matches, but a smartly dressed man in his 40s proffered his Dunhill lighter, and my candle of hope sputtered to life. I looked at that taper like a five-year-old counting his candles at a birthday party, and carefully handed my *houey fai* to one of the boy–otters, as if handing him my destiny. He took the lantern and placed it in the water. It rocked unsteadily, then seemed to catch a current and began surging towards midstream with the confident instincts of a hatchling turtle. All my troubles were heading for Cambodia, and my future seemed assured until, about five metres from the bank, my vessel was snatched up by another of the river boys, who began using it to relight the candle of a boat he was fostering.

There was a certain inevitability about what happened next. The ten-year-old Mekong pirate tilted my craft at a dangerously sharp angle to relight his own candle, in the process setting fire to my boat. Replaced on the water, it flared briefly, then faded to a smoulder. A third boy took pity and doused it with a desultory splash of water. My bad luck wasn't going anywhere.

Ok Phansaa, literally 'the end of the rain', marked the end of a three-month period of abstinence and had become the occasion for big commercial promotions. Young Buddhist novices with freshly shaved heads could be seen along Quai Fa Ngum accepting free cigarettes from the '555' girls and buying Bugs Bunny gas-filled balloons. The Mekong was supposedly a barrier between all that was loud, brash and aggressive—that is, Thailand—and all that was submissive, gentle and quiet—that is, Laos. But it depended on the day.

The next day we returned to the river for another annual event—the boat races on the Mekong. Again the crush was enormous, only now, instead of being crowded with the flickering lights of *houey fai*, the river was clogged with gladiatorial rowing crews, 50 or more men and women to a craft, all contesting the title of fastest pirogue. New teams kept filing down to the river, marching in formation, dressed in team colours and shouting war cries accompanied by pounding drums and clashing cymbals. There was the Marlboro boat, the Pepsodent boat and the Lao Beer boat, and in the sparkling water they resembled serpents on speed. The bank was muddy and squalid after the previous night's party, and US Army parachutes sprouted like mushrooms, shading makeshift kiosks in which women fried meatballs and bananas, popping them into little plastic bags. All around lay discarded coconut husks, chewed sugar cane and plastic bags. The girls on the Lux boat passed, grunting like tennis players. Boy and girl boats cruised each other.

Having lost Felicity, I descended to the bank, its firm mud like a rubberised tennis court, and ordered a bowl of noodles from one of the kiosks. A crone with breasts like withered mangoes, thin hair and betel-rotted teeth sat down on the bench beside me, spitting a regular stream of red liquid into a plastic bag. The chilli in the soup brought tears to my eyes, and I drew liberally from the toilet roll dispenser conveniently placed on the folding-table counter. It was only 9 a.m., but the sun beat strongly. As the final boat race ended, firecrackers began exploding and a momentous roar greeted the victory of the Thanalaeng Warehouse team.

After the races I met up again with Felicity as she boarded a ferry to take some sunset photos. The day had cooled but the river bank still swarmed with a beery multitude. The boat was top-heavy, listing as it struggled upstream. Viewed from here, the river appeared much broader and more formidable, and the waves more threatening. On the Lao side, the buildings of Vientiane crouched low, like so many guerrillas in the jungle. They must have made a hard target for the Thais when they were shelling the city in the late 1980s. Today, though, their inhabitants were flaunting their Lao-ness, thousands of them dancing in a forest of amplifiers and speakers. They were lifting trophies in the air, lifting each other in the air, and the marquees sagged and the plastic tables and chairs toppled over.

A wake was held for the unsuccessful *felang* women's crew after the races had ended. The western women sheepishly prepared food whilst the Lao women belted out boating songs and passed the *lao lao*. Later, I overheard one of the Lao women speaking English with an Australian accent. It turned out she had fled Laos with her family before 1975 and was now back as the manager of a construction project. On the Thai bank of the river, Lao exiles would often come to stare longingly across at their lost homeland, unable to summon the courage to return for fear of government reprisals. This short, stout woman obviously was not in that category. I introduced myself and made an appointment to see her in quieter circumstances the following week.

Soumieng Deajpanyanan's late grandfather was a trader in food and precious stones from the Teo Chew–speaking region of Canton, from which came many of the Chinese people who live in Bangkok, Kuala Lumpur and Penang. He had married a Thai woman during his commercial forays around South-East Asia, and their son expanded the family empire into Laos, marrying a local girl and taking a 'shop house' in the Morning Market in Vientiane. Somsak Ma did not progress beyond the third grade at school, but he taught himself how to raise pigs and market their meat. Laos, he found, was a country crying out for good-quality pork. When there was no more room for his money under his mattress, he began buying land. Somsak noticed that people liked to eat his pork with rice, so he began growing rice too. Seeing that they liked a drink as well, he bought a whisky factory.

Soumieng was the eldest of Somsak's five children. She was sent to a Chinese school where portraits of the king of Laos hung alongside those of Sun Yat Sen, nemesis of the Manchu dynasty and father of the Chinese republic. The shop house was a hive of activity during the week, and at weekends the family would move out to their farm, which boasted not only pigs but a small tiger, a sun bear and many other animals. It was well known among the hill tribes that captured exotic animals were best taken to Somsak at the Morning Market. Did they usually end up in Chinese medicines? Possibly, but several were donated to the zoo in Udon Thani in Thailand. The family itself would later follow the animals into exile.

The Ma family had plenty of servants, which left Sou free to indulge her great love—pond fishing. Most Lao families that can afford it have a pond beside or even under their house—a combined fish market, refrigerator and recreation facility. In Vientiane, the cloying aroma of home-caught fish being barbecued wafts through the streets. 'That's a very Lao thing,' said Sou, pulling her legs up beneath her *sin* in the two-storey bungalow that doubled as the office for the Gateway Enterprise Company, a joint venture building the first modern shopping centre in Vientiane. At 33, she had the brilliant black hair and compressed build of a typical Lao woman. Politely sensuous, she had an earthy laugh and chewed her consonants in a way that made me long for noodles.

'I'm fifth-generation Chinese,' she said, still looking Lao to me. 'Chinese is funny. It doesn't matter how many generations your family has lived in a country, or whether your grandmother is part Thai, or even if you haven't a lot of Chinese blood in you. At the end of the day, you're still Chinese.'

'So you're Chinese. Not Lao? Not Australian?'

'I'm all of the above,' she said, and her belly laughed. 'When I introduce myself here, I usually say I'm Australian. In Australia, I'd say I'm Lao.'

Growing up in Vientiane in the 1960s, Sou was oblivious to the politics. Around November each year, the king would allow his people to feast their eyes upon him at the festival of That Luang. Sleepy children would be shaken from their beds before dawn and dressed in their best clothes for a glimpse of the emperor of Lan Xang. 'My mother kept telling me not to stare at him,' said Sou. 'You were supposed to show respect. But he was just this big guy who looked older than in the picture at school. He also looked as if he wasn't very smart. He didn't have the authority of being a king. He looked really weak. That's what I thought. He was weak and old.' If a ten-year-old found the kingly pomp inadequate, I wondered, how could the rest of the population be impressed?

'We didn't know anything about the king's son or the rest of his family,' Sou recalled. 'Or even his wife. I can't remember what his wife looked like. I think the only reason we remember him is because when you went to the movies you had to stand up for the national anthem. And they always showed a picture of the king.'

In the Kingdom of Thailand, just a few kilometres from

where we were sitting, people were still standing to attention before images of their monarch projected from fly-spotted monochrome slides onto cinema screens. The Bangkok newspapers were full of pictures of the royal family doing good works, and businesses competed to take out the largest advertisements in praise of royalty. But in Laos, the war had undermined respect for the king.

When a coalition of communists, royalists and neutralists took office in 1974, the children of the Chinese schools had farewelled their Taiwanese teachers, who were politically unacceptable to the Pathet Lao. They were replaced by teachers from mainland China, who wrote in a Maoist-approved Mandarin script and led the class in revolutionary songs about the Red sun of the East. It was not unheard of for the children to rise at 3 a.m. to walk kilometres to the Patuxai—Vientiane's Arc de Triomphe—to prepare for mass parades. Communist insistence wore down a jaded aristocracy, almost all of whose members had their parachutes ready and their escape routes well planned.

Then, one day in 1975, Sou overheard her parents arguing about whether to stay in Laos or leave. Her mother, Chou, wanted to take the children across to Thailand, but Somsak was against the idea. 'That's the first time I realised there was a war going on. I was really upset that we had to leave. I didn't want to go. All my friends were here. And I really had no idea why we had to leave. The history taught in the Chinese school didn't relate to the present, and Asian parents don't like to tell their kids about troublesome things. I think kids should know what's going on. At least let them know, "Yes, we do have a war here".'

The family stayed long enough to see the establishment of the Lao People's Democratic Republic, but fled across the river to Thailand a few days later. By that time Somsak was the largest pork producer in Laos, supplying the entire Vientiane market and exporting to Udon Thani and Nong Khai. The family had substantial holdings in property and industry. They left it all behind. In Thailand, where the family stayed for three months, Sou began adjusting to a life without servants. She started doing the laundry and cooking. When the family reached Australia, her parents both got jobs, leaving Sou to look after her four younger brothers. Letters received from old school friends still in Laos painted a picture of revolutionary change. The first Pathet Lao government was determined to challenge the comfortable old ways—above all, the antiquated and oppressive culture of good manners. There were no half measures. To change society, the Pathet Lao knew, they must change people; communist semioticians saw language as the key to thought and attitudinal change, so they embarked on an ambitious campaign to rid the language of vestiges of the feudal past. Lao is similar to Thai, containing only one additional tone. The four forms of saying yes, each denoting a different level of respect, were abolished in favour of the proletarian *jaow*, or 'yeah'. The humble form *doi kanoi*, 'yes, my lord', which children had always used to address their elders, was no longer to be used. For the New Lao, 'yeah' would suffice for all occasions and for all people.

Decades later, Lao like Sou who returned to their homeland found they no longer spoke the same language as their compatriots. 'They told me, "In the old days, we used to have lords, and servants, and slaves—caste structure. That's why people would say 'my lord' and 'your highness'. From now on, we are brothers and sisters, uncles and aunts, nieces and nephews. There isn't a caste structure any more." In fact, it was the wife of a very high official who pulled me aside and said, "Sou, don't say *doi kanoi* any more. You should say *jaow*." I found it really weird that they could suddenly change the Lao we had known our whole lives into a different kind of Lao.'

In Lao homes, however, people never stopped saying *doi kanoi*. As the ardour of the revolution faded, traditional ways slowly reasserted themselves. Ideology wins sprints; culture wins the marathon. Later I learned that there was still one place in Laos where the use of *doi kanoi* was officially encouraged—in prisons.

Laos lost one in ten of its people in the exodus which followed the Pathet Lao victory. Those who left were mainly those with wealth and education. However privileged they may have been in the past, returning Lao started with a handicap; the stigma of having run away. 'You have to work hard to get over that,' said Sou. 'The people who stayed never miss an opportunity to tell you how bad it was in the old days. They're like war veterans remembering their terrible battles. The hardest part was the general lack of opportunities for a whole generation. A lot who stayed feel that there's this gap in your memory and they have to fill it in for you. They look at people coming back from abroad and they say, "You went to Australia. You had a good, comfortable life. You educated your children. Look at us. We didn't even have high schools to go to. No travel. No opportunity." You suspect their motives for telling such stories; that they might want money or something. But generally they're just letting you know who's who, asserting their self-respect. And, of course, those who were loyal are bitter that the system wasn't able to reward them.'

Confiscated land and buildings helped ease the pain of those who stayed; a windfall of houses, cars and valuables. Among the booty inherited by the PDR was the Ma family's pig farm. The government had no idea how to run it, so eventually it invited Somsak Ma to return to Laos and resume pig farming. It would be a joint venture. Vientiane municipality would provide the land, which actually belonged to Somsak, and Somsak would put up the capital. 'Dad really wanted to do it,' said Sou, 'despite the bad terms. But when he asked the head monk in Sydney, the monk said, "You're 65 years old and you've killed enough animals for one life. So no more." After that he decided not to come.'

Sou was back, of course. But gutsy as she was, the difficulty of reclaiming ownership of her family's lands had her beaten. 'It's gone,' she said. 'Let's forget about it. I know that if I go back and start putting in claims for my land, it's a very long and complicated procedure. I mean they're not giving land back on a silver plate. I'd end up really angry and frustrated, with a bad feeling about the country. And I might not do the business I want to do, because of that. So I'd rather just let it go. I know a couple of families who've done it, and we get a lot of Lao coming back with the intention of reclaiming their land. But my advice to them is, Don't bother. Leave it. What's gone is gone. The day you decided to leave this country, you let it go.'

As the five-yearly congress of the Lao People's Revolutionary Party approached, Vientiane's small business community began to realise the odd niche it occupied: that of the necessary evil. Not only foreign business people, but returned Lao experienced the same problems. Their view of the country's future depended a lot on the sort of day they'd had. 'If I've had trouble getting a meeting,' said one returnee, 'I'll tend to question my judgment. You know, did I make the right decision in coming back? Am I wasting my time here? That's a bad day. But then sometimes you just think, well, this country's going to progress, and it's going to change, and I just hope that in a small way I can help it go in the right direction. That's why you bother a lot of the time, because you encounter a lot of hostile behaviour. You sometimes feel you're not welcome here. That you're intruding. A lot of returning Lao believe those who stayed don't really want us back in.'

4

'Six Clicks City'

It was now more than a week since I had written to the government proposing to visit places and meet people associated with the twentieth anniversary of the founding of the republic. So far there had been no reply, so I did the tourist thing, which in Vientiane means visiting *that*s and *wat*s. There was That Luang, the massive *stupa* on a hill north-east of town painted a gaudy gold and surrounded by dozens of smaller *that*s. The stately Wat Sisaket, its scriptures carted off to Bangkok by marauding Thai armies, was impressive, and the forest temple of Sokpaluang, with its sauna run by nuns, inspired and soothed. But there are only so many temples you can take before retreating to the bamboo bars that perch along the Mekong levee, there to enjoy a slow stupefaction of beery sunsets. One such afternoon I realised I was getting bored on holiday, and would go stir-crazy in Laos if I didn't find some work to do.

Then out of the blue I received a telephone call from the Ministry of Foreign Affairs summoning me to a meeting at 9 a.m. the next day. The caller, who did not identify himself, gave no indication of the purpose of the meeting, nor whom

I would be meeting. An expatriate friend warned me to be prepared. 'The Lao have a reputation for being submissive,' he said. 'But among themselves they're quite ruthless. All that gentle stuff is eyewash for the foreigners. If you cross the line, if you're seen as interfering in their internal affairs, the gentility turns to obstinacy, and even hostility.' He told of a recent incident at the Central Telephone Office on Setthathirat Road, when a backpacker tried to argue about the minimum three-minute call charge. Staff had called the traffic police, who'd mildly threatened him. 'The Foreign Minister is interested in your case!' they said, and confiscated his passport. Next day, he was invited to the police station and informed that the Interior Ministry was now aware of two incidents involving him within one week—this argument, and the theft of his camera, which he'd reported earlier. So, for the crime of being robbed, and complaining about it, he was driven to the Friendship Bridge and pointed in the direction of Thailand.

It was a cool morning and the haze was beginning to rise on the roads as I entered the iron palisades of the Ministère des Affaires d'Etrangers, a large but undistinguished building in which men in suits disappeared round corners in clouds of cigarette smoke. In the outbuilding housing the press department, I was met by a stocky young man called Khen who sat me in a reading room lined with the works of the late North Korean communist leader Kim Il-Sung. A copy of *On Carrying Forward the Juche Idea*, by Kim's son Kim Jong-Il, was on the coffee table in front of me.

The work had been published by the Dear Leader in 1983 to mark the 165th birthday of Karl Marx.

After stewing in my thoughts, and those of Kim Jong-Il, I was led upstairs to meet Linthong Phetsavan, a polished diplomat who'd served as chargé d'affaires in Washington. He welcomed me warmly and asked how my visit was proceeding. As always, I had prepared a list of complaints—interviews not organised, a new and arbitrary service charge which had been imposed on journalists for the occasion of the twentieth anniversary of the revolution—something to hit back with in case they had some complaint against me. But Linthong knew the first rule of diplomacy. He never stopped smiling.

'We highly appreciate your efforts to write about our country,' he said. 'We regard you as a friend of the Lao PDR.' This worried me. Many times in Vietnam, a vicious denunciation had begun sweetly. You had to be established as a friend before they could denounce you as a turncoat and an enemy. It had never happened to me in Laos, and I looked at the floor, waiting for the verbal blow to fall. As it turned out, Linthong simply wished to discuss my request to interview the prime minister. 'The government is considering your request,' he said. 'The questions you have submitted are very good, very constructive. We want to do this. But we need your assurance that you will stay with these questions, not other, unconstructive questions which might damage the excellent relations between Laos and Australia.'

Linthong reminded me that if he organised the interview and things went awry, he would get into trouble. Even if the prime minister smiled and was gracious in my presence, the trouble would come later. Concluding that any interview was better than none, I agreed to all conditions, confident that once the bonhomie developed between me and the prime minister, I could ask whatever I wanted and we'd all part beaming and embracing, as always happened at the end of a non-interview with a communist official. In the event, the interview was so useless it never eventuated.

Returned to the custody of Khen, I was informed that Sisana Sisane, a founder of the People's Revolutionary Party, had agreed to meet me. Born in Savannakhet in 1915, Sisana had fought the French and fled to Thailand with the Lao Issara. He'd been imprisoned by the royal government in 1959 and had been with Souphanouvong on the 'little Long March' overland to Sam Neua. Throughout the 1960s and early '70s he'd run the Pathet Lao radio station, broadcasting propaganda designed to undermine the morale of the royalists, and after 1975 was made the first minister for Information and Culture. Being in government, however, did not agree with him—or perhaps it agreed too well. In 1983, he was demoted for expressing 'anti-Soviet sentiments' and banished to Houaphan. Reliable sources had told me this period of re-education had more to do with personal problems than with political ones. Sisana's *faux pas* had been made at a gala song contest he'd presided over as minister. The audience was large and enthusiastic, and Sisana, who enjoyed a drink, decided to perform one of his own compositions. Ignoring shouted requests for a popular Russian tune, he interspersed his rendition with jibes at the crowd, the Russian song and the Soviet Union in general. Apparently it was quite a performance, but the Houaphan hangover proved sobering. In 1985, Sisana was rehabilitated as director of the Institute of Social Sciences and entrusted with producing an official history of the country and the party which, as far as I could establish, he had never completed.

'There's not much time,' said Khen, bustling and flustering like a minion. 'We'll take your car.'

'You mean, my *tuk-tuk*.'

Khen looked at me in disbelief. What was the point of being a government official if you had to travel in *tuk-tuks*?

'*Baw*,' he insisted, getting quite agitated. 'We can't. We must have a car to get in to Sisana's office.'

'Oh, really?' I said, enjoying his irritation. 'Does he live in a garage?'

'No, of course not. He's meeting us at Kilometre Six.'

I was dumbstruck. Kilometre Six had been off limits to foreigners since the revolution. It was the former compound of the United States Agency for International Development (USAID) which the Pathet Lao had besieged in 1975.

When in January 1973 the US decided to cut its losses in Indochina by negotiating the Paris peace agreements with North Vietnam, the fate of Laos, as well as Vietnam and Cambodia, was sealed. American aid to Laos was higher per person than that to any other country and was the main means of support for the 25 000 troops of the Royal Lao Army. In April 1975, as Phnom Penh and Saigon fell, Pathet Lao troops attacked the strategic crossroads at Sala Phou Khoun that linked Vientiane with Luang Prabang and the Plain of Jars, and began to move into the Mekong River towns, the last bastions of the royalists. Pro-American ministers, including the Defence minister, began to flee across the Mekong to Thailand. The deputy Defence minister, Khammouane Boupha, ordered government troops to lay down their arms and not to resist the Pathet Lao. At the celebrations of Constitution Day in Vientiane on 11 May 1975, Prime Minister Souvanna Phouma addressed an audience depleted by the heat and political uncertainty, but which included the king, who arrived in a black Russian limousine. Souvanna had come in a Ford, but his car was the only pro-western statement made that day.

'The upheavals which have agitated our country for twenty years have clearly resulted in a new situation,' he said. 'It is necessary to look at the facts and prepare to arrive at an accord with history. Our population understands the situation well by instinct. We must stop the fighting. The war has reached an end.'

A few days later, communist troops surrounded USAID's Vientiane compound at Kilometre Six on the road to Nam Ngum dam. The compound served as residence for the CIA staff who were then overseeing the secret war in Laos. The siege was lifted only after the US agreed to withdraw the USAID mission and all the personnel by the end of June. National elections scheduled for the same period were postponed indefinitely. More street protests followed, and in August a revolutionary administration took power in Vientiane.

The time of the 'seminars'—communist indoctrination classes—now began. The word had a dual meaning for the Lao. The first was the western sense of seminar, but in Lao *samana* means a gathering of friends. It was to prove a useful ambiguity for the government in persuading its opponents to attend voluntarily. Sisavangvong University in Vientiane, now Dong Dok University, became one of the larger re-education camps, although high-security political prisoners were sent to Viengsai. Members of the Foreign Ministry, tainted by their long association with outsiders, were well represented. 'Last week,' noted the diary entry of a western diplomat based in Vientiane at the time, 'the Ministry of Foreign Affairs was practically empty.'

A cameraman I knew who'd visited Six Clicks City during the 1960s and early '70s had often spoken of the place as a sort of Shangri-La in the midst of the civil war, with sealed roads, bars, restaurants, swimming pools, tennis courts and saunas, a well-stocked commissary full of duty-free booze and, according to him, blue movies on video. 'It was magnificent, mate,' he'd told me, eyes watering over a soda, one sweaty evening at the Lan Xang hotel. 'Magnificent!' Whatever the reality, Kilometre Six had provided what every war needs—a beacon of splendour reassuring people that somebody at least was living it up. It was the last word in luxury, and within its barbed wire barricades was everything you could ever want, or need.

Khen had been a press guide since the early 1990s and had never been to Six Clicks City. No western journalist had been there either. We ran to the *tuk-tuk* and headed for the Morning Market, where we hired a battered Corolla and driver and headed out past the Defence Ministry.

At 6 a.m. on 20 May 1975, the American residents of Kilometre Six received telephone calls ordering them not to attempt to leave the compound. The Pathet Lao had surrounded it and were in command of all exits. Anyone seen leaving or entering would be shot. The following day the Americans paid off their servants, who walked out and were immediately sent to re-education camps. A few days later the first busload of American dependants left Kilometre Six for the airport. Now we were barrelling along that same road, passing Pepsi billboards, shop houses and soup stalls, and beyond them, paddy fields, fish ponds and palm groves.

On the left-hand side of the road, at one of those murals glorifying the drudgery of peasants, we turned onto a short stretch of smooth tarmac bordered by oversized freeway lamp posts bending inwards like respectful serfs. An arched entrance

King Sisavangvong

Souvanna Phouma

*King Savang Vatthana
and Queen Khamponi*

Left: *The Princess Mahneelai, 1961*
Above: *The 'Red' Prince—Souphanouvong*

Wedding of Crown Prince Vong Savang and Princess Mahneelai

Royal Palace, Luang Prabang

Fresco detail, Luang Prabang

*Temple door detail,
Luang Prabang*

Elephants are a common theme
in decorative work

Royal dancer, Peng Dee,
Ban Phan Nom

Silversmith at work

Funeral stupa of King Sisavangvong, Luang Prabang

Stilt house with bomb casings, Xieng Khouang

Above: *Palace of Prince Boun Oum, Pakse, 1994*
Below: *With Sousath, Plain of Jars, Xieng Khouang*

That Luang festival, Vientiane

Standing stones, Hua Muang, Houaphan
Facing page: *Landing strip, Sam Neua*

Number One Re-education Guest House, Viengsai, Houaphan

Wat Phu, Champassak

bearing the words 'Lao People's Democratic Republic' beck-oned. Cautious Khen looked for someone to report to, but perhaps thanks to the awe in which people held Kilometre Six, no guards were necessary, and we passed inside unhin-dered to find a neat but graceless barracks of brick bungalows, painted white and Wattay Blue, lining small streets with severe, almost Calvinist, gardens. Even the gymnasium of the former American school, where the crown prince had read out the king's abdication announcement, looked smaller than I had imagined, the red-and-gold hammer-and-sickle flag of the party hanging limp from a pole outside. How history had magnified all these things. It was clear nobody of great importance lived here anymore. We walked past volleyball courts and a satellite dish on a lawn, and stopped to inspect the sole wooden structure in the compound, which turned out to be a large sauna. Khen stopped several times to ask directions. Eventually we came to a two-storey scale model of the former US embassy in Saigon, one of those strange American diplomatic structures with concrete lattice work shielding the windows from rocket attack, and lots of air conditioners. Inside, it was musty and dark, with parquet floors and narrow corridors.

We found Sisana in an upstairs office which had louvres instead of glass in the windows. He was a nugget of a man, short, with a stance like a boxer's and hard eyes. A German correspondent who met him in 1979 noted Sisana's almost European features—he said he'd been told in Bangkok that the minister's grandfather had been a Corsican living on the Mekong. He wore a dark grey flannel safari suit with epaulettes and two gold pens in the pocket, as if denoting his rank. He smoked Marlboros, holding them between his fingers like a chillum, the ash pointing up between his knuckles. He had the earthy laugh of a survivor, displayed an historian's eye for the past and a reporter's eye for lascivious detail.

'This was Kaysone's bedroom,' he said, 'but he had several houses,' he added, guarding against too much disclosure. He sat us down on a brown vinyl sofa under an oil painting of That Luang and, while coffee was served, made modest small talk suggesting he was perplexed why I should want to talk to a retired historian like him. The older generation of Vietnamese leaders, including former Prime Minister Pham Van Dong, had shown me similar coyness in interviews. But their self-deprecation was simply a charming way of concealing the facts. The glint in Sisana's eye told me he was a hard-boiled type who could be moved to poetry only by the concept of class struggle. He had penned the national anthem, a crusty piece of revolutionary bravado:

> From the beginning, the Lao people
> have brilliantly represented their motherland,
> with all their energies, all their spirits and hearts,
> and as a single force, they have progressed united and
> determined,
> honouring dignity and proclaiming their right to be their
> own masters.
> All Lao ethnic groups are equal,
> never again will they allow imperialists and traitors to harm
> them.
> The people united will safeguard the independence
> and freedom of the Lao nation.
> They are determined to fight and win, to lead the nation
> to prosperity.

The coffee was better than the poetry, one of those clean, deep brews that you only seemed to get these days in the offices of high officials. Etiquette required a long period of pleasantries and small talk, followed by effusive farewells. What normally got left out was the interview. I told Sisana I was curious about the fact, that, before 1975, the Pathet Lao had given no indication that they intended to abolish the monarchy.

'That's right,' he said. 'Our party appointed the king as advisor to President Souphanouvong. In a small country it's unnecessary to say "We won't use the king." So we tried our best to use the king.'

'So the party didn't believe that the monarchy was necessarily a bad thing?'

'Generally the people did not like the king.'

'But it was an ancient institution.'

'Yes, but the Kingdom of Lan Xang only held power in the north. Champassak was different. There, Boun Oum was given rights but was considered only as a prince. The southern provinces came under the French protectorate. There was a declaration of independence in 1949, but the north remained a monarchy. Generally speaking, the Lao people—especially Luang Prabang people—didn't like the king.'

'Why not?'

'Because the administration had no justification.'

'Economically or socially?'

'Mainly economically. The king had teak plots in Paklai. No-one else could touch them.'

'Did he log them or just keep them?'

'They belonged to the king. No-one else could cut them without paying money to the king, like paying taxes. The villages were divided into guilds—weavers, entertainers. The village of entertainment should provide beautiful female entertainers just for the king.'

'Like a feudal system?'

'Yes.'

'But if the king had cooperated with the new regime, maybe today you'd still have a figurehead monarch?'

'Yes. At that time the Soviet Union built two statues of Sisavangvong. One is outside Wat Seemuang. The other is in Luang Prabang. And we still keep those two statues.'

'Because Sisavangvong was a good leader?'

'It's not that. It's the party's policy that what we have, we preserve.'

'But not the monarchy itself. The party forced the king to abdicate.'

'I don't know if that's the case or not, because before the first plenary session of the Congress of People's Deputies was opened, on 2 December 1975, Souphanouvong had a personal meeting with the king and tried to explain to him how the political situation would be. He tried to persuade the king to accept the new system of government.'

Sisana was showing signs of increasing impatience with my line of questioning. He would look at Khen as if to say, 'What is this? Why is he asking that question?' and then Khen would look at me the same way.

'Savang Vatthana was never really king,' Sisana said dismissively. 'The prince did not automatically assume the throne upon the death of his father. There should be a ceremony. The reason this did not occur was that at the time Sisavangvong died, there was still fighting in the country, from province to province, and it became worse and worse later on. He was waiting until there was calm in the whole country.'

'What was the actual event which led to the arrest of the king?' I asked.

'The reason the liberation government arrested the king and his son was because his son Vong Savang, with the French government and several other governments, tried to fight against the liberation government. The second reason was that we knew the crown prince wanted to send his father into exile. We knew of that plan, and that was why we arrested them, and stopped their plan in advance.'

I said that Kaysone Phomvihan, when asked about the fate of the royal family, had stated that Savang Vatthana had died of 'natural causes' but had not mentioned Queen Khamphoui and Vong Savang. I asked what had happened to them.

'The queen died before the king,' Sisana replied, 'but I'm not quite sure whether the prince died before his father or not.'

It struck me as odd that such simple facts of Laos's history were unknown to the country's leading historian. Perhaps I needed to press him a bit more. I told him of reports published in the west that Vong Savang had been killed in an escape bid.

'No,' Sisana replied. 'There was no escape because guards kept close watch on the people sent to seminar, or re-education camp. There were several escape attempts by former high officers, but they were caught.'

I asked whether being a historian was a difficult job in a one-party state.

'Writing is not difficult, but it depends on the politics,' he replied. 'Because it's for the sake of the party. We used to have a dispute with China. So should we write about that? I don't. We may have a dispute with the Thai. Should we write about it? It depends on the future situation. That's the crucial point which I consider difficult. Writing is not difficult.'

I thought briefly about quoting George Santayana's remark, 'Those who cannot remember the past are condemned to repeat it,' but there was no point. Sisana had not forgotten the past. He knew very well that in March 1979, the Lao government had sided with Vietnam in its war against China, asking Chinese road construction gangs to leave the country and protesting against Chinese troop deployments on their common border. He knew about party insiders like Dr Khamsengkeo Sengsthith, a senior official in the Health Ministry who in December 1981 defected to China and said the Vietnamese were using chemical weapons against Laos's Hmong tribes, and Khampeng Boupha, who was arrested in the summer of 1979 for conspiring with the Chinese. But relations with China were good now, so as an historian it was his duty to overlook the inconvenient past. Communist historians preferred to talk about the future, which was always bright and certain.

'Is the old system of monarchy finished for ever?' I asked. 'In 1975, did Laos move irrevocably into a new era?'

'Yes,' he said, stubbing out a Marlboro.

'And Marxism?'

Sisana nodded. At last, a question he was expecting.

'We agree Marxist–Leninist theory is good,' he said. 'But our government is still learning all progressive theories from other countries. The success of a theory depends more on the person who implements it than on the theory itself. The person who studies Marxist–Leninist theory should know the level of his own country's development. If you base your decisions only on the texts, you will die. In the beginning of liberation, we didn't have much experience, so we had to do it according to the way of the existing socialist countries. We wanted to become a socialist country quickly. Lenin wrote that even an underdeveloped country, under the leadership of a Marxist party and with the help of a socialist country, can become a socialist country.

'Now the world situation has changed and the Soviet Union is destroyed. Some other socialist systems have been destroyed. So Laos has to be independent. Also, in Laos the economy is based on the natural economy. We don't produce any goods for export. We have only family production for family consumption. The Lao system is neither socialist nor capitalist. Whether it becomes socialist or capitalist, it should be based on turning this natural economy into an industrial economy. Once we get industries we can export. To become a balanced economy, we have to create several economic sectors, including government, joint-venture and private. We also need to open the door to foreign investment.'

'Why was the hammer and sickle removed from the national crest?'

'In 1986, at the fourth plenary session of the party, we saw that we could not go to socialism. So we have to establish democracy. Once we set up the People's Democracy, there was no need for us to use hammers and sickles, which would create misunderstanding of our policy.'

When our meeting was over, Sisana escorted us downstairs, stopping briefly to show us scores of gold-painted busts of Kaysone Phomvihan made in North Korea for distribution around Laos to mark the revolution's 20th anniversary. He said the building had been the venue for Politburo meetings until Kaysone's death in 1992. The mute conference of imported Kaysones said it all about communism's failed experiment in Laos. Another building, which had housed the leader's office, would be opened soon as a museum. The attempt to create a lasting niche for Kaysone in the hearts and minds of the

Lao hobbled on. In the meantime, his family were, of course, doing well.

On a visit to Vientiane earlier that year I'd met one of Kaysone's sons, Saysomphone, a former governor of Savannakhet, after he became minister of Finance, having ousted Souphanouvong's son Khamsai from the job. He was softly spoken and reasonably direct—until I attempted to garner some biographical detail, notoriously difficult to come by in Laos.

'How old are you?' I asked. 'Where were you born and how did your upbringing as the son of a great revolutionary affect your childhood? Did you have to move about a lot? Was it an unusual childhood?'

A murmur rose from the assembled acolytes. The translator shifted uncomfortably in his chair. Saysomphone laughed and adjusted his Omega watch, then mumbled something to the translator.

'The minister graduated from the Moscow Institute of Economics in 1983. He then became a teacher of economics in Laos. In 1987 he was appointed to Savannakhet as assistant to the governor. In 1991 he became deputy governor. In 1993 he became governor. Recently he was appointed minister of Finance.'

Saysomphone continued to smile as he watched the translator. I fancied he was waiting for him to deliver a punch line. It never came. Perhaps being the youngest member of the party Central Committee was a sensitive issue—if you were the son of Kaysone.

'You avoid mentioning your youth,' I said. 'You don't like to talk about your past?'

He laughed again.

'The minister liked sport,' came the translated reply. 'Football. As governor of Savannakhet he participated in football with others.'

And that was the most he was prepared to disclose to me.

A few weeks after my meeting with Sisana, a small party of foreign media representatives was allowed to visit Kaysone's office but not to take photographs. Before we entered it we sat in the former chapel of the Kilometre Six compound and watched a video of Kaysone dancing the *lam vong*—the national dance, which resembles slow-motion karate—and leading the revolutionary struggle. His bungalow consisted of three small rooms, one of them the screened-in porch, where his appointments were written on a whiteboard in English. I imagined ambitious party men stealing inside to add their names to the list after Kaysone died. A pile of audio cassette tapes on his desk indicated that he'd recorded most meetings and conversations. There was a lacquer painting of Ho Chi Minh sitting on a settee talking to Kaysone and a book by Ho on the desk. The wall clock bore the logo of Tiger Beer. There was a Parker pen and a Russian desk calendar, a book called *Getting on in English*, an exercise bike, and dozens of Johnnie Walker scotch bottles. A cabinet contained several Buddha images, and some incense sticks had been lit on an ancestor altar. Evidently the revolutionary leader had found religion.

I asked our guide what the cause of Kaysone's death had been.

'Health problems,' he said.

Sisana Sisane had alluded to the collapse of communist orthodoxy in Laos. The Pathet Lao had emerged from their hideaways full of enthusiasm to reshape society but with little administrative experience. Their efforts to turn ideals into reality were hamfisted. Beginning in June 1976 the *kip* was withdrawn and replaced, withdrawn and replaced again, each time hugely devalued. Eventually this practice destroyed all wealth in the country. A catastrophic drought in 1977 forced the government to appeal for international aid to avert a famine. Attempts to forcibly collectivise agriculture began the following year but were suspended at the end of 1979 after encountering mass resistance. Regular closures of the border with Thailand took a further economic toll on land-locked Laos, and the Thai embargo on 'strategic goods'—including bicycles and fuel—was in effect a blockade. Pathet Lao troops began selling their units' fuel allocations to supplement inadequate salaries.

The old royal capital also proved troublesome for the new government. Thousands of people took to the streets to protest against attempts to remove the talisman of Lao nationhood, the *pra bang*, from the royal palace. They were also outraged that Buddhist monks were compelled to give sermons endorsing the new government's policies. All monks had to study Marxism–Leninism and the religious hierarchy, the *sangha*, was dismantled. The ceremonial fans carried by senior monks were smashed as part of the general levelling.

Addressing a training course for Buddhist teachers on 17 October 1976, Politburo member Phoumi Vongvichit said, '[T]he Lord Buddha tried to abolish class distinctions. In this way the Lord Buddha became involved in revolutionary politics. Monks should mix current politics with Buddhist politics when they give sermons . . . The policy of the party and government is merely to request Buddhist monks to give sermons to teach the people and to encourage them to understand that all policies and lines of the party and government are in line with the teachings of the Lord Buddha'.

The monks were forbidden to accept donations of food and forced to labour in the fields, thus breaking their religious vows. But after a while the obsession with Marxist purity was abandoned. As a result, you still see old monks in Laos, unlike in Cambodia where they were all exterminated.

Vientiane was beginning to strike me as a city of amnesic misfits: widows, foreign expatriates, Lao returnees, and sidelined politicians, unable to say where they'd come from and unsure where they were going. It was as if the revolution had thrown them all in the air and left them floating. But one thing had settled back into place since then: at least you could get a decent meal again.

I was lunching with a prince at L'Opéra—a converted warehouse which was the first new restaurant to open in eighteen years and which boasted a wine list, an espresso machine, and a Neopolitan proprietor whose mood swings were a reliable indicator of the vagaries of doing business in Vientiane.

Souphaxay Souphanouvong would not have called himself a prince. It was twenty years since his late father had formally renounced the family's heritage and assumed the presidency of the revolutionary republic. I arrived to find him seated alone at the window, a mobile phone at his elbow, smoking a Benson & Hedges and glancing now and then at the Nam Phou fountain outside. We had not met before, but I think I would have recognised him anywhere. He had inherited not only his father's stocky build, moustache and smile but also—you could tell from his confident, brisk movements—the Souphanouvong swagger. He wore a fawn safari suit with epaulettes and two rings, a huge sapphire on his left hand and on his right a signet with the letter 'S' in diamonds. He looked as if he could stand up against a hurricane.

Now, at an age when his father had been a revolutionary, Souphaxay was working at the Committee for Planning and Cooperation, the organisation which controlled foreign investment in Laos, and was involved in a power struggle with conservatives in the lead-up to the party congress.

'They tend to believe that you can solve problems by decree,' he said. 'This is not pragmatic. Laos won't be accepted into APEC or the World Trade Organization if we don't play the game.'

What had it been like to grow up as the son of Souphanouvong, I asked. Souphaxay said his father had never told him and his siblings they were princes or communists. Life in hiding, in the caves of Viengsai near the north-east border with Vietnam, had been the same for them as for other cave-dwelling children. After the war, when the family had moved to Vientiane, Souphaxay had nursed his uncle, Souvanna Phouma, who was dying slowly of heart disease and whose immediate family had fled to Paris.

Souphaxay remembered his father and uncle as old men, arguing to the end about politics as Souvanna Phouma taught his half-brother to play bridge. Souphanouvong was still president then, but he had slowed down a lot since having a stroke in 1983 on his way to a non-aligned nations summit meeting in Zimbabwe. Souphaxay laughed when I suggested things in Laos might have been different if the two men had begun playing bridge earlier. He said Souphanouvong liked to reminisce not about the years in the caves but about the early days of Lao nationalism, at the end of the Second World War. Souvanna Phouma, whom he thought an honest patriot, had simply lingered on, excluded from government but hoping some day to make a contribution to his country.

Now it was the party's authority that was waning, as its role in society was taken over by the military. The authoritarian nationalism that prevailed elsewhere in South-East Asia was seeping into Laos. The black Russian limousines that once scuttled along Vientiane streets with party chiefs hidden behind their dark-tinted windows had been replaced by Toyota Crowns with even darker windows carrying military officers. Six of the nine Politburo members were current or former generals. General Choummaly, the Defence minister, had been pushing for years to build an eco-tourism resort cum casino on the Nam Ngum reservoir. Army-owned trading companies were the biggest and most powerful in the country. Foremost among these was the Mountainous Areas Development Company based at Lak Sao in Bolikhamsay province. The village had been transformed into a go-ahead town of 12 000 people with a modern hospital, schools and an airport. Headed by General Chang Sayavong, the company kept people busy in agriculture, forestry, building, infrastructure, handicrafts processing, tourism and, allegedly, cattle smuggling. One of Chang's pet projects was a zoo staffed by foreign experts, which was constantly replenished with wild animals fleeing his company's own logging activities. But this was nothing new. Judy Rantala, the wife of a USAID official, saw elephants hauling teak logs at Ban Houeysai, which, she wrote in *Laos: A Personal Portrait from the mid-1970s*, was part of the collusion between 'enterprising and unscrupulous foreign merchants' and 'greedy government officials who granted them permissions to log . . . The labourers were paid pitiful wages and forests were irretrievably denuded. Millions of dollars were being realised from these valuable teak harvests, but neither the Lao people nor the Lao economy benefited.'

Some of the forests Rantala mentioned belonged to the king, whose youngest son, Sauryavong Savang, was director of Forestry in the department of Crown Properties. The opium trade, too, had royal connections. During the 1960s it was said to be controlled in northern Laos by General Ouane Rathikone, commander-in-chief of the Royal Lao Army. But according to their enemies the Pathet Lao also engaged in the trade. Just before the arrival of the Japanese in 1945, Phoumi Vongvichit, later a Politburo member, allegedly made off with the entire opium crop of Sam Neua province, which had been stored in the provincial headquarters building.

A document circulating within the Lao exile community suggested a death-bed renunciation by the 'Red Prince' of his life-long commitment to Marxist orthodoxy. (The first sentence was understood to refer to Souphanouvong's Vietnamese wife, Nguyen Thi Ky Nam, or Vieng Kham, to use her Lao name, whom many saw as a tool of the Vietnamese.)

> Because of my worship of women's beauty, I was a deaf and blind person in my youth. Now I reflect on this and I recognise my mistakes. I have never thought that Vietnam is capable of committing so many brutal crimes against our country and our people. In the past, we have agreed that once the war is over, Vietnamese will stay in Vietnam and Laotians will stay in Laos, although the two nations would continue their friendship as brotherly countries. I personally don't know when they will cremate my body, but the crimes I have committed against our country will never disappear with the cessation of my breath and my crema- tion. Before I could not say anything. I wish to leave something behind, and I urge all the children of Laos of all ethnic groups and genders to unify, and to resolve to wash the crimes I have committed against our country and

our people. I just realise now that I am not a decent and patriotic person towards our country; it has only dawned on me when my bones are about to be boiled. All comrades, who are still healthy and strong, when you hear my call, please change and reform your thought so that you could guard our nation and the national treasure of our people, of which the most important is your life. Dear brothers and sisters, all the children of Laos, those in foreign lands in particular, are the true patriots. They are far-sighted and intelligent. Their love for our country surpasses all. You must not let Laos die. My children, especially those still in Laos, you must reform yourselves and embrace a new way of thinking, particularly the thinking of all Laotian children in foreign lands, so that you all would be fruitful and helpful to our country and our people. I believe that if you all understand the situation as I do now, we shall remain immortal. Before I die, I urge you all to do as requested and, for this, I am sure Laos will always be Laos.

This text had been sent to the exile newspaper *Sieng Lao Seri*. According to overseas Lao, it had been reprinted in *The Vientiane Times*, but the editor, Somsanouk Mixay, told me he'd never heard of it. I suppose it's not uncommon for old men to blame all their mistakes on sex, and regrets are an unavoidable feature of old age. But this recantation seemed to me a crude forgery. Souphaxay agreed, saying his father had never expressed any such doubts: 'Did he regret his role in the abolition of the monarchy? It was never an issue we spoke about. He simply believed that it was an anachronism.'

On 9 January 1995, Souphanouvong died of a heart attack. He was cremated on That Luang esplanade in Vientiane. The monks accorded him full Buddhist rites, as they had done for Kaysone in November 1992. The pall-bearers wore the traditional *sampot*, but the red flag of the party was also flown. A witness told me that as the flames began to consume the coffin, a black limousine pulled up and an hysterical woman leapt out and rushed to the pyre as if to throw herself on it in what Indians call *sati*—the ultimate act of wifely devotion. The woman was Vieng Kham Souphanouvong. Bodyguards bundled her back into the car, which drove off at high speed.

Rumours had it that Souphanouvong's body was not even in the coffin but had been cremated several days earlier.

The 'Red Prince' and his wife had helped deliver Laos to Marxism–Leninism, but their children seemed not to have been born with collectivised genes. Partly thanks to their father's power and the opportunities it provided, they had been well educated and given senior positions. As long as the system had rewarded them, they supported it. Now, with their father and mentor gone, they had to survive on their own in the political fray. At the 1996 party congress, Khamphoui Keoboualapha, the leading reformer and Souphaxay's boss, was dumped from the Politburo. Souphaxay's brother Khamsai had earlier been dropped from his post as Finance minister and dumped from the party's central committee. But like all the sons of powerful families—except the family which once was most powerful of them all—they were still players.

5

Riding with the colonel

In April 1976, the Pathet Lao newspaper *Sieng Pasason* reported a ceremony in Luang Prabang at which King Savang Vatthana handed over his palace to the state for use as a national museum. The previous month the British ambassador had been denied access to the palace and had noted anger among the townsfolk at the treatment of the king.

Even before the revolution, on 21 July 1975, the *Vientiane Post* had reported that more than 100 military personnel from the rank of lieutenant to general had been involved in re-education 'seminars'. 'They have had their eyes opened,' it said. 'This has given them greater confidence in the provisional government and taken away the fear they may have harboured of the patriotic forces. All fear and distrust has disappeared thanks to the direct and meaningful exchange of views.'

After taking power, the Pathet Lao targeted social undesirables for reform. Vientiane's prostitutes, drug addicts, gamblers and lost children were rounded up and sent to two islands recently formed in the rising reservoir of the Nam Ngum dam, Don Thao and Don Nang—literally, Gentlemen's Island and Ladies' Island. Sisana Sisane, then minister for Information and

Culture, was quoted as saying the round-ups would 'teach the city dwellers how to follow the revolutionary line'. But many would die. Soon the numbers of seminarists had reached tens of thousands—160 000, according to the Union of Lao Organisations in America—and dozens of camps had sprung up across the country. The highest-security facilities were located around Viengsai, near Vietnam. In a speech on 6 January 1977, Politburo member—Phoumi Vongvichit said, 'Those former bosses who never worked with their own hands must learn how to do so, because under the socialist system everyone must engage in both mental and physical labour. Some persons have asked me when they will be allowed to return home. I cannot answer this question, nor fix a definite time for their return. It is like asking a doctor how long he is going to keep his patient.'

Officially, the 70-year-old king was still 'supreme advisor' to the president, but since giving up the throne, Savang Vatthana had taken no part in politics. His main concerns—to maintain Wat Xieng Thong and the orchard at Pak Xuang—were frustrated by the loss of his property and royal stipend, and the need to obtain permission to travel outside Luang Prabang, which in his case was not given. The king and his immediate family remained in the royal capital under house arrest for fifteen months.

The most detailed account ever published of the circumstances surrounding their removal from Luang Prabang appeared in the Vietnamese Army newspaper *Quan Doi Nhan Dan* in January 1984, almost seven years later. Savang Vatthana, the paper said, had almost escaped to Thailand during a revolt which was only crushed after heavy fighting. The former king had been placed under house arrest after turning down the Pathet Lao's offer to act as advisor to President Souphanouvong. 'Reactionary forces directed from abroad' had tried on several occasions to arrange his escape, most daringly in March 1977, when 'pirates' attacked Luang Prabang with the aim of taking the king to a helicopter in a nearby town and then to Thailand, where supporters wanted him to lead a government in exile. The paper said this attempt had the support of the chief of communist forces guarding the king, a General Chantalansi. It took four hours for government troops to fight off the rebels. 'Thus ended the last days of the king of Laos in Luang Prabang.'

The Soviet newsagency Tass had reported on 16 March 1977 that a plot to overthrow the government had been organised by Prince Sisouphan Tharangsi, the ex-king's brother and former secretary-general of the royal palace, with the support of the ex-king, Crown Prince Vong Savang and members of the former King's Council. As a result, it said, the king had been sent to a 're-education centre'.

A diplomat who was based in Vientiane at the time told me: 'The government made no formal announcement of what had happened to the king. We heard it first from one of our local staff in the embassy, the daughter-in-law of Sisouphan Tharangsi. She'd had a phone call from Luang Prabang on 12 March, saying that on that morning they'd taken away the king and his family, including her father-in-law and several other senior officials. Ministers we met socially gave the impression that the king had outlived any useful purpose, but they insisted they had no intention of executing him. They'd say "We want to cure the patient, not kill him."'

By late March, Deputy Foreign Minister Nouphan Sithphasai was telling people in Vientiane that the king was 'in a safe place, a long way from the Mekong'. Since his abdication, the king had been allowed to work and was given Pathet Lao personnel to help him. However, he had proved uncooperative. His brother had been in contact with the rebels, who had attacked the airfield a few days after the king was taken away. The government now regarded the king as a security risk and had acted just in time. Stories of a rebel attack on Muong Nan, 50 kilometres south of Luang Prabang, were published, even in the foreign media. But I had met the village head man, and he denied there was ever any trouble there.

During those early months of 1977, the king's former right-hand man, deposed Prime Minister Souvanna Phouma, was still a fixture on the Vientiane cocktail circuit, with his penchant for good cigars and bow ties. Since the revolution he had tried to help the new government where possible, most notably in February 1977, when he had been dispatched to Luang Prabang to urge the former king and crown prince to go to Vientiane for a meeting of the Supreme People's Assembly, the rubber-stamp parliament which had replaced the National Assembly. Three months later, Souvanna recalled the trip at a dinner hosted by the British ambassador. The king, he said, had rebuffed his entreaties, more or less telling him to mind his own business. According to a fellow dinner guest, 'Souvanna said that shortly afterwards, the king had made contact with the rebels by radio, asking them to rescue him.'

Boun Kham slurped the last of his aromatic *foi*, wiped his mouth with a napkin and placed his chopsticks across the top of the bowl. He picked up the photocopied article I'd passed him across the outdoor cafe's table and read impassively while picking his teeth. He frowned and shook his head. 'Thus ended the last days of the king of Laos in Luang Prabang,' he read. He snorted. 'This newspaper prints fairytales!'

I had to admit that during my term in Hanoi, the army newspaper had impressed me more by its accuracy in reflecting the party line than by its regard for the facts. 'Look at this,' Boun Kham continued. 'It says nothing about what happened to the king. Nothing about Viengsai. Why doesn't the Vietnamese army know about it? They have soldiers in the camps, advising the Lao government. They know everything, but say nothing.'

But if they wouldn't, then who would? By March 1977 the last independent correspondent had been expelled from Laos and the Tass correspondent was no doubt a KGB colonel.

'There was no big rescue attempt,' Boun Kham said, sighing. 'His family told the king many times to leave Laos, but he refused! His youngest son, Sauryavong, swam across the Mekong to Thailand in November 1975. Before he left he met him. His father told him it's OK to leave. But he himself would not leave. He wanted to stay with his people.'

According to the Vietnamese report, the Lao army had besieged the traitorous General Chantalansi at the old royal palace. But why there? Savang Vatthana no longer lived there. So what had happened on that day? Boun Kham turned up his nose, as he always did when discussing difficult matters.

'There was some shooting across the Mekong. Behind Chompet temple. But it's nothing! Some shooting in the air. By the Pathet Lao soldiers themselves. They wanted to make people think somebody was coming. Some Thai soldiers or something. That night, an army truck goes to the king's house, and Savang Vatthana and Queen Khamphoui are put in the truck. The same truck gets the crown prince and his brother Sisavang, and the king's brother Sisouphan Tharangsi, and the chief of protocol Tongsouk, and the chef du cabinet Manivong Khammao, and also Bovone Vatthana, the king's half-brother, who used to be governor of Sayaboury. When they are all together, the truck takes them to the airport, and they fly—two helicopters—to Viengsai.'

'Did they resist?'

'Of course they cannot! The Pathet Lao have guns. When a man has a gun, you cannot do anything.'

Not all of those taken to Viengsai were high-ranking family members. The second son, Sisavang, was a farmer who tended the garden at Pak Xuang and was not in the direct line of succession. Second in line to the throne after the crown prince was Mahneelai's eldest son, Soulivong. He was left behind in Luang Prabang and put to work planting rice and cutting bamboo like the rest of the population. After years in the jungle the Pathet Lao didn't know who was who in the royal family.

I tried to imagine the scene as the Pathet Lao troops took them away. Did they excoriate and lambast them as they made their accusations that Sisouphan Tharangsi had made contact with the rebels—or was that charge for public consumption only? Whatever the circumstances, the king would have remained calm. But the crown prince? How would he have coped with the insolence of sullen, bayonet-wielding Pathet Lao soldiers?

When the army truck had deposited the king, queen and the six princes at Luang Prabang airport, they were led to one of the two Russian-built helicopters, which took off through the smoke haze of fallow rice fields being burnt off ahead of planting. It was the last time any of them would see Luang Prabang. The helicopter flew high over the Plain of Jars, where pockets of Hmong resistance still held out against the government, then over the rugged Annamite Range, setting down again amid the limestone karsts of Viengsai. The former stronghold of the Lao communists had by then become one of the largest prison camps in South-East Asia, and these members of the oldest royal family in Asia were its newest inmates.

Boun Kham had disappeared into the coffee shop's kitchen. He thought nothing of marching into restaurants big and small, inspecting the standard of hygiene and ordering the staff around. He would even send them off to the markets to buy fresh produce. In Lao, the English verb 'to eat' is translated by *gin khao*—literally, 'to eat rice'. But Lao cuisine is much more than that. It was Boun who introduced me to the delights of green papaya salad with cabbage, dried pork skin and sour eggplant—a mango version of which we ate with chilli and small crabs caught in the rice paddies—and *laap*, a delicate envelope usually filled with minced meat and chilli, but sometimes with eggplant, onions, mint, and peanuts. Then again, we could subsist quite comfortably on sticky rice, rolled into balls between our palms, dipped in a chilli paste and *padaek*, fermented fish paste, and washed down with Lao beer. With Boun Kham even the humble *foi*—noodle soup with beef, chilli, basil, bean sprouts and fish sauce—became ambrosia. But he drove me nuts by constantly declaring the food was better in the old days. And for a former pilot, he had a strange fixation with fish, ordering them at every opportunity. Once I joked that in a previous life he must have been an *anabas*—a freshwater fish capable of leaping from the water and climbing trees. He loved that, and cracked us both up by saying 'I am an *anabas*!' every time he ordered a meal.

It was two weeks now since my return to Vientiane, and I had adjusted to Lao time, saying *baw pen nyang*—doesn't matter—each time some arrangement went astray. Vientiane was a sleepy town, slumbering most profoundly around Nam Phou fountain, which was overlooked by the shattered, weed-infested former Information Ministry building. The fountain, which at night was a popular drinking spot, was turned off during the day, adding to the area's deserted air. There were more traffic lights and cars than at any time since 1975, but the biggest development project in the city centre was just six storeys tall. In Vientiane, it was almost impossible to believe in change, until it overwhelmed you. They say it was like that in the early 1970s, even as the kingdom shrank in towards the capital and the government gave way.

Straddling the seat of his Honda Dream motor scooter, with me clinging to his back, Boun Kham had picked up an old scent and was shedding the decades. Gone was the maimed re-education camp inmate. In his place rode the dashing young colonel of the Royal Lao Air Force. As we rolled down Lan Xang Avenue, past the Patuxai, he gave a running commentary. 'You like Patuxai? Like Arc d'Triomphe, no? Arch is stolen, you know? The Americans gave Laos concrete for the airport, but we build arch instead . . . Here they had student demonstrations. Stupid! Some students even came from Thailand. They said they didn't want to live under the dictatorship. They went back later. Sure! They got a degree in dictators. Ho, look! Green Latrine . . . Vienglatry. It's an old nightclub, only it used to be on Rue Circulaire. Now they call it Viengratry. No "l", see. They've changed the language.' The colonel pointed out the old National Assembly building opposite, and the green building on the next corner, which was the Lycée. He said the *tulaat saow*, or Morning Market, had formerly been built of wood, and that the traders were mainly Indians and Vietnamese: 'Vientiane has always had too many Vietnamese.'

Racism is par for the course in South-East Asia, but he had a point. To satisfy its need for clerks, the French colonial administration had imported large numbers of Vietnamese. As late as 1943, they comprised the majority of the capital's population. The proportion of Vietnamese in Savannakhet was 72 per cent, in Thakek 85 per cent, in Pakse 62 per cent, in Xieng Khouang 72 per cent.

As Boun Kham told it, there were no *tuk-tuks* in the Vientiane of the 1960s, just indefatigable, colonial-issue Renaults that worked as taxis. The distant hum of B-52s on their way to bomb Sam Neua could be heard in the evenings, and the government depended entirely on foreign aid. It still did, of course, to the tune of 44 per cent of the national budget. In Vientiane, gaudy high-walled villas belonging to rich traders and corrupt government ministers were sprouting again as the gap between rich and poor—a gap the party had promised to abolish—approached pre-revolutionary levels.

Building by building, Boun reconstructed the city, veering left and right to favour his good eye. The Pathet Lao compound had been near the post office opposite the Morning Market, and what was now the Asian Pavilion hotel had been the notorious Constellation, nest of hard-drinking journos. Where I saw a sleepy, shabby town, my Virgil saw history.

From Samsenthai Road, we could see the bristling barbed wire and antennae of the American embassy, my destination. Not wishing to be seen outside those particular gates, Boun Kham dropped me at the scaffold-shielded That Dam, the Black Stupa, a short stroll away. Inside the embassy's cipher-locked doors, portraits of Bill Clinton and then Secretary of State Warren Christopher hung on a wall of the foyer. The building had the look of a radio studio of the 1940s, its rooms sound-proofed with particle-board panels. A map on one wall was peppered with pins showing MIA cases the Joint Task Force had worked on—searches for pilots lost over the Plain of Jars in the early 1960s, or in the south until 1971, when the Americans had flown about 340 sorties a day out of Saigon, Udorn and Guam, and from aircraft carriers in the South China Sea. When it came to detective work in the remote provinces of Indochina, the Joint Task Force Full Accounting were the A team.

I had decided to head up country again, this time to the north-eastern province of Houaphan, and thought it might be useful to talk to members of the Vientiane-based POW–MIA search teams who had worked there. I was to meet Jack Dibrell, the Texan who commanded the detachment, and William Gadoury, whose full title was 'Casualty Resolution Specialist Joint Task Force Full Accounting'. Each handed me a business card with Lao script on the reverse. Of the hundreds of US pilots shot down over Laos, Jack Dibrell said, only one remained officially listed as a prisoner of war—Colonel Charles Shelton, who went down in April 1965. This status remained for 'symbolic reasons'. Intelligence reports indicated he was dead, as was Colonel David Hrdlicka, who had been shot down the following month. I read later in *Time* that the US Air Force, at the request of Shelton's family, had changed his status to 'killed in action' after his wife Marian committed suicide.

Dibrell introduced Gadoury as the 'institutional memory' of the MIA search in Laos, a man who'd been 'on the case' since the early 1980s. Gadoury said the task force had located the initials 'CS' scratched on the wall of a cave near Ban Nathene, a few kilometres north of Viengsai. 'It was 1994, but two witnesses remembered that he'd died of ill health and they took us to where he'd been buried. We dug up the whole side of a hill. These guys were certain of the location to within 10 to 20 metres, and they seemed credible. But lots of years had gone by.'

Three years earlier, on their first visit to the area, they had met a guard who remembered an American. 'He called him "Mr David"—Hrdlicka we assume, but he couldn't remember the surname. He said the prisoner had become sick and died. They stayed in the caves most of the time. They had no fire, so they couldn't boil water, and they just got sick. This David was never chained up. I said, "Weren't you afraid he'd escape?" They said, "Escape to where?" We went part way into the cave where "Mr David" was held, but they cautioned us not to go further for fear of rock falls.

'We returned a couple of years later with Senators John Kerry and Christopher Smith, and they pressed on with the aid of flashlights. We went up a spiral staircase at the rear of the lower chamber. This led to a large auditorium-sized room, complete with a stage. At one time I'm sure it would have been the meeting and entertainment hall.'

Gadoury's matter-of-fact, almost deadpan account of his adventures in the Lao labyrinth was enough to make you break out in a cold sweat. He seemed unaware how weird the whole enterprise sounded. He believed the Joint Task Force had done just about all it could in the cases of Shelton and Hrdlicka.

The MIA search is replete with many ironies. Among them is the fact that Americans risk their lives searching for the remains of other Americans in the jungles of Indochina, but can't find them because bombs dropped by still other Americans have destroyed all trace of them.

'In David's case we had two witnesses to his burial,' said Gadoury, picking the mud off his mountain boots, 'the guy who buried him, and the village chief who watched. They took us to where they recall it happened, a place called Ban Bac, also in the karsts around Viengsai. When we excavated the site we saw evidence that the area had been bombed, and were unable to locate a grave site or any remains.'

The task force had even scaled the terrible heights of Phou Pha Ti, thought to be impregnable until it was overrun by the Vietnamese. 'You can't walk up that mountain,' said Gadoury. 'You need to be lowered down from a helicopter on top. We spoke to the military commander—Colonel Muk from Vietnam—who'd led the sapper team that overran the place. We got him up there and he pointed to the spot where the

Americans were killed. We searched for them but didn't come up with anything.'

The talk around Vientiane was that the whole MIA show would be wound up in two or three years, but pressure in the US to obtain the 'fullest possible accounting' was huge, and Gadoury was hedging his bets. 'As of today, estimates of how long it will take us to complete the excavations of sites we've already found range from three to six years,' he said. 'The most important thing is that we will continue to try to develop new leads.'

I wondered what the Lao thought of this activity. After all, the Americans had bombed the hell out of the place, and they had not always been so polite about the MIA issue, either. In March 1981, a CIA team secretly crossed the Mekong from Thailand, heading for the Nhommarath camp, 65 km from the border, where intelligence reports strongly suggested that American airmen were held. The team was pinned down by Lao army fire for a week, and got no closer than 500 m from the camp. On the basis of their observations from there, they reported that no Americans were held at the camp.

To help end decades of mutual suspicion, a Lao Army delegation was taken to Hawaii to see the Joint Task Force laboratories. I could just see them walking along the beach at Waikiki, festooned with *leis*.

'It was kind of hard breaking in,' said Gadoury. 'The Lao had lots of concerns. But when we showed them our labs, they realised we're really doing this. It's not a cover for something else.'

From the embassy, it was a short walk across town to the offices of Lao Survey & Exploration Services, a small company set up by a laconic Australian called Harold Christensen. The former Perth stockbroker, who was later convicted of improper share dealings, operated from a two-storey villa a stone's throw from the presidential palace. His business was doing well, due mainly to the interest of foreign mining and hydroelectricity companies.

Harold was in his office, surrounded by dozens of maps

held down at the corners by rock samples. He had a way of letting his hands fall on a map before swooping down to peer closely at it, his thick bifocals apparently unable to help him with the fine lines of topography. We were searching for villages. 'It's a bit difficult because the villages keep shifting,' he said.

'Why do they shift?' I asked.

'Slash and burn,' he said. 'They're a bit like you. Only settle down for a year or two at a time. I once had to go across to Samarkan . . .'

He pointed to it. 'It's not far, but because of this bloody mountain range you have to go all the way up here to get to it. Well, between Ban Dong and Samarkan, there are about 50 villages on the map, but I reckon we passed two.'

What a country! Not even cartographers could pin it down. But if maps were elusive, I thought, could history ever be portrayed accurately? Had the trail of the Elephant Kings already disappeared in the amorphous memory of the unmappable land?

The *Vientiane Times* had just reported the re-opening of scheduled flights to Sam Neua, the capital of Houaphan. The airport there had been out of use for five years because of 'damage', and I was to be on one of the first flights into the Pathet Lao heartland. My travel preparations continued at the Service Géographique National, located in a back street off Lan Xang Avenue, which sold maps produced by Soviet cartographers in the 1980s. Not surprisingly, perhaps, in the unmappable country, maps were freely available. These were Russian maps, after all. From the standpoint of national security, there could be nothing to fear. Its foyer was lined with glass cabinets containing compasses and set squares. The Soviet Union remained triumphantly in existence on a map of the world stuck to the wall. Behind a high counter stood a woman who diffidently took the scrap of paper on which I'd scrawled the reference numbers for maps of Sam Neua and Viengsai. Disappearing into a room behind the counter, she soon returned with all five maps. I checked them carefully, while she stood impassively waiting. 'You can have all the maps under the sun,' her expression seemed to say, 'for all the difference it makes.' I waited in vain for an official to rush into the room, horrified at the ease with which I had obtained the maps to these once secret areas, but was instead handed an invoice and pointed towards a hole in the wall marked 'caisse' where sat a plump, grandmotherly lady who did needlepoint with one hand and counted out my change with the other.

It was closing time, which meant a rendezvous with Harold at the open-air bar at the Nam Phou fountain. To sit around Nam Phou, watching the late-afternoon dust settle and washing it down with plastic jugs of *bia sot*—fresh beer—was one of Vientiane's timeless pleasures. The buildings around the Nam Phou circle spoke of competing cultural influences. There was the Italian restaurant L'Opéra, where I had lunched with Souphaxay Souphanouvong, and the Scandinavian Bakery, with its pine-panelled interior. Between Stockholm and Naples, the Vietnamese had occupied a tumbledown terrace with the yellowing pamphlets of their Cultural Centre. Here at the bar were hydro-electricity workers, World Bank consultants and even the odd United Nations apparatchik who'd decided to slum it.

One Nam Phou habitué was a pilot called David who flew choppers for a charter company. On every flight he was accompanied by an officer from the Defence Ministry, who made sure he didn't stray over sensitive areas. He'd covered most of the country, but occasionally, he said, he would still fly into villages where people had never seen a helicopter. 'The kids rush out, all wide-eyed and friendly. That's good, but it's a bit of a worry when they get close to the tail rotor. We pay a guy just to run around and shoo them away. There are so many kids out there in the villages. No electricity, no TV, nothing else to do but procreate, I suppose.'

David spoke with an enthusiast's affection about the ageing Lao Aviation fleet, which included Antonov biplanes with radial engines and the gigantic Mi-26, the largest production helicopter in the world. He said my friends Bill Gadoury and Jack Dibrell of the MIA task force chartered more choppers than anyone else in town.

One had an uncanny sense of the past sitting around the white plastic tables at Nam Phou: all these foreigners working on their projects in the provinces, returning whenever possible to drink and swap tall stories. One fellow had been working on a hydro project on the Ma River, which ran into Vietnam and met the sea at the beach resort of Sam So'n near Thanh Hoa. He told me an American aid project in the area had been badly delayed because some sites were so badly littered with unexploded bombs that they were no-go areas. Half the aid promised for irrigation and opium substitution had been spent on mine clearance, and the money had run out before the projects were completed.

He was with a bird-like American woman who had taught in Vientiane in the 1960s and 1970s and had returned in 1993 to pick up where she had left off. Vientiane was much the same as she'd left it, except that the statue of King Sisavangvong outside Wat Seemuang had been overgrown by an unkempt thicket. She went back to her old school, the former Lycée Vientiane, 'just to have a look'. 'The same maps of the US and Laos are still on the wall,' she said. 'The curtains in the director's office are the same as in 1975.'

I told her of my plans to visit Houaphan. To my astonishment, she said she had already been there. 'I loved Viengsai. Absolutely. I would like to have stayed a week.'

'Why?'

'Peaceful, quiet. The mountains were beautiful.'

'You're pulling my leg. You think it's got tourist potential?'

'Oh, absolutely. If someone picks up that hotel—it's an absolute mess at the moment—but you should stay there. I think it's called the Number One Hotel.'

Next evening I set off for the Champa Lan Xang, a kind of theme park-cum-restaurant, where Boun Kham had gathered a few old-timers to brief me on the bad old days in Sam

Neua. The place looked like a reconstructed labour camp, with huts built of thatch and set around a pond. Only the paddle boats—and the beer—would have been out of place in 'seminar'. Boun Kham's pals were a mixed bag. There was Ounheuanne, a middle-aged man from Sam Neua who'd risen to a senior position in the Vientiane military police under the old regime, and Anou, a shy man in his 40s who now worked for a private company. And there was Michael, a thin, bespectacled Englishman who shook and shivered a lot. He said he was a businessman being held over a barrel by the bribe-seeking deputy prime minister. 'My impression,' he said, 'is that people in the government know they haven't got long left, and are just st-st-stuffing their pockets as fast as they can.'

Over Tigers, and urged on by the colonel, Ounheuanne told how in 1975 he'd been 'invited to have new ideas' on a fact-finding mission to Sam Neua—presumably arranged to show him how police should operate in a people's state. Sixteen years later he was allowed to return to his wife and family in Vientiane. He had spent those years in re-education and labour camps at many different locations, rising before dawn each morning for hard labour until 9 a.m., when classes in the Marxist–Leninist theory began. It looked to have done him no harm, but then he was one of the survivors. He wore a striped shirt with a T-shirt underneath, and had single *baci* strings on each wrist and a chunky silver watch.

'We built a lot of roads and houses in the villages,' he said, 'but we never complained. We always tried to win the confidence of the local people and make them realise that we were good men. Anywhere, anyplace, we could survive like that. They would bring us extra food, or herbal medicines, and sometimes we would sit down and have a drink with them. That's how we survived.'

I had heard elsewhere of officials of the old regime being similarly hijacked. Some were told they were going on government business to China, and were surprised on landing to find local officials speaking Lao.

'*Sabaidee!*' they would greet their hosts, 'You speak excellent Lao.'

'Of course,' came the reply. 'We're Lao.'

'Ah, so what are you doing in China?'

'We're not in China.'

'We're not?'

'No. Welcome to Viengsai!'

It was more or less that way for the last commander of the Royal Lao Army, General Bounpone Makthepharak, who in 1975 visited China and was invited to tour a remote part of the country to inspect the People's Liberation Army activities there. His plane landed in Viengsai, where the general was handed over to the Pathet Lao. The Lao ambassador to Australia in 1975, Khamchan Pradith, belonged to Souvanna Phouma's neutralists. He was persuaded it was safe to return to Laos after the revolution. Soon after he arrived, he boarded a plane to Viengsai and was never seen again. In May 1979, Souvanna Phouma told the *New York Times* that between 10 000 and 15 000 officials and military personnel who had served in his government had been detained, but he knew only what the Pathet Lao told him. In the same interview he claimed Queen Khamphoui was still in Luang Prabang—in fact, she had left the former royal capital two years earlier—and that the seminar prisoners were not held in camps.

I noticed Boun was getting the wild-eyed look of excitement that often preceded a terrible recollection. 'All the time in seminar they would ask you, what is your idea about the government,' he said, indignantly. 'But I'd say, "I don't know. I have no opinion." This made them very angry. My friend said, "Oh, I think the new government is very nice, very good." He left Sam Neua a long time before me.'

'Many friends got depressed in seminar, very depressed,' he said.

A mosquito dive-bombed his ear. He dispatched it with military efficiency. 'They would always be thinking, thinking how high up they'd been, in the army, or the government, before 1975. But now they were nothing! They started to get crazy! They lost their mind, and then they got sick, but they got no medicine in the camp. So they died.'

He opened his hand to reveal the swatted mosquito. 'Just like mosquitoes,' he said. 'They died.'

'We tried to keep healthy in the mind,' added Ounheuanne, who was now in his 60s. 'I used to run up and down the hills in the morning, and chop wood. They gave you weekends free. You could travel around the province and see people, stay overnight in friends' houses. Some men took local wives, especially those whose real wives had fled overseas or forgotten them. That was actually encouraged by the regime—to take a wife from Long Ma.' Long Ma meant 'the valley of the River Ma', on whose banks stood Sop Hao, a former French colonial army camp, and later, the most notorious prison in Laos.

Anou sat quietly, saying little. He'd been involved in the demonstrations against the monarchy outside the palace in Luang Prabang in 1975, and seemed to regret it. 'When the king came to Vientiane for That Luang, he was welcomed by the students,' he said, studying his beer can. 'They lined the road all the way from the airport. They were shouting, "Long live the king!" The party organised the demonstrations. Just a few weeks later, the party changed its line. Then we were shouting, "Down with the monarchy! Out with the king!" After the revolution, Luang Prabang people could see that they had been mistaken. We were very comfortable with the king, even if he was not very good at running the country. We knew him, but we didn't know what would come after. We were afraid of tomorrow.'

Anou's education continued after the revolution, but in the late 1970s he left Luang Prabang for Vientiane. After the abdication and the founding of the Lao PDR, he said, there had been a wave of arrests and forced deportations of Luang Prabang residents to the countryside. Among the first targets were all those who had been working at the court at the time of the revolution. They were rounded up, put on buses, and sent to camps all over the country.

'They sent some people to Muang Noi, and the more senior officials . . .'

'Muang Noi is for small potatoes!' interrupted Boun. 'Big potatoes go to the south or to Sam Neua. Some place where the language is different, and the people are different, so you look different. You can't talk to anyone. Easier to watch what you're doing.'

'They sent the entire military police academy, 750 men. Arrested them in July 1975 and sent them to Xieng Khouang without charging them,' Ounheuanne chimed in. 'Anyway, it's better now. The party only has 60 000 members, you know. And with all this foreign investment, things must change.'

Michael, looking pallid and nervy, swallowed a burp as he intervened. 'My impression is that there is rising discontent among the people,' he said. ' They are fed up with corruption and rising prices, among other things. Of course, not many are willing to stand up and be counted. But the complicity of western governments gives them little encouragement.'

They were big words to be using before an audience for whom English trailed a poor third behind Lao and French. But Ounheuanne, who had the best English of the Lao present, understood enough to disagree.

'I think the west is being clever,' he said. 'They make their investments, and they get power. They can buy these old communist leaders.'

'But what about people like Thongsouk?' said Michael. 'He speaks up against the government, and they send him to rot in Houaphan. And the west keeps investing.'

Three senior officials in the government—Thongsouk Saysangkhi, Latsami Khamoupoui and Feng Sakchittaphong— had been held at re-education camps in Houaphan since 1990. Thongsouk was a former deputy minister for Science and Technology who had resigned in August 1990 after criticising the government for 'restricting popular liberties and democracy'. Latsami, a former deputy minister for Agriculture and Forestry, wrote a letter to the government criticising the political and economic system. Together with Feng, a former official in the Justice Ministry, they had also written an article calling for more democracy. The three had formed a Social Democracy Club and held meetings at which a multi-party political system was advocated. They'd been detained without charge until November 1992, then sentenced to 14 years' jail after a trial at which no defence lawyers were allowed. The charges included 'making preparations to stage a rebellion and conducting propaganda against the Lao PDR'. The three men had been declared prisoners of conscience by Amnesty International.

'I don't agree with Thongsouk's way,' Ounheuanne responded, dismissing Michael's point with a friendly wave of his hand. 'A mouse should not think it can crush an elephant. The mouse must be clever.'

Michael cast me a sidelong glance and whispered that he could introduce me to some enduring critics of the government—as if these ones weren't good enough. Boun managed to close the gap between them by hitting on everyone's favourite bugbear—the Vietnamese.

'Hanoi still controls this country,' he said.

'Absolutely!' said Michael. 'And the west wants to keep these communist governments in power because they're more easily corrupted so as to exploit their resources. Look at what the Thai are doing in Sayaboury province!'

Since Anou had been in Luang Prabang in 1975, I thought he might know something about the fate of the king. I wished I hadn't asked. He looked from face to face, breathing deeply, before answering: 'Most people never knew they had taken Savang Vatthana. You say it happened in 1977. That is correct. But most people don't ask about it. Most people don't talk about it.'

The atmosphere was suddenly strained. Anou seemed to be choking. The others studied him intently. 'B-but I know,' he said finally. 'I know, and I cried when the king was taken. I cried because my father was taken with him.'

Anou tried hard to swallow. So seductive had the student movement of the 1970s been that even the children of those who worked inside the palace were swept up in it. Many, like Anou, had lived to regret their naivety. We all sat there, stunned into silence by Anou's anguish. 'Once, my father was able to write to me,' he went on. 'The letter was carried by a pilot who had flown some Pathet Lao officials to Viengsai. He pleaded with me to send medicine. He had a problem with his toilet. Some infection. He said there was not enough food and life was very hard there. My family immediately sent him several packages of food and medicine and clothing. But we never knew whether he received those things, and we never heard from him again.'

Grave-faced Ounheuanne broke our silence. 'I knew where he lived,' he said, picking at one of his *baci* strings. 'But I was never able to visit him. He was in the same camp with the king and queen. Sop Hao, we call it, the lips of the Hao River, where it meets the River Ma, close to Vietnam. It is an old military camp from the French time. They moved them there because they feared Kong Le, the neutralist general who staged the 1960 coup and who had come back to Thailand, might try to rescue the king. I spent some time in Sop Hao, in the mid-1980s, but by that time the king was dead. It was just a few wooden barracks and a fence, across the river from the village. The prisoners there said the royal family lived in great hardship. There was only a handful of rice per day for each person. No medicine if you got sick. The king was not allowed to speak to other prisoners at Sop Hao. Not even allowed to have any contact. After leaving Viengsai, the king and queen were separated. The king and his son lived alone in one hut. When the king died, they wrapped his body in cloth and tied it to a bamboo pole and it was carried like that by two men to the burial spot.'

Ounheuanne reached inside his jacket and took out a photograph. He handed it to me. 'This was taken in Viengsai,' he said.

The photo showed two elderly people, a man and a woman. I knew who they were, but had never seen them looking so wretched and bedraggled. Savang Vatthana and his queen, Khamphoui, were kneeling on the ground in the Lao style, legs tucked behind them and to one side. Their hands were clasped in prayer and there was a rudimentary flower arrangement, a poor man's *baci* bowl, in front of them. The queen's hair was not held in her characteristic bun, but fell dishevelled over her shoulders, and the king wore a plain black tunic.

'They put him in some kind of uniform,' Colonel Boun said emphatically. 'This was in Viengsai, before they took him to the camp.'

'Kaysone is to blame,' volunteered Michael.

'No,' objected the colonel. 'Khammouane Boupha is to blame. He took our guns away so there'd be no fighting. Then the Pathet Lao came in and started sending everyone away. They lied!'

Twenty years on they were still arguing about who was to blame. 'Henry Kissinger came to Vientiane in January 1973,' said Ounheuanne. 'I helped arrange his security. Big job, but he only stayed here for two hours. He met the cabinet and asked them, "When will you agree to sign a peace deal with the Pathet Lao?" The Defence minister said, "But we have no concessions from them. We know they allow six to seven North Vietnamese divisions to operate on our soil." And Kissinger said, "Well, it's up to you to sign or not to sign. But we, the US, have agreed to stop all aid to Vietnam, Cambodia, and to you."

'When we went to the US embassy and Kilometre Six to ask for fuel and ammunition in May 1975, when the Pathet Lao began their final advance, the ambassador had already gone. The chargé said he had no authority to release any supplies for us. They forgot their best allies, the Hmong, left them to fight their way overland, carrying their injured with them, to Thailand. One group of 2500 Hmong arrived in Nong Khai in December 1977. Eight thousand had left Phou Bia, but the Vietnamese and Pathet Lao gassed and bombed them all the way.'

The government had arranged for me to meet the Minister for Justice, the very same Khammouane Boupha, now 62, who had served in senior government positions since before 1975. He was one of the very few to make a smooth transition to life under the Pathet Lao. The waiting room of his office, housed in a building opposite Vientiane's grand arch, was the size of a broom closet, just large enough for me and a fax machine. After a short wait I was ushered into the office, in which all curtains were drawn and the air-conditioners were on full throttle. The colour scheme was, inevitably, Wattay Blue. The furniture was chipped, a bathmat doubled as a doormat, and the original plastic covering had been left on the sofas. Khammouane was an imposing figure, solidly built, yet he was strangely defensive, with a nervy, impatient way of speaking. His smile was more of a wince, and he wrung his hands. With him was a thin man, the *chef du cabinet* and ministerial translator, who sat perched on the sofa's edge. Khammouane began our meeting by reading from prepared answers to questions I had submitted in advance.

'We're trying to take the state under law,' he said. 'Our system of law is based on the democracy of the people. We have a criminal code, a civil code and an economic law.' He rattled off the nostrums. The revolution had made Laos free and the people the owners of the country. The government had brought peace and was developing the country, paying special attention to the highland people, increasing everyone's rights so that they could be free to make their own choices and decisions. It was a better system which would make everyone equal. When Khammouane had finished reading his answers I asked whether I could ask some more questions. He looked at his pencil-thin assistant, who smiled non-committally. I took that as a yes.

'I had a part in getting rid of the old system,' he said modestly, when I asked why he had ordered his troops to lay down their arms. 'I helped to create the new system successfully without bloodshed, just by campaigning and meeting with officials from the other side. Some people were sent to Sam Neua to understand the ways of the party and also the new government. Afterwards, they were put into the workforce, depending on their knowledge and ability.'

'What happened to the king?' I said. 'You're the Minister of Justice. Was it lawful?' Khammouane looked again at his assistant, apparently disbelieving the translation. I repeated the question.

'They've made a film about twenty years of the Lao revolution,' he said. 'You should look at that.'

'Did the king do something illegal?'

Khammouane took a deep breath.

'In 1977 it was the idea of the government to invite the king to Sam Neua. Some countries were trying to use him.'

To my question about political detainees, Khammouane responded with a trump card; his *chef du cabinet*. Houey Pholsena was the brother of Quinim Pholsena, a former minister whose assassination in the early 1960s had convinced the Pathet Lao that it was too risky to stay in Vientiane. 'Dr Houey spent thirteen years in seminar. Now I have made him the director of my office. When I'm away, and the vice-minister is not here, the director takes on the role of head, with all responsibilities.'

'To mend the damage of war,' he went on, 'people needed to change their way of thinking. Feelings of hatred must be forgotten. When a person fully understands the situation, he can come back. This is the Lao way, the Lao system. Some countries use weapons, but Laos doesn't use that sort of system. If the attitude of the person changes then the sentence is quickly reduced. Those that understand the new situation are given jobs—like Dr Houey.'

The interview ended with handshakes and salutations, but it had not been a meeting of minds, much as we might have liked it to be.

The colonel had his motorcycle with him and invited me to spend the rest of my last night in Vientiane with his family. I settled awkwardly again on the pillion seat, and we rode carefully along Tha Deua road, turning left into the alleyways around the southern Talat Souan Mone district. Boun Kham's family—his mother, second wife Laoly and their baby daughter Noi—lived in a stilt house with thatched roof and walls. The walls were decorated with a gallery of photographs of handsome young men and women, dashing lieutenants, ministers in former royalist governments. Nowadays Laoly was the family's main breadwinner, working a small patch of land on the banks of the Mekong and selling her produce in the market. Noi was looked after by Boun's mother, leaving the colonel free to roam around all day. He was too old to be rehabilitated in the air force and unwilling to demean himself by doing manual work. He'd graduated as a pilot and navigator from the French Air Academy outside Marseilles and flown missions over Indochina for both the French and the Americans. As a former forward air guide, for bombing runs, he was a collaborator and war criminal as far as the Pathet Lao were concerned.

Laoly greeted me warmly, and soon I was seated with a cup of green tea on the comfy thatch floor, watching Thai television. A clock on the wall bore the words 'Wel' and 'Come' in gaudy, flashing lights. The old woman was lying in a cot under a mosquito net. She smiled at me, and beautiful three-year-old Noi found me an exciting novelty. She rolled around on the floor, grappling with a brightly painted plastic duck. Then she showed me her book of the Roman alphabet, and we ran through the names of various things in English and Lao. 'Sabaidee, bonjour,' she said at one point.

Laoly spoke a little English. Boun had taught her and was also teaching Noi. They laughed at the way she had said, 'Mummy, I'm here,' when Laoly had returned to the house that afternoon. Boun was always playing with his languages, cross-referencing wherever possible. Even teaching his daughter English was a form of disobedience for the old rebel. 'Patron!' he'd say, out of the blue. 'Same in English and French!' At 57, he was still a handsome man, scrubbed clean, lean, but well built, trained at the French air force academy at Salonde Provence, but who had spent the best years of his life in re-education. Nobody could return what had been taken away—like his first wife, who was faithless in adversity. But he had his consolations, and they were in the thatched stilt house with us that balmy evening.

6

Sam Neua

Houaphan was the cradle of the Lao revolution. Here the Pathet Lao had burrowed underground to survive American bombardment. It was an experience they never forgot. Here, too, might lie the answer to the fate of the last king.

A cold wind lashed the dirt airstrip at Sam Neua, sending eddies scurrying into the thatched shacks that encroached upon the runway. Toppled fuel tanks labelled in Russian fringed the cratered, one-lane road which led into Sam Neua past stilt houses, free-ranging turkeys and Lao men in army windcheaters and fur hats. The town squatted obstinately in a small valley on the northern arm of the Sam River, about 35 km from the Vietnamese border. The market hugged the river, and beyond it a couple of wide, featureless streets made a vain stab at a town grid before surrendering their order to the hills. All but two of the place's pre-war French villas had been flattened by bombing. The rubble had now been replaced by simple austere timber and concrete structures, none higher than two storeys. Some buildings consisted of little more than sheets of metal pinned together. It was very quiet.

The Dok Mai Deng guest house had bare wooden floorboards, low ceilings and room rates of $1.50 a night—which consoled me for having been charged double the normal airfare because I was a foreigner. The Foreign Ministry's Khen Sombandith had vomited theatrically several times during the flight from Vientiane. Accompanying me was apparently a plum assignment, and he'd spent the previous evening celebrating. 'Too many bottoms up,' he explained. 'Four people, two bottles of cognac.'

Khen suggested that we drop our gear at the guest house, then head for the provincial headquarters, overlooking the bridge across the Nam Sam. When we got there, a shiny black Russian car and some weather-beaten jeeps were parked outside. Inside, an aide to Governor Somphan Penkhammy, sporting a Russian-style fur hat and reading a volume by Korea's Kim Jong-Il, said the governor was out of town, but that he would organise a meeting with one of his deputies. I asked him what people in this chilly, spartan outpost did for fun. Football and 'chatting', he said.

The people of Sam Neua are predominantly T'ai, and their colourful tribal dress enlivened the dour street market. Carrying babies in slings on their backs, Hmong and T'ai women browsed among the meat and vegetables; one cooked strips of marinated squirrel's brain, another sold lottery tickets. One stall holder said she paid 50 *kip* a day rent. To move into the new undercover market taking shape behind her would cost twice that. A dog stiffened by rigor mortis lay in the road until a man picked it up, balanced it across the bar of his bike and cycled off. There was one beggar, an elderly man who said he'd lost his foot in the war against the French and had been dependent upon the generosity of others for 40 years. Several stalls proffered medicines—Marwitt's kidney pills, large jars of pink chloroquine for malaria, and bubble packs of Fansidar, for the more lethal cerebral malaria. At the state-run store, a spry woman in a blue cardigan sat among plastic bowls, batteries, sheet metal, screwdrivers, and nuts and bolts—everything except customers. Next door, a shop run by the Trade ministry sold garments from Oudomsai, but again there were no buyers. The man in charge said this was 'normal'. Khen, meanwhile, had found a cure for his hang-over—fertilised chicken egg, the only egg that's crunchy even after it's been shelled. He swallowed the solid grey-green oval whole, insisting it was delicious, burping loudly and flexing his muscles in a vain effort to get me to try one.

Eating out in Sam Neua put a new twist on the term 'bring your own', because here you had to bring your own food. The proprietor of Joy's was unwilling to risk any *kip* investing in food which no-one might order. Instead, he advised cus-tomers to fetch their ingredients from the market outside his door. We bought a pumpkin, a carp-like fish and a chicken, delivered them to him, and promised to return to eat them that evening.

Loitering in the market, I felt less noticed than on the streets of Hanoi or Vientiane, even though outsiders rarely came here. People seemed instinctively to mind their own business. Minding foreigners' business was the task of the Committee for Planning and Cooperation. In its grey concrete building I met chairman Chan Dee Onlat Bounmee, a small man whose neatness was disturbed only by crooked teeth, clutching at paperwork as it blew off his desk. Mr Chan Dee frankly admitted there was no foreign investment in Houaphan province. 'We'll welcome it,' he said. 'Tourists as well. But we have no decent hotels, and our roads are very bad.'

Twenty years of socialist rhetoric had failed to provide a decent healthcare system in Laos, and Sam Neua's only hospital was a dirty, dangerous place which showed how little progress had been made since 1975. The iron bed frames were covered not with mattresses but with pieces of plywood, and the wind howled through paneless windows. At least there were mosquito nets, but these were little consolation for the patients, most of whom already had malaria. There appeared to be no staff. Families nursed their own sick. It was easy to see why the average life expectancy in Laos was only 50 years, and why almost one child in five died before reaching age five. The bronchial cries of babies on Fansidar stabbed the air. A boy on a drip was being fed sticky rice from a basket by his father. The grandmother of one child was a 63-year-old T'ai farmer called Yeh, whose gnarled face and elephant-skin ankles and toes were covered in a head cloth, black tunic and embroidered blue *sin*. She wore large silver earrings in elongated lobes, and had walked 40 km from Long Ma, carrying the baby in a sling.

If you tire of seeing monks in Laos, go to Sam Neua. I hadn't seen a *bonze* since arriving, although the drab streets could have benefited from their dazzling orange robes. At the town's only *wat*, which had been badly damaged during the war, I met Maha Thong Phone, who had arrived in Sam Neua in 1978 and said renovation of the temple began the following year. The government had provided the labour—work gangs formed from the ranks of re-education camp prisoners. 'The carvers were very good,' the monk said. 'They'd obviously worked on *wat*s before. I think they were from Vientiane and Luang Prabang. There were some very skilled people in the camps.'

The doors of Wat Phosai had survived the bombing, and were old and deeply carved. Two battle-scarred *stupas*, one of them leaning alarmingly, stood in the centre of the town. A solitary French-style villa, a two-storey ochre-stucco building with an iron roof, had served as a flop house since 1977 but had just been taken over by private interests, who were renovating it. The Hotel Pan Xai, named after the new owner, would charge at least $5 a night, making it the most expensive hotel in town.

Back at the more modest Dok Mai Deng guest house, I discovered there was no running hot water, but the friendly owner produced five full thermos flasks. Standing on a bare concrete floor by the light of a candle, I poured the steaming water into a large plastic bucket, diluted it with cold water, and began ladling it over myself. The bucket wash revived me, and my spirits rose another notch when Sam Neua's town generator kicked in and the Dok Mai Deng lit up. Come dinner time, I found Khen seated at the bottom of the stairs, putting on a pair of leather slippers. He said slippers were designed for people who get drunk a lot.

The night air was cold as we crossed the main street, dimly lit by household light bulbs suspended over the road every 20 m or so. Flashlight beams played on the road as a few people moved about in the semi-darkness. Twenty years after leading Laos to liberation, Sam Neua was still getting only three hours' electricity a day, from 6.30 to 9.30 in the evening. The market was deserted now, and rats foraged among the vegetable waste in the street. It was a relief to reach Joy's, where a television set and open hearth created a cheerful atmosphere. Cases of fish sauce, Ovaltine, Johnnie Walker Red Label and orange crush were stacked against the walls beside a small Buddhist altar with burning joss sticks and Chinese calligraphy. The cook was splitting garlic cloves with a mallet and frying them with the skins on. We hadn't bought garlic, so these were his contribution. The wooden tables were set with cheap vinyl tablecloths and blue plastic toilet-paper dispensers. Khen brightened when the beer came. It was Lao beer, flown all the way from Vientiane and sold here at double the price. Houaphan province had been too busy liberating Laos to build its own brewery.

A group of local men who'd already eaten sat picking their teeth with blunt toothpicks, engrossed in the Chinese TV show 'Dragon Sword'. Another table was neatly set for six diners whose arrival was awaited. Dinner came in the form of a stew containing our *panai*, or carp, a watery chicken curry, rice and steamed pumpkin. But before we could begin Khen jumped up to greet a dark-haired man who walked into the restaurant with his hands dug deep into the pockets of a light-grey suit, his shirt buttoned to the neck. This was Lamphan, the representative of the local authority, who would accompany us everywhere we went in Houaphan.

Lamphan had been informed by the provincial headquarters of our arrival and had come to discuss our itinerary. A former organiser of the Youth Union, he was born in Sam Neua and had worked in the local government since 1977. His thick black hair was swept back off a dual-purpose face—grinning from the mouth while the eyes watched the room. Through Khen, I explained my purpose; to collect material for stories about the twentieth anniversary of Pathet Lao power. Lamphan nodded that it was no problem. I proposed we begin with a day in the countryside, followed by a day in Sam Neua to meet officials. A good plan, Lamphan said. As to the day in the countryside, I suggested we start by driving early in the morning to Viengsai, then continue along Route Six to the village of Sop Hao, at the junction of the Ma and Hao rivers. Khen's translation faltered, and he asked me to repeat what I had said. When I had done so, he paused, smiling a weak, frozen smile. Lamphan took advantage of the delay to begin eating Khen's dinner, doing so in a serious, professional way which suggested he was quite practised at helping himself to other people's food. But when Khen finally stammered out a constipated translation of my suggested itinerary, Lamphan stopped eating and looked me straight in the eye.

His gaze was distracted by the arrival of five well-dressed Asians and a red-bearded European in mountain gear, who took their seats at the set table, nodding politely in our direction. Lamphan, his eyes now glued to the newcomers, whispered something out of the corner of his mouth to Khen. The European called for drinks in fluent Lao, then, having made sure his guests were settled, stood up and approached our table.

'Hi!' he said, with an open smile and an American accent. 'I'm Tom Love. What brings you to Sam Neua?'

Tom had been working for the aid group Food for the Hungry in Houaphan since 1990. Others, like the Quakers and Mennonites, had come and gone, he said, but only 'the Foodies' had stayed, working on small irrigation–hydroelectricity projects for remote villages. The invitation, or rather the order to work in the revolutionary province, had come from President Nouhak himself. 'When we came, he made a speech saying that since the revolution, nothing had happened in this area. We were assigned to work here. We didn't have a choice!'

So far, Food for the Hungry had built 30 weirs costing $7000 each. Tom's guests were journalists from Seoul inspecting a South Korean-funded project in Xieng Kho district on the River Ma. 'Xieng Kho was the first liberated district in Laos,' he said, mainly for the benefit of Lamphan and Khen, I gathered. 'You're a true patriot if you're from here.'

As he spoke, he juggled a flashlight—standard equipment, he said, for living in Sam Neua. He was called back to his table by the arrival of dinner, a plastic colander full of *nok seet* and *nok peet*—sparrows and rice birds—chicken claws in soup, beans with chicken liver (our chicken didn't have any) and deep fried pork ribs.

Continuing to watch the foreigners' table, Lamphan told me there was a fuel shortage in Sam Neua so it might be difficult to venture outside the town the following day. Houaphan, he explained, was dependent on Vietnam for salt and petrol. Petrol from Vietnam was yellow in colour, whilst that used in Vientiane, which was from Thailand, was red. The only storage facility in Houaphan, at Nathen, was now moribund, so fuel had to be trucked in from Vietnam as needed. During the rainy season the road would get cut, but even in the dry season it was difficult to estimate the need correctly, which led to frequent shortages.

'Our problem is we're isolated,' he said. 'It's expensive to get here and our roads are lousy. The weather's often bad, so planes can't land. Before the airport was fixed we could go two to three months without a flight from Vientiane and then only Antonovs could land at Viengsai, or helicopters at Sam Neua. Cups and saucers cost twice here what they do in Vientiane. A bottle of beer costs 850 *kip* in Vientiane, here it's 2000! In Sam Thai and Xieng Kho they get two rice crops a year. Here in Sam Neua we get one. Electricity is too expensive. I have three lights, an iron, and a TV and it costs me 4000 *kip* a month. In Vientiane, Khen has a refrigerator, fan, hot water and TV and he pays 2500 *kip*.'

Still, as an official, Lamphan was much better off than most people. I told him I knew I could trust him to come through with the petrol, and I wouldn't mind paying a little extra if necessary. He disappeared into the night, ostensibly in search of fuel.

Tom, meanwhile, had finished dinner and waved goodbye to his Korean friends. I suggested Khen turn in, then joined the American for a nightcap. I asked what he knew about the re-education camps. Were any still operating?

'This province is very sensitive and cautious about outside involvement,' he said, squeezing his lumberjack hands. 'One of our best Lao workers was a man from Vientiane who was very good at motivating villagers to contribute to projects. You know, he'd go around telling the Lao to help themselves, how the old days when they could live off Soviet aid were gone. But by the time word of his speeches reached the provincial headquarters, those talks of his had become anti-Soviet propaganda, and we were told in no uncertain terms that our man was no longer welcome in the province.'

Tom had been too busy building weirs to notice much else, but he did tell an interesting story about a royalist army officer who'd spent sixteen years in detention. In 1991, there was still a functioning re-education camp on the main road between Viengsai and Sop Hao. It consisted of a dozen or so buildings and held about nine prisoners, the numbers having been reduced greatly over the years. Not wanting to get involved, Tom had been careful not to stop there, but one day the local crew he was travelling with decided to pause in the village for lunch.

'After a while, we noticed this guy nearby, who obviously was not a villager. He was just too sophisticated, you know, he spoke English. Turns out he'd been there for sixteen years. We got talking to this guy, who had worked with the Americans during the war. He took us to his house and it was incredible. He had built himself this fully functioning bar there, with bar stools and army memorabilia on the walls. But he didn't want to speak in English in case there were any misunderstandings. You know, "They all think I'm CIA or something." So we spoke in Lao.

'One year later, another of our trucks was passing through that camp when this guy runs out on to the road, waves down the truck, sticks his beaming face inside the cabin and yells, "Guess what? In two weeks, I'm going to Chicago!" They had finally decided to let him go.'

Returning to the Dok Mai Deng, I settled down to enter some notes in my laptop. I'd been at it only a few minutes when the faint blue screen suddenly flickered and died, along with the room light. It was 9.37 p.m.: lights out in Sam Neua. On the street outside the only illumination was provided by flashlights groping about like blind men's sticks. I finished my notetaking on paper by candlelight.

Houaphan had changed hands many times since the defeat of the Vietnamese armies by a people called the Ai Lao in 1337. Early Vietnamese accounts referred to Laos as a lethal desert, and the emperors of Hue had difficulty persuading their troops to fight in a region believed to be teeming with ghosts and debilitating diseases. But fight they did, regaining and losing control of Houaphan sporadically until the 1830s, when Thai armies helped the king of Luang Prabang take it back from the Vietnamese. The area slumbered under French colonial control until 1953, when the communist Viet Minh forced French and royalist forces to vacate the province. The Pathet Lao were then allowed to set up their government in Sam Neua while the Vietnamese used it as a base for thrusts into the Plain of Jars and South Vietnam. Kaysone Phomvihan, the half-Vietnamese Pathet Lao leader, stayed in Houaphan while his comrades were in Vientiane participating in coalition governments. Later, when US bombing forced him into the caves at Viengsai, he would travel once a week by truck to Hanoi for meetings with Ho Chi Minh, Vo Nguyen Giap and the other Viet Minh leaders. In the 'liberated zone' the Pathet Lao ran a parallel government and disseminated propaganda via Sisana Sisane's radio station, staking their claim to national leadership. After the revolution they signed a treaty with Vietnam which would bind Laos's fortunes to those of its larger neighbour for the next 25 years. Several secret protocols in the agreement provided for close military cooperation and set the location of the common border.

In Sam Neua, the dawn is red. At 6.30 a.m., the Ministry of Culture loudspeakers mounted on lamp posts began their ritual scourging of the population, bellowing distorted music and messages. Fiery streaks darted across the sky as the sun came up over the mountains, and the greyness of the main street was highlighted by the impossibly pink tracksuit of a lone jogger.

The lure of making a few dollars had apparently outweighed Lamphan's concerns about the threat posed to national security by taking me to Sop Hao. He arrived twenty minutes late driving a jungle-green Russian jeep for which he'd scrounged a litre of petrol here and there from local households. Crossing the bridge, we headed north-east past the airport. The sun flashed on crowds of yellow *dok khom* flowers and signs allotting firewood rights to individual villages. Black pigs with coarse hair were everywhere, the sows so heavily pregnant that their stomachs scraped the ground. Each pig wore a yoke-like wooden collar up to a metre long, as if for pulling a plough. The collars were designed to stop the pigs slipping through vegetable garden fences. Khen said the bigger the collar, the 'naughtier' the pig.

The road descended past a Hmong village called Ban Houakhang and into a broad valley dotted with dozens of limestone karsts reminiscent of those in Guilin, China. The descent continued through hairpin bends for about 4 km, ending at the village of Hang Long, meaning 'end of the tail'. Lamphan said that during the war people would drive at night without headlights, as any movement would attract the unwelcome attention of American reconnaissance planes and the bombers that followed them. The Forward Air Guides (FAGs), often Lao with local knowledge, would drop flares at the sight of any road traffic, illuminating the area sufficiently for a strike. When a flare went up, the driver had no option but to stop and run to the foxholes, which still punctuated the hillside every 50 metres or so. Gaping holes in the karsts formed the entrances to caves up to several kilometres deep which during the war had housed schools, hospitals and prisons. A quarter of a century after the event, Lamphan knew the 'statistics' of people killed by American bombing at each locality: a family of eight blown up here, a hospital blown up there. But at the end of the day, the bombs were no match for the caves. Some entrances were open, but others burrowed between mountains at angles so sheer that even today's 'smart' bombs would have trouble finding them.

Before the battle of Dien Bien Phu, Vietnamese army units had moved into the Sam Neua area and begun reinforcing and enlarging the natural caves for themselves and their Lao comrades. Initial construction ended in 1963, but the caves were constantly being improved and enlarged. Throughout the war, as Sam Neua was pounded into dust, they formed the secure heart of the 'liberated zone', and after the war the party seriously considered moving the capital of Laos from exposed Vientiane to the cave country around impregnable Viengsai.

A small airfield, and some barracks painted ochre and green, announced that we had reached Viengsai. Officially it was a mere district capital, but its role in the Pathet Lao's history gave it disproportionate status and power. Lamphan prided himself on having influence in Viengsai as well as Sam Neua. Being important in the provincial capital, he pointed out, didn't necessarily carry weight here. The first monument you see in the town makes its affiliations pretty clear. It's a statue depicting a soldier, a worker and a peasant, their hammers, rifles and sickles hoisted in the air, their feet crushing bombs inscribed 'USA'. The next thing you notice is the relative emptiness of the place. There were few people about, even in the market, where we stopped to put in an advance order for lunch. The yellow two-storey building housing the district headquarters looked quite grand from a distance, set at the end of an open square, but upon closer inspection it was decrepit, with broken windows, collapsed ceilings and plants sprouting from between the terra cotta roof tiles. All the town's buildings, constructed by Cuban, North Korean, Russian and Vietnamese work brigades with the help of seminar labour, looked decayed.

The interior of the district headquarters was decorated with a set of antlers, a bust of Lenin and a portrait of Ho Chi Minh. A man in jungle greens, one eye clouded by cataracts, sat listlessly on the front steps beside an old man in a Pathet Lao uniform and floppy cap. Soldiers wielding shovels and brooms seemed to be making an effort to spruce up the nearby office of Military District Five. Viewed from the steps of the headquarters, the grand square resembled an unkempt paddock. We were met by Pengsone Lovankham, chairman of the local Kaysone Museum project. He said plans were afoot to make Viengsai a permanent revolutionary memorial to attract tourists, but a survey was needed to determine transport, infrastructure, and accommodation needs. 'Houaphan is an historic province for Lao people,' Pengsone said. 'There are many caves where the different leaders hid during the war. We would like to show other people.'

'What does Viengsai mean?'

'"*Vieng*" is Lao for "fence". And "*sai*" means "great" or "glorious". Glorious fence!'

Unlike Khen and Lamphan, the owlish Pengsone was old enough to have personally experienced much of the area's history. During the war he had trained in propaganda at Sisana Sisane's Ministry of Information and Culture, and had met Souphanouvong many times during the ten years, from 1963 to 1973, the 'Red Prince' and his family had spent living in the caves. He proved to be the ideal guide, accompanying us the short distance to Souphanouvong's cave. The first thing we saw at the cave site was the large cream and lemon-coloured villa constructed for Souphanouvong after the Paris peace accords ended US bombing in 1973. The two-storey brick building, and a garden of poinsettias and pomelo trees, had been built around a former bomb crater transformed into what Pengsone called a 'peace pond'. The president's car had a little cave of its own in the base of the nearby cliff. A path led into the karst behind the villa, where a group of villagers was hacking away at the undergrowth with machetes. Jungle covered the gorge, and it was a full-time job to prevent nature reclaiming the revolution's history. A cleared area revealed a *stupa* Souphanouvong had built to house the ashes of his eldest son, Souphaxay's brother, who'd been assassinated during the war.

The cave entrance was perched about 10 metres above the ground and was protected by a concrete bunker. We waited for a generator to provide light inside the cave, but when it failed, Pengsone fetched a hissing gas lantern. The cavern was divided into rooms by wooden partitions. Small signs in Lao, French and English identified Souphanouvong's office, a living room, and bedrooms for his ten children. One room in particular stood out, the only one formed of metal rather than timber walls, and the only one with a false ceiling. It was accessed through a riveted metal doorway similar to those on ships and submarines, and contained what looked like an electric pump. Pengsone described this as the emergency room, into which oxygen could be pumped in the event of a gas or chemical weapons attack. As Souphaxay had told me, the cave was damp, but it was lighter and airier than I'd expected, and all openings were screened off to prevent bats and birds getting in. The kitchen, with an open hearth and a meat safe, was outside on a natural patio overlooking the ravine, protective cliffs towering hundreds of metres above.

There was little in the bare rock surfaces to give any sense of warmth, or the real life of Souphanouvong, as cold and hard as the official portrait of a one-dimensional revolutionary. Marxism–Leninism helped solve his many grievances: the slight of being given a position lower than his half-brother Souvanna Phouma in the colonial civil service; the injustice of being born into the lower echelon of the royal family, destined to play a secondary role to the intellectually inferior sons of the king.

Souphanouvong had good personal reasons for despising a system of governance by birthright, even as he used the advantages it offered him. In the 1930s, while working as an engineer in the Vietnamese beach resort of Nha Trang, he'd met Nguyen Thi Ky Nam, an innkeeper's daughter who shared his detestation of colonial rule and belief in socialist ideas. The motto of the bride's family was 'Jointly, the family finds happiness; unified, it reaches prosperity.' But Souphanouvong subjugated the unity of his family to the solidarity of the revolutionary struggle. In 1957, he signed an agreement with Souvanna Phouma ending the civil war and committing the Pathet Lao to participation in the first coalition government. The communist rank and file were dismayed, thinking the struggle against Vientiane had ended in a miserable compromise, but in a speech to Pathet Lao cadres and soldiers, Souphanouvong explained that although national liberation could not be accomplished immediately, the Central Committee of the Lao People's Party was not relaxing its revolutionary effort in any way: 'The purpose of the revolution and the goal of our struggle is to liberate totally our homeland by expelling the imperialist aggressors; to bring about peace, independence, freedom and national unity; to progress until the overthrow of the puppet regime, the abolition of the monarchy, and the establishment of a genuine democratic regime in its place.'

Yet the Souphanouvongs were not averse to royal hobnobbing for the cause. In March 1974, Cambodia's Prince Sihanouk was their guest at Viengsai. A joint communique denouncing American imperialism was issued and Madame Souphanouvong hosted a banquet for the Cambodian royals.

We moved out to the natural terrace overlooking the gorge to talk. Pengsone spoke eloquently about the days of revolutionary struggle, mentioning as an aside that after 1975 in Vientiane, he had been Souphanouvong's unofficial barber.

'Was he the kind of man who shared confidences with his barber?' I asked.

'No, not really,' said Pengsone. 'He'd joke around, or discuss what a man should do in order to be respected. How he should work hard.'

'Souphanouvong was a prince, a member of the royal

family. Did he ever give the impression of being different from other people in that way?'

'No, never. He was just like ordinary people.'

'There were also other members of the royal family up here. But they were prisoners. Were they kept here in this general area as well? Was the old king, Savang Vatthana, here?'

Khen stammered out the translation of this one. My ears pricked up at Pengsone's reply, which included the words 'Long Ma'.

'They were in seminar in the Long Ma area,' Khen confirmed.

I was glad I had taped the conversation. It was the first public statement by a Lao official regarding the precise whereabouts of Savang Vatthana since the king's arrest and internal exile to Houaphan in March 1977.

'Did Savang Vatthana die there?' I asked.

'I don't know,' said Pengsone, reverting to the stereotypical Lao historian.

Returning to the market, we ate a lunch of boiled chicken, small fish, green vegetables and rice. I was given the prized chicken head, its expression frozen at the moment of slaughter. Including the beer, lunch for the four of us cost the equivalent of $3. The only stalls doing any business in the almost deserted marketplace were those selling lottery tickets.

We drove off east on National Highway Six. Gradually, the landscape underwent a transformation. Horizontals became verticals, from brooding peaks to broad terraced valleys. At Ban Ban Hai there were fields of sugar cane, at Ban Nam Mau only the second *wat* I'd seen in Houaphan. The road followed the Keng River, a shallow stream of wide sandbanks on which buffalo lazed. River sand was being sold at the roadside in several places. Boys carried long-bore hunting rifles and machetes, women struggled along with babies on their backs suspended in slings from their foreheads. Men with limbs missing, veterans of the many wars, hobbled along in jungle greens. Also in green were the Vietnamese road gangs, distinctive in their pith helmets. They were heading for Sam

Neua, leaving a line of concrete power poles neatly dotted behind them every 30 metres or so. Sam Neua soon would have power 24 hours a day, supplied by the Russian-designed Hoa Binh hydroelectric dam in neighbouring Vietnam. This, in a country embarking on massive hydroelectricity projects of its own. The Vietnamese secured the deal by offering to build the power line free of charge. Only electricity consumed would be paid for. But Laos would pay a higher price for Vietnamese power than Thais paid for electricity generated in Laos.

After 90 minutes we crossed from Viengsai into Xieng Kho district, and the Nam Keng became the Nam Hao. 'Now we enter the hot zone,' said Lamphan, and within minutes the temperature did seem to rise. There was also more light as the river valley opened out, with palm trees clustered in groves and a vista of blue mountains way in the distance. 'Pears won't grow here, but coconuts do,' Lamphan continued, his face lit up too by his Big Smile. 'They don't have frost here like in Sam Neua.'

The road, however, was getting worse, dwindling at one point to a narrow dirt walking track across a saucer of badly eroded rice terraces. Yet the size and prosperity of the villages seemed to increase. Small dams provided local hydroelectricity to run rice mills. The rice was stored in what looked like houses, but were really rice 'banks'. Farmers with a surplus made deposits, while those with a deficit made withdrawals from their account or took out loans, all paid in rice, rather than money.

Soon we would be in Sop Hao, a name of dread in Lao history. The only outsiders ever admitted to the re-education camps of Houaphan were the Vietnamese and Russian advisors who helped set up and run them. The number of camps in Houaphan, and their names, had been the subject of many contradictory reports. Some said the camp at which ministers of the old regime and the royal family were held was known as Camp 01. Others referred to it as Camp 05. It is rare in Laos to meet members of the French-educated former elite who did not undergo 'seminar'. Indeed, after the vast majority of the government's political opponents had been either jailed or forced into exile abroad, members of the new government began putting each other away. They were now as vulnerable as their victims had been. Government officials claimed in 1980, 1985 and 1987 that all such camps had been closed, but each successive claim was subsequently shown to have been untrue. According to the US State Department report on Human Rights, 'In 1992, three men detained since 1975 were sentenced to life terms for crimes allegedly committed during their tenure as officials under the previous regime.' The government claimed three other officials released the same year had chosen to remain in the province.

Sop Hao turned out to be a disappointment. Getting there seemed to have been my main achievement. The village was large and well ordered, with dozens of stilt houses and even a couple of small shops. First stop, as always when travelling with minders, was to the local government representative. Phoui Tong turned out to be from Sam Neua and was staying in the Lao equivalent of an Indian circuit house. There were postcards of Hanoi on the thatched walls. Already Khen and Lamphan were bustling around me, saying we'd need to leave soon if we were to make it back to Sam Neua by nightfall.

We visited Boua Sy at the local store. He said he was 50, had been born in Sop Hao, and had opened his little shop by the main road in 1987, when the New Economic Mechanism reintroduced private capital to Laos. He had papered the walls of his shack with pages from the *Far Eastern Economic Review*. One of the covers read 'US in Asia'. 'It's just for decoration,' said Boua Sy, who neither spoke nor read English. The best thing that had happened in recent years, he said, was the advent of shops. The health of business depended on the size of the harvest. Good harvest, good business. The Vietnamese electricity was the next big thing. Politics, he said, was irrelevant to most people. Boua Sy had an old black cash box. Covered in leather, it looked decades old, a relic of the French time. A passing aid worker had offered him 15 000 *kip* for it, but he'd refused to sell. The shop displayed the usual array of biscuits and soft drinks, and as we spoke a small group of bystanders gathered, including one young man in a 'Keith Richards' Expensive Winos' T-shirt.

Were there ever any seminar camps around Sop Hao? I asked.

'Never heard of them,' said Boua Sy.

Was it known that the king died in the vicinity?

He didn't know what I meant by king.

Frankly, had a complete stranger accompanied by translators and minders from the government wandered into my village and started interrogating me about state secrets, I would have said nothing too. Boua Sy was all tense looks and sly smiles. I could have sworn Khen was winking at the poor man. With all avenues of serious inquiry evaporating, we ended up talking about fishing. They were catching whoppers in the Ma River, apparently.

Khen and I argued in the jeep on the way back to Sam Neua. Displaying obvious irritation with my line of questioning throughout the day, he suggested that if I wanted to know what had happened to the king, I should ask his family.

'I have,' I said. 'They don't know.'

'So ask those Lao living overseas,' he said peevishly. 'I'm sure they'll give you a good story.'

'I don't want a good story, Khen. I want the truth.'

He laughed, and that made me angry. 'What's the point,' I said, 'of asking the family of someone who's been kidnapped, or someone who's been murdered, what happened to them? If you want to know, ask the kidnapper. Ask the murderer.'

'So, that's it!' he shouted. 'You accuse the Lao government of being murderers! Murderers and kidnappers, you say. Well, I hope you have evidence of that. Can you prove it, eh? Can you?'

I realised I had overstepped the mark and would score poorly when Khen wrote his report. It was odd the way we'd been brought together. Khen had lived in Australia for a few years, having gone there on a government scholarship in the 1980s. He'd studied at the same college I'd attended, and lived in the same dormitories. We enjoyed many of the same things, yet we remained products of our own cultures. We drove on, plunged into a black and moody silence, absolved at least of the need to shout to be heard above the whining Russian engine. I contemplated my back pain for the rest of the three-hour drive to Sam Neua. A bucket of steaming hot water awaited me at the guest house, where I slept deeply.

Sunrise illuminated a new street mural on a billboard outside the Dok Mai Deng guest house. A squiggle of multi-coloured script, stripes and flowers, it greeted the twentieth anniversary of the People's Democratic Republic. A ruler and paintbrush rested on a 44-gallon drum to one side, but the artist was gone and the mural was unfinished. At the provincial headquarters, Khen and I were greeted by deputy governor Cheu Ying Vang, a Hmong from Ban Houakhang, which we'd passed on the way to Viengsai. As usual, there was a phalanx of note takers, fixers, photographers and minders sitting on the fringes of our meeting. The deputy governor was pudgy, with thick hairy fat forearms, and the whole room was the brighter for his lovely flower-embroidered shirt. He personified the fact that not all Hmong had thrown in their lot with the Americans.

In response to my ritual questioning about seminars and kings, Cheu said there were still four people in detention, all of whom had been convicted by a court. One had married a local girl. The king had died in Houaphan, but the issue 'belonged to Vientiane'. 'We just implement their policy,' he said.

The province was considering a foreign proposal to develop a tourist resort in the Long Ma area. In principle, he was in favour of it, Cheu said, although transport would be a problem.

At the end of our meeting, he leaned over and asked a favour. 'Some overseas Lao have the wrong idea,' he said, applying charm as if it was ointment. 'They think Vietnam dominates Laos. Here you have seen the truth with your own eyes. You should explain to them that we are really independent.'

It was Saturday afternoon, and boys and girls promenaded on the main street of Sam Neua, stopping to observe the mural painter, who was now adding green leaves to his flowers. The concrete billboard was attracting the sort of attention accorded to the slab in *2001: A Space Odyssey*. A curious boy scratched it. A woman sniffed it. By 4 p.m., shadows enveloped the town, the sun touching only the high peaks around it. The loudspeakers started up with a cough, a burst of static, and a flood of advice, the words 'doll-aar' and 'Ameri-caa' interspersed with distorted music from *khene* bamboo pipes. A rooster crowed and a woman threw slops onto the street. The flag of the Lao People's Revolutionary Party stood in the lobby of the Dok Mai Deng, waiting to be unfurled on 2 December. From the window of my packing crate of a room I saw the deputy governor returning home in the gubernatorial Toyota, one of the few modern vehicles in the town. With no electricity to run my laptop, I was listening on my portable shortwave radio to the BBC reporting on the strife in far-off Bosnia. Was it the European focus that was so comforting, I wondered, or the economy of language and reverence for fact? It was a relief to know that independent reporting existed somewhere, and that I'd soon be leaving the claustrophobic atmosphere of Sam Neua.

At 5 a.m. next day, loud music began blaring near the hotel. It transpired that two young townsfolk were to be married that morning, and preparations for the party had begun in the house adjoining the Dok Mai Deng. The green parachute of a long-lost American airman was put up, creating a canopy under which several dozen chickens were being slaughtered. By 10, the *lao lao* was flowing, and a *baci* bowl, decorated with poinsettias and marigolds, anchored many lengths of holy string held by relatives and friends. A despondent bride and groom stood together as a shaman shouted mantras on a practice amp and rice was thrown. Earlier, the young man had gone to the house of his bride and bartered for her symbolically. Later they would be sequestered in a bedroom amid much bawdy sign language.

In the lobby of the guest house, Khen was getting into the spirit of things, knocking back *lao lao* with a girl of thirteen. Lamphan joined in while three small boys and I looked on, disgusted.

At the airport, the Yuen-12 squeezed between a gap in the hills and raised dust as it hit the runway. My passport was checked—even without the *laissez passer* Big Brother was still watching—and I walked down to the landing strip, past a small open-air meat market which had sprung up for the benefit of travellers. On display were bunches of dead squirrels threaded together through their noses and selling at 800 *kip* a kilogram. One of the passengers bought a live bamboo rat, a beaver-like creature, for 2000 *kip*. The sharp-toothed rat was not a good traveller and would pose a threat to all on board. So after pocketing her money, the vendor bashed the hapless animal in the mouth, breaking its prominent front teeth, before tossing it on the grass for the buyer to pick up. It stumbled about, drunk with pain, blood spattering its furry face.

A short distance away, two European men were installing what looked like some kind of radar beside the runway. The device was a radio beacon to help guide aircraft onto the mountainous strip in bad weather.

One of them, a Frenchman, was complaining bitterly about his 'otel, which had 'terrible mouses'. I asked him if the beacon would make a difference to pilots trying to reach Sam Neua. 'I don't think so,' he replied, gazing balefully at the misty mountains beside the runway.

7

The Plain of Jars

Back in Vientiane, the street murals invoked the 'spirit of Sam Neua', but the people were still partying. Tens of thousands of them thronged the city's temples on the nights leading up to the full moon. Wat Seemuang was engulfed by a sweaty human sea, as families seeking merit carried silver *baci* bowls and swaying *phasat peung*—wax castles decorated with palm leaves, money, and marigolds—in a procession around the six-pillared temple. The sky was full of fireworks, and their acrid smoke mixed with the fragrance of incense, and the pervasive odour of chicken and bananas grilling on charcoal braziers along the road. Under normal circumstances, Wat Seemuang would have been a fine place to meet up again with Boun Kham, but given the crowds, I found it an odd choice for a rendezvous, unless he wanted camouflage. But even amidst the thousands of people milling around the base of the statue of King Sisavangvong, I could see his billiard-ball head from metres away.

The colonel was impressed and disgusted. Impressed that I'd made it to Sop Hao; disgusted that, other than getting official confirmation that the king had been held in Long Ma,

I had seen and heard little which might throw light on the fate of the royal family.

'You must have seen the Vietnamese!' he shouted above the sound of nagging loudspeakers calling out the names of people who'd made donations to the *wat*, and how much they'd given in dollars, *baht* and *kip*.

'Only the workers building the electricity line.'

'Aha!' he cried. 'They take off their uniform to work on the road. But their guns are never far away. Those Vietnamese you see, they are commandos. They occupy my country!'

The colonel fiddled with his collar, as if to let out steam.

'You did good,' he said. 'But the communists are very clever. They know how to hide everything. But don't worry. Don't give up! Boun Kham knows how to beat the communists!'

He told me it would take time. If I could stay on in Laos, he would try to contact an old friend who'd worked for the regime in Houaphan. As a chain-gang prisoner, Boun had helped build a house for this man, whom he'd eventually befriended. He was a committed nationalist who'd been on the Pathet Lao side but disagreed with many things the regime had done. Boun wasn't sure whether this man was still working for the government in Houaphan, but he was certain that he would know details about the last days of the royal family. His 'brother' would never betray Boun Kham nor any friend of his. The only problem, from the colonel's point of view, was how to contact him. For me, it was a more serious matter.

'I'm not going back there,' I protested. 'What's the point?'

'Relax. Maybe there's no need. Maybe my friend will write you a letter.'

'They'd never allow me to go back there, anyway. Not this soon. Not after the questions I was asking.'

Boun's closed eyes and pursed lips patiently absorbed my reaction. When he spoke, he was a sage advising a rookie.

'Take a break, guy,' he said, slipping into the US Army-speak he used in lighter moments and slapping me hard on the back. 'Go see That Luang.'

The celebration at Wat Seemuang was only the curtain raiser to a much larger act of devotion two days later—the festival of That Luang. According to legend, the original *that* was erected by the Indian Buddhist emperor Ashoka in the third century BC and contained relics of the Buddha. The great esplanade leading to the monument disappeared beneath vast crowds caught up in a fever of giving. Long lines of monks, carrying begging bowls in crocheted slings, accepted sticky rice, boiled eggs, candy bars and 100-*kip* notes as the sounds of pounding drums and cascading xylophones punctured the air. Above the fray, crowned with a slouch hat, rose the statue of the city's founder King Setthathirat, who'd built the present *that*.

The crowds were attempting the impossible feat of squeezing inside the confined space of the cloister, which already groaned with devotees, monks and flowers. Through it snaked a current of beautiful women, their necks swathed in gold chains and ornate sashes, their hands sweeping rhythmically as they danced the *lam vong*, and men carrying bamboo staves which they beat in a warlike manner on the ground. One man of especial dignity preened and fussed over his antique tunic and brooch of the emerald Buddha and cooled himself with a courtly mauve hand fan. He fairly pranced about in the baggy pants known to the Lao as *pa nong* and to foreigners as *sampot*. This traditional costume was being worn by more men than at any time since the revolution. The *Vientiane Times* saw the trend as perhaps a 'renaissance of interest and pride in Lao culture'; but just like the crowds choking the entrance to That Luang, it was creating a bottleneck, a head of creative cultural steam with few outlets in a society still dominated by the party.

Extracting myself from the crush of the cloister, I returned to the esplanade to see a young boy buying a finch in a small bamboo cage. A new pet, I thought, until he opened the cage door to release it. Releasing birds was, it appeared, a traditional way of obtaining merit, and this one darted away in an arc across the top of the great *that*, remembering how to fly just as the Lao remembered how to live.

Parallel to the religious pilgrimage route was the government-organised trade fair. Security guards frisked people entering the improvised arcades promoting satellite technology, cars, telecommunications equipment and computers. There was a fun fair with bumper cars, where demure Lao girls worked off the year's accumulated tensions, and a deserted Tourism Authority stall displaying a photo of Souphanouvong's cave at Viengsai. The longest queues led to the official American stand, where one of the staff said 1000 people an hour were passing through. The trade fair had been a feature of That Luang under the royal government as well, but one important aspect of the festival was different. *Thi khi* is the local version of hockey, a mad melee played with bamboo sticks and a root ball on the vast That Luang square, with hundreds of people taking part. But whereas before 1975 two teams—one representing the people and the other the regime—battled in the presence of the king, now the distinction between government and people had been deliberately blurred, and the contest was confined to two municipal teams. Under the king, the people's team had always won. Now the government could not tolerate even a symbolic contest.

That Luang was part religious festival, part commercial hard sell, and part village fair. There were even freak exhibits—a four-horned buffalo, and a white elephant, which was believed to live under high security at the home of Mrs Kaysone. Albino elephants had long been prized in Buddhist South-East Asia as talismans. Pregnant women would walk beneath them for good luck, and nations had been known to go to war over them. In *The Life and Lore of the Elephant*, Robert Delort wrote that whenever a white elephant was spotted in the forest, 'it was captured with the utmost care, ministered to by a host of attendants and adorned with exquisite jewellery. It was served luscious delicacies in the hope of prolonging its life and with any luck it lived to a ripe old age. Its death prompted consternation, grief and fear, from the king down to his humblest subject.' The Thai believe people of great merit can be reborn as white elephants to live among men and help them in times of trouble, unless you are a convicted criminal, in which case a white elephant is usually the one trained to carry out the death sentence by crushing you underfoot.

If Laos had ever truly been the land of 'one million elephants' it was, sadly, no longer. Logging and clearing for agriculture and development threatened their continued existence. Their hides were coveted for making shoes and bags, their teeth were used in medicines, and ivory poaching—which targeted only the tusks of bulls—had severely upset the male–female ratio.

Leaving the festivities, I hopped a rickshaw down to the Agriculture and Forestry Ministry, near That Dam, where I found Sivannavong Sawathvong, a field officer so dedicated he was at work during That Luang. His office was crowded with ring binders, meticulously arranged in glass-fronted bookcases. An old Russian air conditioner banged away overhead, and the light was a flickering fluorescent. Sivannavong had been involved in surveying wildlife in areas of the Nakai Plateau in central Laos before the flooding of parts of the region by the Nam Theun 2 dam. Logging had gone ahead parallel with environmental impact assessments, and now one of the heaviest concentrations of Asian elephants had been decimated. Although the government had established the Nakai Nam Theun National Biodiversity Conservation Area, which stretched across Bolikamsai and Khammouane provinces east of Thakek, logging continued at a steady pace.

Sivannavong said there were about 250 elephants in the protected area, in herds of sixteen to twenty, each with a leader. 'Sometimes, the leader is a female' he said. 'They can fight, even without tusks.'

The Lao elephant was confronted not only by rising waters but by alienated and angry villagers, who regarded the big beasts as pests because of the damage they caused to buildings, fences and crops. Illegal poaching also took its toll. A

village guardian—a man armed by the government—had shot
an elephant after accusing it of repeatedly trampling his crops,
and had been awaiting trial since 1994. Sivannavong said he'd
once found an elephant with its ears cut off, although tusks,
tails and feet were more usual targets. In 1993, 40 elephants
were killed in a single hunt by Vietnamese poachers. For
centuries the desire for them had persuaded the Vietnamese
to overcome their traditional fear of the strange land of Laos;
emperors like Minh Manh needed elephants in the same way
that modern armies need tanks.

Sivannavong reached for a file like a preacher reaching for
his Bible: Poachers 1:3. He produced a photograph of several
men in pith helmets carrying huge chunks of meat suspended on poles across their shoulders. They were
Vietnamese. 'They've been coming in large armed groups for
years now. Ever since the war,' he said. 'There's nothing
anyone can do about it.'

The office seemed a pathetic place; a library of the
doomed. Under-resourced scientists like Sivannavong were
unable to describe, let alone save, the many endangered
species of the Nakai. Juggling a bunch of keys, he opened a
filing cabinet and took out some photos. The *kouprey*, a sort
of white ox with swept-up horns and a hunted face, stared
back at us. Extinct. The *sao la*, one of only two new mammals
discovered this century, again in perilously small numbers,
looked coy. I asked about the white elephant said to be kept
in captivity in Vientiane.

'We have only one,' was Sivannavong's reply. 'Villagers
found it. And because they believed it would make the country
lucky, they gave it to the government. The animal was caught
near Sepon in 1984. The man who caught it was worried that
someone might take it from him, so he used mud and painted
the elephant brown. I went to check reports about it in 1986
and confirmed its existence. Then the party heard about my
report, and the provincial governor asked for it. The villager
and his family brought the elephant to Vientiane and were

given a house. They're still here. Officially, the elephant is under the control of the Council of Ministers.'

I was beginning to tire of Vientiane, city of stolen arches and white elephants. Boun Kham was still awaiting word from Houaphan, so I headed back to Lao Aviation and bought a return ticket to Phonsavan, on the Plain of Jars. Like Sam Neua, this place retained many secrets.

As we landed at Phonsavan airport, a Soviet-made MiG fighter aircraft screamed overhead on a dummy strafing run, before barrel-rolling over the horizon. Trees sprouted from bomb craters, marching in straight lines across a denuded landscape that evoked images of Ulan Bator.

The sky was Wattay Blue, and the stiff, cool breeze was bracing after the heat of the Mekong plain. We were now 1000 m above sea level and there were pelicans, as well as MiGs, in the air. Men wore woollen caps with ear flaps and relieved themselves on piles of dirt near the tin-shed terminal. There were gold-toothed Tajiks in stale uniforms left over from the Russian time, small brown women in football socks and Lakers caps. It felt good to be back on the frontier, all improvised and half-finished and changing.

In the car park I spied a young European man haggling for a taxi.

'Five thousand? You must be kidding!' he whined. 'I mean, fair's fair. That's outrageous.'

Richard's prominent chin gave him a disdainful air. He had long hair, grey drill trousers and a stained pullover that told me he'd been on the road for some time, like a well-spoken English tramp. We introduced ourselves, then someone called to him.

'Richard! Over here.'

The summons came from a lumpen-looking character who towered over a small Lao man beside a Russian jeep. This was Damien, an Australian. They had met on the plane. Damien had apparently negotiated a deal with the Lao, a local tour guide called Sousath. Soon the four of us were bumping along the ramshackle streets towards the Dorg Khoune Hotel, where the lobby was decorated with rusting bombs and landmines and the room key-rings were spent bullet casings—unexploded ordnance being Xieng Khouang's tourism trademark, along with its huge and ancient stone jars. You could imagine the car number plates of the future: 'Xieng Khouang—Explosive State'.

Phonsavan was an upstart village turned capital, its predecessor, Old Xieng Khouang, having been destroyed in the war. Its buildings, too impatient for style, rose rough and ready, with reinforcing rods protruding from their flat upper floors, ready to rise again as soon as funds permitted. The broad main street was the stage for a comic opera of overladen buses groaning to and from Nong Het on the Vietnamese border, dusty black Volgas, and packed *tuk-tuk*s. A new photo lab shone like a gold tooth in a mouthful of decay. Satellite dishes now sucked information from the stratosphere, the town cinema had been bankrupted by the popularity of videos, and the city's first fax machine had begun operating the previous day. Unfettered by a past, Phonsavan was headed for a future which its cantankerous *tuk-tuk*s could not reach quickly enough. It was only a matter of time before all the land mines and bomblets were melted down for scrap or sold as souvenirs, and the people of Phonsavan embraced their destiny. Only the dogs, dozing in the gasoline haze, seemed oblivious to the opportunities.

That evening the four of us met at Sousath's 'bar', the basement of his home, which he planned to turn into a restaurant. He began the evening's entertainment by producing a bottle of *lao lao*, made to his own recipe from fermented sticky rice, honey and ginseng.

Sousath had a mop top of black hair and wore an Australian football jersey. Having started a brush fire in our bellies, he lit up our imaginations with other props—maps, photographs and stories. Xieng Khouang had been the key battleground in the Lao theatre of the Indochina wars, and the Ho Chi Minh trail was only a few hours' drive away. The

Hmong general Vang Pao, who with American support came to represent a greater threat to the Pathet Lao than the Royal Lao Army, was based at the isolated mountain settlement of Long Cheng. America's support for Vang Pao was supposed to be a secret, but Judy Rantala—whose husband was a USAID worker—had written of how regular civilian flights to Luang Prabang were sometimes diverted to remote airstrips where GIs in fatigues, but with no identifying insignia, milled around. A soldier had boarded one such diverted plane at Long Cheng to announce to the startled passengers: 'You have not been here. You have not seen anything, and you will not talk about this to anyone!'

Time had softened the edges of Xieng Khouang's many bomb craters, and the footsteps of heaven's wrath were being absorbed by wind, grass and rain. But danger still lurked in the earth in the form of 'bombies', the lethal contents of the cluster bomb. Vietnam's military mastermind, General Vo Nguyen Giap, had worked hard to ensure Viet Minh and Pathet Lao control of the plateau, allowing him to bear down on both Vientiane and Luang Prabang. Although his fate was being decided upon its rolling hills, King Savang Vatthana rarely ventured onto the plain, apart from a couple of morale-boosting visits to Long Cheng.

Sousath and Richard hit it off right away, sharing an interest in the archaeological mysteries of the plain. Richard was doing postgraduate work at the School of Oriental Studies in London and had written a thesis on transport policy in landlocked states like Laos and Afghanistan. Excited by his subject, he would launch into theatrical dissertations about the history of the ancient stone jars of the plain, with Sousath chiming in. 'I heard about a village north of Old Xieng Khouang. Completely deserted!' said Sousath, tossing back another rice wine. 'No westerner has ever been there. Around this town, you've got hundreds of statues of dogs, made of stone. Everybody fled this town because the shaman, you know, the holy man, had a dream that a big bird would come from the sky and eat the village. So everybody moved to Old Xieng Khouang.'

Perhaps the villagers had misread the shaman's premonition. It was Old Xieng Khouang, the busy provincial capital of 1500 buildings, that would be obliterated by bombardment.

'Un-believable,' said Richard, his adrenaline rising. 'Have you been there? To Dogville?'

'I've never been there,' said Sousath. He did, however, know Old Xieng Khouang and several jars sites. He also had a jeep and spare time. Richard and Damien wanted to explore immediately, but it was not until Sousath revealed some of his own history that I committed to the enterprise. 'My family name is Phetrasy,' he said. 'My father was Soth Phetrasy. You're a journalist, you should know him!'

'The Pathet Lao representative in Vientiane . . . during the war,' I said.

'Exactly! He was the one who decided whether to fight, or whether to shake hands. You know what my name means? Pillar of the nation! We lived in a compound in Vientiane guarded by 100 Pathet Lao soldiers. I played volleyball with them. They were my friends. No-one could touch us. But I had to go to school at the Lycée, and I fought with the French kids. The Pathet Lao always won. The French fought only with their fists. But I kicked!'

He mimicked the wince of a Frenchman holding his balls, then exploded in laughter.

'My family even had a cave in Viengsai. You know Viengsai? Here, look . . .'

He dug a photo album from the pile we'd been looking at and turned to a dim image of himself pointing to some rock graffiti.

'*Hasta la victoria siempre!*' Richard read aloud. 'Victory is coming, always.'

'That's my family's cave. You know who wrote that? Fidel Castro himself!'

Sousath's father Soth Phetrasy was the public face of the Pathet Lao. While his main role was to liaise between Vientiane and Sam Neua during the civil war, he acted like the ambassador of a foreign country, and the presence of his detachment in the capital, only 300 m from the American embassy and guarded by a company of Pathet Lao troops, undermined the confidence of many royalists. The delegation staff were the only customers for the light aircraft service between Vientiane and Viengsai operated by Aeroflot. A short, rather stocky man, Soth had a difficult life in Vientiane, being subjected to petty harassment by the royal government and the constant threat of assassination by right-wingers egged on by their American advisors. He did, however, get invited to all the best parties, and was a guest of the King at the New Year celebrations in Luang Prabang in April 1975.

'He was in the communist style,' a Lao exile later told me. 'Not open. Watched everything. Said very little.'

We left Sousath's that night having agreed over a final toast to engage his services and to visit the Jars, Old Xieng Khouang, and a place he called 'the secret city' near Phou Khout. This was a fortress built by the French in 1953 to defend the western approach to the Plain of Jars in the event that the Viet Minh overran Luang Prabang. American bombing obliterated the fortress after it was overrun by the Pathet Lao in the 1960s.

At the 'Sangah' restaurant, I learned more about my companions. Richard came from Newbury outside London. He was a vegetarian but loved fishing for pike. He had a special interest in unexploded ordnance and the Black T'ai tribes, which had fled communism several times, moving from Dien Bien Phu to Sam Neua, Xieng Khouang, and finally Thailand. Richard had dozens of obscure facts at his fingertips. He knew the going rate for old bombs—10 *kip* per kilogram—and when Sousath had mentioned the Han dynasty, he noted casually that they'd ruled from 206 BC until 500 AD. He reminded me of a nineteenth-century English archaeologist, transplanted into the information age.

Damien was a complete contrast. His ruddy face, golden earring and hirsute neck and forearms gave him the look of an apprentice butcher. He was actually a software engineer, but he seemed an easygoing, adventurous type, and his hefty build might help if we got into a tight spot.

We ordered coffee, which came in glasses, with a layer of condensed milk undisturbed on the bottom. It was brought by a neat Lao woman whose *sin* was woven with flashy gold thread. She seemed impervious to the dust which in Phonsavan was everywhere. From the street, a youth appeared and made straight for Damien, who seemed to know him.

'I met him walking in town this afternoon,' he said. 'He's going to take me to an opium den.'

The young Lao man smiled his assent. Richard did a double take.

Opium was nothing new in Laos, but successive generations insisted on rediscovering it. For the Hmong tribes who left China in the early 1800s, it was the economic basis of their hopes for an independent homeland, and large parts of the Hmong tribal lands above 1000 m still depended for their living on poppy cultivation, which is not illegal. In some hill areas the number of people addicted to opium is greater than the number who can read. The French protectorate was largely financed by it, with the opium output of northern Laos being sent to Luang Prabang's *bouillerie*, or boiler, and the output of southern Laos being sent to Saigon. The processed product was sold to Ho traders travelling with mule trains from Yunnan in China. So vigorous was the industry during the Second World War that Luang Prabang became 'rotten' with silver, the currency in which the Ho paid, and the solid silver necklaces worn by Hmong women to denote status and store wealth weighed up to 2 kg each. In the 1960s, Air America—the CIA airline—financed the secret war partly by flying opium out of the country for processing into heroin in Saigon and subsequent sale to US troops, among others. For the Hmong resistance, opium meant weapons—6 kg of it was enough to purchase a light machine gun and ammunition; a rifle cost 2.5 kg.

On a previous visit to Laos, I had visited the opium-growing areas on the slopes of Palavek Mountain, south of

Long Cheng in an area under direct military supervision called the Xaisomboun special zone. The local Hmong king was a toothless, nuggety old man who claimed to be 106 years old. His name was Nau Her Tor in Hmong, but he was better known as the Phia Luang. In the 1920s he'd been given the area by King Sisavangvong, but he had no time for the old king, saying all he did was lie around all day 'like a castrated pig'. The Phia Luang was one of the few Hmong leaders to side with the Pathet Lao, and had been rewarded with the only brick house in the area and a Japanese jeep. He'd led his people through the Japanese, French and American wars, and said the last one was the worst because Lao killed Lao and Hmong killed Hmong.

'People came to me and offered me money to fight on their side,' he said, his words punctuated by giggles, 'but I've never wanted to take sides. I've always said, "I'm on the side of the winner, but I want to stay by myself and look after my people." But they came and told me to kill the Pathet Lao. Because I refused, they killed my daughter, my princess, and they killed my people and shot me. So we had to take up muskets to defend ourselves. That's how I became a hero of the revolution. Not because I wanted to kill anybody, but because we had to defend ourselves.'

The Phia Luang, who'd never been interviewed by a foreign reporter, said the war now was against opium. 'It's not the man eating the opium, it's the opium eating the man,' he said.

Opium traders had been coming to Palavek with packhorses to buy the local crop for a very long time. The sticky dark-brown substance itself could still be used as money in the Hmong homelands, and was the only widely available painkiller, but high levels of addiction wasted the upland communities. The United Nations Drug Control Program had, at the king's request, built a new road to the mountain, making it more economic for Hmong to grow cash crops like coffee and chilli for the Vientiane market. Opium production had been cut from more than 5 tonnes a year to 100 kg. One of the UN people showed me a poster painted by a Hmong girl featuring a sick man lying on a bed. 'My daddy is an opium addict,' read the caption. 'He is yellow, and he does no work. And he smells like a goat.'

The Phia Luang's son, Sathor, had himself cultivated opium until the arrival of the UN project. 'It's very difficult work,' he told me. 'You have to grow it high in the mountains, and you have to leave the village and go and live in the opium fields. And there's a lot of weeding to be done, because grass grows very quickly among the poppies. Then, when people get addicted, they lose their health, they can't work well and they start to steal because they have no money. There's no peace in the village.'

While he didn't like opium, the Phia Luang swore by his own version of *lao lao*, to which he credited his advanced years. It was fragrant and warm, and contained a root which he called *sarsee* and which resembled ginger.

In the market at Palavek, the baguettes recalled the French and the turkeys the Americans. A live monkey cost about 50c, including the bangle round its neck. The lofty peak of Palavek soared to 2000 metres from the valley floor, a big broken nose swathed in gossamer. In the Phou Nyom escarpment, working elephants hauled logs, and drivers avoided using their horns for fear of spooking them. Boys shot game with rifles and slingshots, and men carried AK-47s. The week after I visited, four Palavek people died when Hmong bandits attacked the town.

Now, more than a year later, I was walking the dark streets of Phonsavan with Damien, towards the other end of the opium food chain, a chain which remained intact despite two decades of Pathet Lao rule. Damien's young Lao friend led us to a mud-floored house on the outskirts of town where an elderly Lao man lay on a double bed base in a corner. Removing his shoes, Damien climbed on and lay down beside him on a grass mat. Our young Lao friend sat on a pew along one side of the bed, and I sat on another at its foot. The only light source, a small oil lamp standing on the bed base, shone on the old man's face, which was pale and almost entirely free of wrinkles. He was extremely thin, but not unhealthy, and wore a ponderously heavy gemstone ring. When he moved, it was with great economy, and in the warm light his face was suffused with a child-like expression. He began preparing Damien's pipe as a matter of course, watching the opium intently, as a tranquil lover regards a treasured partner. He cupped the lamp over the bowl of the long bamboo pipe as Damien inhaled deeply several times, then rolled over on his back and stared at the ceiling.

'You smoke opium?' he asked me, lifting his head.

I felt suddenly dry-mouthed and inarticulate.

'Not me, no,' I giggled like a Lao. I almost said 'soh-reee' or 'baw mee'.

The old man ignored us as he smoked a pipe and began the intricate ritual of preparing another for Damien, without raising himself from the bed. The process involved the use of several implements arranged beside him on a wooden tray. His eyes possessed an unearthly concentration and calm as he removed a small dark pellet from a plastic film canister and placed it in a small, ornate spoon, which he held over the flame of the lamp. As the opium began to boil, he stirred it with a silver needle, to which it began to stick. He kept turning the needle in the spoon, spinning the coagulating substance onto the needle. Then he grafted the resin onto the bowl of the pipe, and turned a lighter on it. As Damien began to suck with great inhalations, the old man scraped the bowl, turning the resin over as it bubbled and disappeared.

'It tastes sort of strange,' said Damien, holding his arms above his prostrate body. 'I mean smoking a joint is one thing. But this is a different sort of situation, you know what I mean?'

In an adjoining room lit by another oil lamp, an old woman sat at a table. She was drinking from a cup, raising it to her mouth with extraordinary slowness, and lowering it the same way, then slowly taking a bite of some kind of bread. She stared fixedly at the lamp in front of her. She was either an opium addict too, taking the drug as a tincture, or an opium widow. The young man who had brought us to the place continued to sit beside the bed, watching intently, like a dog at table. The atmosphere was solemn, like that in a temple.

I took the canister in which the opium was stored and breathed from it. I'd expected it to have a rich aroma, like hashish, but it smelt of nothing. When it burned in the pipe, though, there was a slight fragrance of caramel.

When it came time for reckoning, Damien calculated what he owed at five hundred *kip*, or about fifty cents, per pipe. No sooner was the money handed over than the young Lao man leapt onto the bed for his 'commission', a single pipe, and when that was done, the old man began packing away the utensils with the same deft movements and mild smile.

Next morning, the plain was buffeted by strong winds which drew patterns in the straw-coloured grass. On the hill where we stood, the huge stone jars were scattered like pantry pots from a giant's kitchen. There was an Easter Island quality to the place—the jars told of an assertive and powerful culture existing on the plain centuries ago, but that was all.

'Actually,' Sousath announced solemnly, 'we have six plains of jars.' The limited literature referred only to three. I'd read that all the jars had miraculously survived the wartime carpet bombing. Yet at my feet were several large bomb craters with shattered jar fragments dug into their rims like broken teeth. The intact jars sat at angles, spilling down the hill, across a flat, and up the other side. There were about 300 of them, carved from stone and clothed in lichen.

'We believe they were transported by elephants from Sam Neua to this area,' said Sousath, elongating the '*neuuua*' so it sounded very far away. 'The elephants carried the rock, and the rock was shaved here. We don't know what was the purpose of the jars, but there are two stories: for keeping rice wine, and also as burial jars.'

Even if the jars had been made for purely ceremonial purposes, it was hard to believe their obvious potential as storage containers had been ignored by subsequent genera-tions. An old Khmu song, the 'Call of the Khmu Soul', seemed to point to the existence of a great restaurant—somewhere in Laos:

O soul spirit, return and drink
the beer of the great jar,
Eat the white egg, drink the strong beer,
Eat the fat pork, eat the hard head,
Eat the fatty brains.

'How old are they?' mumbled Damien, bleary from his adventures the previous evening.

Sousath paused meaningfully.

'Actually, we don't know about the age,' he said. 'But we have proof. Maybe you know about the Shang Dynasty in China. The first Shang dynasty sent some people here. They made notes on bamboo pages. That was about 3000 years ago. The jars were here then.'

A MiG flew low overhead, mocking the ancients as it swooped down on the airport. From where we stood, we could see about twenty fighter jets lined up beside the runway of the main military airbase in Laos. The proximity of the base meant the government had been reluctant to open the jars site to tourists, and Sousath claimed credit for having persuaded them. In the early 1990s, surveying, fencing and mine clearance had begun, and hotel plans were approved. But five years later there were still no hotels, only a handful of English-speaking guides, and still not many tourists.

Back in 1968, royalist troops supported by their American advisors had briefly occupied the site. 'They won the Plain of Jars and they drank beer here,' Sousath said. 'They had a large group here. Tents. Everything. All the people moved to Vientiane. But then in January 1969, the Vietnamese pushed their tanks from Nong Het. They didn't start them so nobody heard the engines. The Americans never knew the Vietnamese were going to have a tank war here. And they didn't have enough anti-tank guns. So by about February, the Vietnamese had about 100 tanks here. They overran the Vientiane troops here, and they won.'

We were standing on the edge of a line of trenches dug by the lost armies. Graffiti on one of the jars read 'BOMB USA'. There were bullet holes in it. Sousath said the land mines had been cleared from the main trail.

'This area we're standing on here . . .' Damien began, but Sousath interrupted him. 'It's safe,' he said.

A snake was coiled up, hibernating, in one of the jars. Another one, full to the brim with water, gave a perfect reflection of the sky. On the higher ground behind us were what Sousath called the 'king's cups'; around us, 'the place for normal people'.

'Their king was not a Lao,' Sousath said of the jar makers. 'He was too big. Maybe 2.5 m tall. He was like an American.'

I found myself seeing Sousath differently, more in the way that I imagine he saw himself; a bold explorer on the frontier of Laos. He wore a denim vest with little loops for bullets or pens, a world time watch and brown leather moccasins. He was short, stocky, had the face of a teenager, and he claimed to have written the tourism plan for one of Laos's most important heritage sites.

'Some guard jars, in the forest, are still sealed,' he told us. 'Local people don't want to open them because they're afraid of spirits inside. They never touch them.'

Sousath longed to meet western scholars who could bank-roll a big expedition that would keep him in *per diem*s for years. But there was another side of him, the childlike side, that loved high jinks and capers, even if it meant going down to Phonsavan airport every second day and waiting for the planes that brought in the tourists. In the new free market of Indochina, Sousath lived by his wits. He attributed much of his information about the jars to a Frenchwoman he called 'Miss Coronee'. We thought she was one of his western girlfriends, until he said she'd been there in the 1930s.

'Colani?' said Richard. 'Madeleine Colani. Of course! The French archaeologist. She worked in Indochina between the wars. There were those big digs: the Dong Son culture in Vietnam.' Richard explained that Colani had worked mainly around the limestone karsts south of the Red River, before being drawn to Laos by the jars. She had found ancient crematoria, human remains and bronze and iron tools. Sousath said photos she had taken showed the position of the jars today was unchanged.

We spent the afternoon crawling through toppled forts, robbed *stupas* and a ghost town. And as the eye adjusted to the dun landscape of the plain, it revealed its colours: electric green pines standing like a trimmed mane on a neck of freshly ploughed brown earth; a mirrored lake beneath a leaden sky; a teak tree growing from a jar on Salatuk Mountain covered in avocado-green lichen. We stepped carefully on a narrow trail up a shale hill to visit a crumbling French observation post. A foot misplaced could become a foot amputated by a buried bomblet. As we inched down the mountain, there was a loud thud. A mine casualty beyond the next hill, we thought, but it turned out to be a deliberate explosion in a nearby shale mine. The bomblets, dropped in clusters of more than 600, infested villages, schools and farmland. Many people were still being killed and injured by simply lighting fires in the open, for the heat triggered the buried explosives. We found the bleached bones of international socialism—a Russian beef farm, stranded and ramshackle, its rusting iron walls flapping in the wind. The hills were scarred by scapula-shaped clearings where the Lao practised the art of catching finches and sparrows. The clay bricks of neglected *stupas* like the six-teenth-century That Phuan were so soft they could be eaten by worms—or invaded by thieves. A tunnel burrowed across the base of the *that*, then reached upwards into the *sanctum sanctorum*, where Buddhists often buried votive offerings of gold. Grass held the facade together, and tap roots drove deep into the cracks. A rusty mortar was half buried in the ground nearby.

Before its destruction, Old Xieng Khoang, now renamed Muang Khune, had boasted many grand buildings and mon-uments. It was, in fact, another royal capital, the seat of the Chao Noi Muang Phuan, the king of Xieng Khouang, who in the 1800s had been captured by the Vietnamese and executed in Hue. The ruined palace of the French legation resembled a Mediterranean villa, designed to catch the sun, with wide balconies and ornate balustrades. But the roof was missing, and doorless doorways gaped at grand vistas—rice paddies on one side, mountains with high meadows on the other. The old floor tiles, with their angular-motif borders, were identical to those in my home in Hanoi, some smashed, others intact. Of the town's main temple, Wat Phia Wat, there was nothing left bar the foundations and a large stone Buddha meditating on the ruins. The sculptor had given him a spiky scalp like the skin of a durian. Young novices with similar scalps crowded into the windows of a wooden dormitory building beside the *wat*, laughing as we picked through the rubble. Life was stirring again in Old Xieng Khouang.

Damien had been distracted and withdrawn for most of the day, but he came to life when some villagers invited us to join their game of *kator vai*, the local equivalent of volleyball, played with the feet on the dry, rectangular bed of a paddy plot which had been harvested and drained. Our incompetence took the edge off the competition. The Hmong children delighted in outspinning us with their wooden tops, which they whipped onto the dirt with the aid of sticks. They were practising for the local top-spinning festival, in which first prize was a pig, second prize was a duck and third prize was a chicken. We swung across a few bamboo footbridges, tried in vain to eat the local peanut brittle without consuming its newspaper backing, and watched a boy fishing with a net weighted with chains. Another boy looked on, holding a country-made rifle with brass trigger and fittings and a slender iron rod for cleaning the barrel, which was tethered to the wooden stock with blue cloth. Yet another useful antique.

That evening we dined again at Phonsavan's Sangah restaurant, where a long table was occupied by *felang*, macho types who turned out to be a de-mining team working around Phonsavan. Sousath wanted nothing to do with the foreign experts. They were paid $200 a day, he said, to watch Lao de-miners on $200 a month do the dangerous work. The foreign experts did seem rather full of themselves. I supposed their egos had been boosted by regular visits by foreign journalists, whose stories suggested that unexploded ordnance (UXO) and dams were all that mattered about Laos.

'Give me $1 million, I can clear all the UXO in one month,' Sousath boasted.

Money and foreigners were sore points with him, especially where the two intersected. On several occasions he'd acted as guide for Americans revisiting old war sites. He'd helped the first American POW of the war, Lawrence Bailey, return to Sam Neua, and claimed to have had contact with the teams searching for US servicemen missing in action. The Americans avoided offering rewards for soldiers' remains because whenever spurious rumours swept Laos that money was available, the embassy was besieged by unwelcome vendors of old bones. Sousath, it seemed, was one of those who had been spurned. 'They want the bones, but they won't pay money,' he said, grimacing. 'So they don't get bones.'

The old Pathet Lao fire was still in Sousath's belly: he thought of himself as a David defying a morally bankrupt Goliath. Yet he also coveted the giant's wealth. Communism had convinced him that there was only a limited amount of wealth to go round, and that only the morally pure should have it.

Sousath had bought a bottle of Johnnie Walker Black Label with him, and after we'd eaten he picked it up and moved to a table on the open terrace facing the street. Richard was talking ordnance with the de-miners and Damien had gone off again to the opium shack, so I followed Sousath, and we settled in with the passing traffic and the whisky for distraction. As the drinks passed, I told him about my interest in Lao history, especially the untold bits. He looked sceptical, tracing the lip of his glass with his forefinger.

'My father could have been president of this country,' he said suddenly. After his years as the Pathet Lao representative in Vientiane, Soth Phetrasy joined the third and final coalition government of leftists and royalists in 1974, becoming minister for Economy and Planning. But the following year, when the People's Revolutionary Party took power in its own right, he was conspicuous by his absence from the cabinet. What had happened to him, I wondered?

'He was sent to Sam Neua to oversee the cases of re-education,' Sousath replied with a bitter smile. 'The Pathet Lao did not know who the people in the camps were. Only my father could tell them, because he spent many years in Vientiane mixing with the royal Lao government. So he told them, this one is OK, that one is a fascist.'

It was an article of faith with the Pathet Lao and their Vietnamese comrades that proximity to decadent westerners could lead to contamination. A sobering stint in Viengsai, I imagined, would be a most efficacious antidote.

'My father got nothing from the revolution,' Sousath said. 'After that they made him ambassador to Moscow. We lost everything because we believed. One day my father thought he was dying, and he called us to his bedside and said he would look after us like Souphanouvong looked after his children. I used to have to go to the hospital all the time because my father was there. At that time Souphanouvong was also in there, and he looked pathetic. You know in the communist system the individual is not important.'

Soth Phetrasy and Souphanouvong were the same age, both educated in France, both committed communists and confidants. But Souphanouvong had advantages of birth and intellect, and when it came time to choose a president, these were crucial. Political struggles became personal ones in the hot-house atmosphere of the little revolution. Sousath's first marriage had ended on the rocks when the son of a party leader was seen leaving the Phetrasy home late one night. When the party learned of his nocturnal activities, it sent the young man to Sam Neua for three years re-education. Sousath's wife fared worse, being sent to Don Nang, the women's-prison island in Nam Ngum reservoir. The new prison on the previously uninhabited island was rudimentary, and she died there among what one visitor to the camps called the 'sad-eyed girls and listless young men'.

'I visited there once,' Sousath said. 'All the guards on that island are women. They haven't seen a man for months. They look like they could eat you!' By the early 1990s, security on the island prisons had become so slack that male and female prisoners could be seen swimming to each other's islands. One such gallows romance even produced a marriage.

Sousath himself was restricted for several years to the Sam Neua–Viengsai area after returning to Laos during the war from studies in China, where he had misbehaved. We had given the whisky quite a nudge, and I was emboldened to ask if he knew about Sop Hao, and what had happened to the king.

'Sop Hao? No, I don't know,' he said. 'But I know where the king stayed in Viengsai.'

'Where?'

'In my father's house.'

'What?'

'Why not? You want to go there? When my father was in Moscow, the house was empty. At that time the king came to Viengsai. So he stayed there with his family.'

'Do you still own the house?'

'No. Not really. My father lives in Vientiane, and anyway the house has fallen down. You can't live there now.'

Richard came over to us and drew up a chair.

'How would we get to Viengsai?' I asked Sousath.

'Easy, we drive there. I've been many times. Over the mountains. Takes about twelve, maybe thirteen hours.'

'Over the Annamite Range?' cried Richard. 'Wow! Let's go!'

The nineteenth-century archaeologist in Richard was further excited when Sousath mentioned a Bronze Age site in the mountains, lost to science since the days of Madeleine Colani. The Hua Muong site consisted of standing stones arranged in circles around large stone tables.

'Like your Stonehenge,' said Sousath, 'only Lao version. Smaller.'

We spent the rest of the evening raking over the details—money, available time and Sousath's commitments. I wondered how my return might be greeted by local officials, even if I was travelling as a tourist.

'Don't worry,' Sousath ordered, 'You'll be travelling with Sousath! I am your passport!'

We decided to leave within the next few days.

The next morning Richard and I sat huddled around a candle in the militaristic lobby of the Dorg Khoune, drinking green tea. Richard had been unable to arouse Damien, who'd come in late. I'd agreed to return to Viengsai, but I wanted to talk to Boun Kham first. In the meantime we had decided to spend the morning investigating Sousath's 'secret city' near Phou Khout.

In the early 1950s, convinced the Viet Minh were intent on taking Luang Prabang and hoping to lure them away, the French began building up their forces at Dien Bien Phu, where they would meet their Indochinese Waterloo the following year. As a fallback position, they also began to build up fortifications at Phou Khout mountain, on the western approach to the Plain of Jars. At the same time, they urged King Sisavangvong to leave Luang Prabang. The journalist Bernard Newman arrived in Luang Prabang to find three Viet Minh divisions threatening the town. He also found the king—by then ill with a liver complaint—to be quite stubborn. 'I stay here,' he said. 'I do not budge!'

Crown Prince Savang Vatthana told Newman he was in favour of a general mobilisation, but few others in Luang Prabang shared his sense of urgency. The town was defended by only a single company of Laotian infantry, 'no man of which had ever fired a shot in anger, or ever wished to do so'. The reason for their inexplicable calm was that a blind *bonze* had prophesied that, because the Vietnamese were not good men, spirits would annoy and terrify them and they would not enter the town. And he was right. The Viet Minh did not take Luang Prabang, nor even attack it. They 'faded away as swiftly as they had come', heading for Dien Bien

Phu. Newman must have been impressed, because he began making his own long-term predictions. The Pathet Lao had little hope of victory, he opined, because the favourite pastime of the Lao was 'to lie in the shade watching his rice and coconuts grow. A less promising recruit to Communism can scarcely be imagined; appeals for higher production would be treated as comic.'

Richard had taken a public bus up Route Thirteen to Luang Prabang some weeks earlier, via the strategic crossing Sala Phou Khoun. It was a risky trip, traversing country in which rebels and bandits still operated with impunity. The Australian embassy advised that travel in parts of the country 'may still be dangerous', and the US State Department Report on Human Rights in Laos listed twenty killings in 1995 as a result of ambushes of motor vehicles. It was often unclear whether the ambushers were politically or economically motivated. Richard's bus had been accompanied by an armoured personnel carrier. He'd ridden on the roof with Lao men who told him that in the event of a rocket-propelled grenade attack or mine explosion, he'd have a better chance of survival there than if he rode inside. The option of bus surfing was not available to women passengers, because the men considered it disrespectful to have women above them. The bus and APC had travelled at night.

En route to Phou Khout, the sky over the Plain of Jars was as beautiful as the road was vile. We got bogged and had to be winched out by a passing truck, and then a shock absorber broke, which made life even more uncomfortable. Richard sat shivering in the rear seat, wearing every piece of clothing he had and trying to tape a map over the missing window to stop the wind rushing in. A Russian T-76 tank stood abandoned and rusting by the road where it had been since the Indochina wars, when furious B-52 bombing reduced the height of Phou Khout Mountain by seven metres.

In 1987, war broke out again across the Mekong. Since the sacking and depopulation of Vientiane by Thai armies in 1828, Lao attitudes to their south-eastern neighbours had been summed up by the saying, 'To listen to the Thai is to have your granary burnt down.' The feeling was mutual. In 1988, former Thai Prime Minister Kukrit Pramoj was quoted as saying, 'We should cross over and burn Vientiane once more. There is no need to declare war—just go across and burn it.' A Thai decision to build a road in the disputed Ban Romklao border area preceded the hostilities. Outnumbered and ill-equipped, Lao troops fought tenaciously, and early casualties ran five to one against the Thai. Worried they might not be able to sustain their good early showing, the Lao leadership faced up once more to the vulnerability of Vientiane's location just a few hundred metres away from Thailand. In 1939, when the French had been in conflict with the Thai, the colonial authorities had moved their base from Vientiane to Xieng Khouang. Now the Pathet Lao considered once more the possible relocation of the capital. Viengsai had served this purpose in the past but was now considered too well known. According to Sousath, Phou Khout was their choice, although Lao officials later told me no final decision on relocation had been made.

The village looked like any of a thousand others until the road turned to bitumen, street lights sprouted and an elevated building with a steeply raked roof appeared at the end of a straight boulevard. In the square in front of the building stood a Kaysone pagoda, gleaming red and gold and topped by a multi-tiered parasol. It was missing only the North Korean bust of the great leader which would be installed before 2 December. Cows grazed on the long grass that formed a moat around the deserted building. The surrounding land was dotted with concrete bunkers which, upon closer inspection, proved to be flooded. A local official said the bunkers had been fitted with the same life-support systems used at Viengsai. He said that in the early 1990s, when relations with Thailand had improved, the Politburo had presented the complex to the local district. The downstairs section was being used as a kindergarten. Upstairs was a 'conference' room.

It was the realisation in concrete and iron of the Pathet

Lao's worst fears and best memories. Under threat, they had reacted instinctively and re-created the burrow that had saved them, making a new Viengsai, with a similar layout and concrete bunkers replacing limestone caves.

Later that morning I managed to get a telephone message through to the colonel. At 4 p.m. I went back to the public call office in Phonsavan and rang Vientiane. Boun Kham picked up the phone.

'I've got good news for you,' he said without waiting. 'I got a telegram from my friend in Houaphan. He is willing to meet you.'

'That's fantastic, Boun.'

'Yes, yes. He says you can go any time. His son is there from Vientiane and he speaks English very well. Now, you know the market in Sam Neua, don't you?'

And he proceeded to give me the name of my contact, and simple directions to his home.

'One more thing,' he said. 'You should take a bottle of whisky.'

8

The Re-education Guest House

Early the following day, Sousath's Jeep creaked to a halt, raising dust at a truckstop junction north-east of Phonsavan. Damien was leaving us. He'd been slumped in the back of the truck with his parka zipped up to his prominent nose, hood tightly drawn, ever since leaving the provincial capital.

'What day is it?' he mumbled, agitated because he couldn't find his cigarette papers, then, realising it was sunny, stripped down to his Angkor Wat T-shirt and a moneybelt large enough to hold a camera.

'I smoked ten pipes last night,' he said with a huge yawn. 'An addict smokes fifty.'

'That's a lot of lying down,' said Richard.

We were in a rudimentary settlement called Xieng Klao and Damien's plan was to hitchhike north towards Muang Noi. The road would take him across the Rivers Khan, Xuang and Ou, all of which joined the Mekong near Luang Prabang. From Muang Noi he could take a riverboat down the Ou to the former royal capital. We were at the intersection of two great colonial roads built by the French—Route Seven, connecting Luang Prabang with the Vietnamese border town of Nong Het, and Route Six which traversed the mile-high Annamite chain to link the Plain of Jars to Sam Neua. Japanese troops had marched past this point entering Laos from northern Vietnam during World War II. It had been a strategic crossing during the American war too, when the settlement was known as Ban Ban. The baguettes we'd packed, together with some tinned mackerel, made a lunch, and we sat by the roadside chewing on them and drinking beer, until a truck came by heading for Muang Noi. Damien dumped his backpack into the tray and climbed in, donning his parka while holding a floppy baguette between his teeth.

'Reckon I ought'a get outta here,' he said, a momentary twinkle enlivening his glazed eyes. The truck disappeared, taking Damien with it, like a quick, thin wisp of opium smoke.

Route Six took Sousath, Richard and me north-east to the Soviet-built bridge across the Nam Neune river. The former Russian construction camp was now a neat, prosperous village. Ahead of us lay a stark, wild landscape. The jeep became a bucking bronco, and we got used to landing hard on its niggardly seats. The first four hours passed without sight of another vehicle. Then the daily Sam Neua–Phonsavan bus came careering around a blind corner, almost pushing us off an unfenced precipice. There were the same foxholes, evenly spaced like those on the road to Sop Hao, but the road was soon to be widened and the foxholes buried. At one point I climbed head first into one of them, flashlight in hand, only to leap out again when I found myself face to face with a snake. On a particularly spectacular bend, from which we could see the thickly wooded Annamites towering above several vast valleys, we piled out of the truck to whoop and yodel and listen to our amplified voices echoing across the abyss. Further on, we passed Hmong men with long-barrelled guns, and saw their thatched homes cascading down hillsides. In the interludes, we amused ourselves with our own stories. Sousath claimed to have shot a tiger the previous year in Houaphan. Richard was appalled.

'Why not?' Sousath said. 'It tried to eat me.'

The incessant groan and clatter of the truck tended to kill conversation, and we would lapse into long silences, Sousath hypnotised by the road, Richard retreating into his Walkman. Somehow I fell asleep but was rudely awakened by Sousath shouting 'Honey! Honey!' He had stopped the truck, pulled a revolver from the glove compartment and run into the foliage of the hillside.

'What the hell's he doing?' said Richard, lunging at the hand brake to stop the truck rolling off the cliff. 'Where'd he get that gun?'

Sousath had spotted a large golden-brown formation under a rock overhang, and was galloping through the bush towards it. Even 50 m away, you could see ripples of movement flowing through the swarm covering an enormous beehive.

'Jesus! Look at that,' said Richard, as we followed Sousath, and then, 'My God! He's shooting at it.'

'But won't the bees get angry?' I asked Richard, who'd hit the ground as two gunshots rang out.

'I think they're getting ready to attack,' he said.

Sousath had actually been firing at a second hive which the bees had deserted, trying to dislodge it or cause a honey flow. He'd holed it, but the hive was dry. Still, he seemed to walk taller back to the car. Richard and I, though, trod the path back as if it were a minefield, recalling the warning of one of the expats at Nam Phou fountain. Surveyors working in this area had expected to find up to 800 metal fragments— the remnants of bombs both exploded and not—per kilometre beside the road. They found 4000.

A group of Hmong from the next village had gathered. They said these bees were bigger than average and produced excellent honey. But if angered, they would follow you for a kilometre or more through the jungle, and they had killed many times. The only way to survive a mass attack, the Hmong said, was to cover yourself in honey and lie very still. Their village was a spartan settlement in which everyone wore black. There was a primitive stone grinding wheel on open ground, and animal hides were strung up tight as drums on vertical frames, forming primitive motifs against the sky. Chickens pecked at the earth between mud-floored houses with thatched roofs, and some dusty buffalo chewed calmly and watched. There was a simple yet ingenious reticulated water system, consisting of elevated bamboo aqueducts connected to a common weir. A little girl, who couldn't have been more than three years old, was alone at the weir, scrubbing pieces of black clothing from a pile taller than she was. The village looked settled—it had been there five years—but could easily be abandoned when the time came for the Hmong to move on. No-one knew when that would be. Some nomads lived by the motto, 'Seven times around the mountain'—a full cycle of shifting agriculture before the soil was exhausted by slash and burn. Others, like the Kha Tong Luang (Khmu Banana Leaf Yellow) moved on when the banana-leaf roofing of their huts turned yellow. A gnarled old woman approached us, proffering scratched pebbles of aquamarine. Sousath assayed them with an expert air, weighing them on a miniature set of brass scales belonging to the woman. But the scales were what caught my eye; they were freakishly small, precise in every detail and obviously very old. When Sousath had handed over some money for the stones, the old woman produced a smooth wooden wallet, like a small spectacles case, which had been carved to hold the scales.

It was almost sunset and we'd been on the road for about ten hours when Sousath turned off Route Six and found traces of the Americans. The road itself, wider than Route Six, had been pushed through this remote district of Hua Muong, about 70 km from Sam Neua, only two years earlier by the US government. Poppies grew prolifically in the dark-brown earth of these hills, and the local Hmong people saw opium as an essential commodity, both as a medicine and as a trade staple. The principle of the American project was the same as at Palavek—open up the area to nearby markets and provide alternative crops so the Hmongs' need to grow opium would diminish.

We followed a ridge for several kilometres and eventually

reached what looked like an overgrown cemetery, its head-stones standing at different angles amid trees and low scrub. Approaching on foot, we saw that they were not headstones in the conventional sense, but rather large, jagged shards of a grey, flinty stone which had been carved or unearthed centuries before to form a kind of sacred site. There were at least 50 in the one spot, and they sparkled, as if containing fine particles of silica. The wafer-like structure of the rock which formed them was like that of slate, but its texture was more like that of andesite or basalt. They were up to 2.5 m tall and 1 m wide, but some were only 2 cm thick. They were warm to the touch, having absorbed the day's sun. Some of them were gathered around circular tables 2 m across, carved from the same stone. Silhouetted after sunset, the stones seemed to be conferring in groups, giving an eerie sense of community. Sousath said they were older than the stone jars of the plain.

An old Lao Loum woman carrying a hoe appeared, walking home from her day's work in the gardens. She said she had heard of 'Madame *Felang*', as she referred to Madeleine Colani, and said the stones were spread out from the mountain of Phou Chalay to the Peun River. When we asked what the purpose of the stones had been, she laughed and said she didn't know. Women, she added, did not have the right to discuss such things.

'I've seen things like this before,' said Richard, staring hard at the shards, as if the intensity of his vision might burn their secret from them. 'They're quite a bit like the Standing Stones of Stenes in the Orkney Isles. That lot are 5000 years old. Norse influence. These are smaller.'

'Lao version,' said Sousath, who seemed to have nationalised his 'short' complex.

Richard climbed a small hill on the other side of the road and found more of the stelae there. The American road, part of an $8.7 million foreign aid project, cut along the ridge only a few metres from the main cluster. One of the tables had collapsed as a result of the road widening, and any further erosion would directly affect the standing stones, which were already toppling like dominoes. The forest in which the stones had been situated had recently been cleared, and some of the shards were daubed with graffiti.

Richard was choking with outrage.

'If you can't bomb it, put a road through it.'

At a nearby house, there was further evidence of the Hua Muong site's destruction. One of the stone tables was being used as a chopping board in the yard, and some of the shards served as steps and fence posts. We saw an old man supervising construction of a new kiosk which, he said, would cater for an expected flood of tourists to the place, which he called Pha Kouk. Po Lah was 75 years old and he too remembered the French woman who had been here when he was a teenager—but not, perhaps, as she would like to be remembered.

'She used to ride on an elephant,' said Po Lah. 'All the way to Sam Neua. The local men would follow her. She wore no underwear. We could see right up her skirt!'

We had brought with us some sticky rice and chilli *padaek*, and we sat down on the floor of the half-finished kiosk to eat. According to local folklore, a man called Hart Unh had erected the standing stones, using a diamond scythe to shape them, and they were named after him. I asked if the local animists believed the stones contained *phi*, or spirits, but Po Lah had never heard of any such association. He said the road had not stopped opium poppies being grown in the area, and that the Hmong had simply moved their gardens nearer to it for easier access. He said he believed the tables were not sacrificial altars but dining tables, or oversized mortars for preparing food. He said Colani had paid villagers to help her excavate the sites, and had moved some of the tables. Beneath them, in holes more than 2 m deep, they had found human remains. Po Lah said Mount Chalay, about 2 km away, was the main site, with many more stones, and he mentioned other places where 'madame' had not been. He offered to take us up there for 3000 *kip*, but we were still several hours' drive from Sam Neua, so we had to press on.

We wandered for the last time among the stones. On one of them, I read a scrawled name: Lamphan.

'Oh, shit!' I said.

'What?' asked Sousath. 'You know him?'

'I'm afraid I do. And it seems I can't escape him.'

'Hmmnnn,' mused Sousath. 'Seems like you got important friends.'

The closer to Sam Neua we got, the more the road deteriorated. We passed Ban Don, one of only two or three remaining villages of the Sam Moi people, according to Sousath. During rainstorms, when the wet, uncovered rock sparkled, excellent aquamarines were mined in the forest here. Thai gem hunters had already discovered the place.

I wondered what the Foreign Ministry in Vientiane would think if they knew where I was. What would Lamphan think? And where would we stay? How to be inconspicuous in a town like Sam Neua? Such thoughts made me anxious. The rough journey was also getting to me. We'd been on the road since 6 a.m. Now it was dark and cold.

'How far now?' Richard would ask Sousath. 'We must be close.'

'*Baw*,' Sousath would reply. 'Another 20 kilometres or so.'

Eventually we rounded a bend and saw the lights of Sam Neua glistening in the valley below. The sight inspired more foreboding in me than relief. Soon we were passing along the wide, cheerless streets that I'd been so happy to leave so recently. The few feeble street lamps glowered, and there was nobody around.

'Ghost Central!' Richard exclaimed, his voice uneven with the chill.

The Dok Mai Deng was shuttered, but we found another small guest house on the same street and took three rooms. They gave us black coffee for dinner, supplemented by the sticky rice, *padaek* and some sausages Sousath had brought from Ban Ban. After dinner we briefly made plans for the following day. It was necessary to register our arrival in the province with the local authorities, but tomorrow, Sunday, the government offices would be closed. So we agreed simply to drive to Viengsai the next morning, visit Sousath's family cave, spend the night in Viengsai, and return to Xieng Khouang early on Monday. We were all exhausted, and Richard and Sousath turned in. When I detected no more movement in their rooms, I took a bottle of whisky and a flashlight from my satchel and left the guest house.

A foreigner walking alone on the streets of Sam Neua late at night would surely attract unwanted attention, so I wore a baseball cap with the brim pulled down, but in the event, there was no-one around to notice me. The directions the colonel had given were clear and simple, and led me straight to a typical stilt home, which I identified by an unusual feature on one of the fence posts. A tall, grey-haired man in a woollen cardigan answered the door at the top of a flight of stairs.

'*Sabaidee*,' he said in a low voice.

I said 'hello', realising he could not see my face. He peered into the darkness and, still standing in the doorway, called out to someone inside. In a few moments, a younger man appeared in the gloomy light, running his hands through his hair and putting on his glasses, as if he'd been woken.

'Yes? Can I help you?' he said.

The clarity of his pronunciation comforted me.

'I'm a friend of Colonel Boun Kham,' I said, and they bundled me inside.

Kinship in Laos is based on obligation as much as blood ties. Debts owed and favours done often forge relationships which transcend familial ones. Boun had described this man as his 'love brother', and had complete faith he would do anything Boun asked in the name of that brotherhood. The man had a cat-like, sensitive face, but with a distinct military bearing—rather like an Asian Sir John Gielgud with a thin moustache—so I immediately christened him 'Sir John'. Sitting on the floor of the thatched room, he poured green tea and asked how the colonel was doing.

'Undefeated,' I replied, and he smiled knowingly.

'He is a good man,' said Sir John through his son. 'On the wrong side, but a good man all the same.'

We cogitated on that for a while, nodding and smiling. Sir John never took his gaze off me. He said something to his son, who looked at me with his bright, intelligent eyes and translated.

'He says you can ask him anything. What is it that you want to know?'

'I would like to know . . . what happened to the king,' I said.

Sir John took a thoughtful breath, straightened his cardigan, then let it go. He asked how long I would be staying in Houaphan, thought a bit more, grimaced slightly, then spoke again through his son, who translated simultaneously in small phrases.

'I will tell you what I know but it was some years ago. I'll need to check a few things . . . Go to Viengsai in the morning . . . But before you visit the caves, go to the Number One Hotel and take a room . . . then stay there in the evening. At six o'clock on Monday morning I will send a car for you. Be ready in the lobby of the hotel. We can have breakfast at a friend's house . . . Then I will tell you what I know. If you cannot get a room at the Number One Hotel, return to Sam Neua and come here in the evening, after dark, about this time, and we will talk then.'

I ran through the arrangement again for safety.

'*Krop chai lai lai*,' I said, and got up to go, producing the whisky bottle from the folds of my parka. Sir John held it in his hand, as if weighing it, then handed it back to me.

'*Krop chai*,' he said.

His son looked startled, as if he'd never seen his father return a bottle of good whisky.

'Give it to your friends tomorrow evening,' said Sir John, with a wicked smile. 'Drink only a little yourself, but make sure they enjoy it well.'

The following morning, Richard and I breakfasted on eggs

and coffee at the Hin restaurant, where I enjoyed an anonymity no longer available at Joy's. At the Hin we met a young Australian called Colin, who had ridden his motorcycle all the way from Vientiane. His multicoloured bike had commanded attention all along the route, and a small crowd of men and boys had formed outside the Hin, gawking at the vehicle. Colin had been to Viengsai the previous day, but was unable to get into any of the caves for obscure bureaucratic reasons, so he'd decided to follow the road beyond Souphanouvong's cave to see where it went. After only a few kilometres, he was flagged down by villagers and turned back.

'It was like a citizen's arrest,' he said. 'There was no way I was going to get past them.'

The week before, the representative of a well-established travel guide had been turned away as well, this time by officials, who refused to show him the caves. Earlier, a British backpacker who'd made his own way to Viengsai had been arrested and held for a week after trying to enter an unmarked cave whose entrance had been covered with iron sheeting. The Tourism Department's plan to showcase the heroic province of Houaphan was clearly having teething problems.

'You've got to wonder what they're hiding,' said Colin, who wanted to marry a Lao woman and had been waiting more than a year for the Interior Ministry to officially sanction the union. Bureaucrats were demanding that the Australian host a *baci* ceremony for 600 of the ministry's staff and their families before they processed the paperwork.

To help that night's party along I purchased some of the Lao beer on sale at Hin. I had just put the case on my shoulder when a Japanese four-wheel-drive pulled up outside the restaurant and Lamphan disembarked along with four Asian men in suits. He hadn't seen me, so I looked for an escape route. There was none. But I had the advantage of surprise, at least.

'Lamphan!' I yelled, exploding with fake joy.

He was confused at first to hear his name. Then he saw me, and a look of shock seized his face.

'What the hell are you doing here?' he seemed to say.

Suddenly, his smile returned, but it never reached his eyes. Making every second count, I unleashed a blizzard of chumminess, foreign words and local names, knocking him off balance again: Tourist. Viengsai. Go. Vientiane. Today. Lamphan's eyes betrayed the impotence of a man who desperately needed to ask a question but couldn't frame it. The language barrier was working in my favour.

'Vientiane?' he said, then, 'You go to Vientiane today?'

'Vientiane,' I said, smiling and nodding, and pointing at the beer. 'Viengsai. Vientiane.'

He nodded but didn't look happy, and his guests were beginning to scrape their feet. I could tell by their suits they were Vietnamese—Chinese communists have better tailors these days—and they were probably suspicious of Lamphan's relationship with the foreigner. Finally, I let go of his hand, which I'd been pumping furiously, gave him a big '*sogdee*', and got the hell out of there.

'What was that all about?' asked Richard, following me up the road.

'You don't want to know,' I said, an awful taste in my mouth.

It was as if all the urgency and tension I usually discarded in Laos had actually been stored in some secret location, where it had been compounding. Now it had erupted again. I suddenly realised how little time I had left. Within minutes we were headed for Viengsai.

'Oh, here we are,' said Sousath, guiding the jeep past a small lake and football field into the driveway of a compound dotted with pines. 'Welcome to the Number One Re-education Guest House!'

On 26 April 1974, two helicopters landed at Viengsai, one of which carried King Savang Vatthana. Accompanying him were the cabinet, members of the National Political Consultative Council, Buddhist monks, and members of the king's personal staff. Prince Somsanith, the father of my guide at the

Luang Prabang palace, represented the King's Council. They had flown from Luang Prabang at the invitation of Souphanouvong, who welcomed them warmly to the liberated zone.

'You should visit your people and see how they live,' Souphanouvong had told the king.

It was the first visit Savang Vatthana had made as king to this part of his country, and he reviewed Pathet Lao troops and visited Sam Neua during a week-long trip. He toured the scenic limestone karsts, marvelled at their austere splendour, and was moved to comment that he regarded the population of the province as his children. Since the Paris accords had put an end to US bombing, construction of public buildings and houses had been under way in earnest. One such building, a two-storey brick and stucco structure, was referred to as 'the king's palace at Viengsai'. It was there that the king stayed during his visit, which was designed by the Pathet Lao to win royal endorsement for all that had been done in the communist-controlled north-east, and to reassure the rest of the country as to their intentions. On both counts, it was a great success.

Savang Vatthana had been excited by the invitation, seeing his visit as a public affirmation of the unity of the nation under the crown, and as a way of gaining the trust of the Pathet Lao. Villagers thronged Sam Neua. Some of them had walked for four days to see him, carrying their children on their backs. Many Lao wanted to believe that the visit indicated a change of heart by Souphanouvong, who in 1957 had told his cadres that the purpose of the revolution was 'to progress until . . . the abolition of the monarchy'. But the ideologues in the party believed in class justice. For them, it was not enough for Savang Vatthana to visit his people. He should live among them permanently, and the royal visit to Viengsai was a dress rehearsal for his final relocation and re-education there. Ironically, it was to the same building that Savang Vatthana returned as a prisoner in March 1977.

It stood two storeys high at the base of a limestone karst

near Military District Five, an unlovely block, all vicious angles and grim corridors. Where you might imagine balustrades, you saw prison cell bars. The windows were punched out at random, some boarded up but most broken. It had been painted by committee, in a patchwork of white, aqua and dirty yellow. But the thinness of the paint, the paltriness of the stucco and the erosion of the bricks had spawned a multitude of blotches and eruptions which gave the entire structure a diseased air. It had that unmistakable combination, unique to the architects corps of the Vietnam People's Army, of authoritarian lines marred by poverty and slovenly execution.

They showed us to our rooms. The plaster had fallen from the walls. The wood had fallen from the banisters. Nothing worked. Miserly light bulbs hung down on nooses, and red plastic chamber pots from China lurked beneath thin mattresses. In a vain effort to keep the savage winds out of the bedroom someone had tried to tape newspaper over a shattered window, but the glue had evaporated and both the tape and the newspaper flapped uncontrollably. The newspaper looked familiar. It was a copy of *Nhan Dan* (*The People*), the daily paper of the Vietnamese Communist Party. It was dated 11 July 1975, and the front page carried a photo of three men in a motorcade: Soviet Party Chief Leonid Brezhnev, his Vietnamese counterpart Le Duan, and the former Vietnamese Prime Minister Pham Van Dong.

'Nice place, eh?' Sousath said, fiddling with something under the bonnet of the jeep, when Richard and I presented for our caves tour.

He took an appraising look at the old dump.

'This was where the political education was given to people from the old regime. They learnt all about Marxism here. Then we sent them into the villages to practise what we taught them. Over there was the seminar room, where the dining room is now.'

We went and looked. It was a long room with pillars supporting the ceiling and overhead fans. The tables were arranged in two long lines down either side of the room, and there were girlie calendars on the far wall. It looked like a classroom for reprobates, only set for dinner. Richard came in behind me.

'It's incredible,' he said. 'We're actually staying in a former gulag.'

The blaring horn of the jeep beckoned, and we headed off. I was alarmed when our first stop was the home of a local policeman.

'Do we have to?' I whimpered. 'Can't we just visit your family cave in private?'

'We cannot!' said Sousath. 'In Viengsai, you need permission for everything.'

The policeman turned out to be a reasonable chap. It was his day off, and he was just sitting down to large meal. Without much difficulty, he persuaded us to join him. Our last decent meal had been at the Sangah restaurant in Phonsavan. After lunch he took a large machete, walked us down to the base of a karst, directly beside the district military headquarters office, and began hacking away at vines and creepers choking the path.

'This was the area of the Foreign Affairs caves,' said Sousath, waving a neon-green flashlight at the rock face. 'Here there used to be a kind of supermarket for all the Foreign Affairs staff. And here, here is Castro's graffiti.'

Along with the message from Fidel, who had visited Viengsai when American planes were still bombing the area, were words of encouragement from communist delegations from France, the Soviet Union and Germany. After taking the obligatory photos we climbed higher, and soon reached the gaping mouth of a cave. It was the family cave, little used by the Phetrasys but remembered well. Sousath had lived there from 1971 to 1973 after blotting his copybook in China.

Long after I left Laos, a western diplomat who'd served in Vientiane during the 1970s told me a story which said much about the strange nature of Sousath's family. He recalled going with Soth to Wattay airport to meet several of the Phetrasy children returning from abroad. It had been ten or more years since Sousath had seen his parents, and there was speculation as to whether they would recognise each other. As it happened, they didn't.

Now, as we moved around Cavern Phetrasy, Sousath wore a glum face. There was a drawing on one wall done by his sisters. In the living room, which had a stone table and shelves, he brightened momentarily, standing behind the table and mimicking the action of a cocktail waiter. But it seemed an old joke, dismal like the cave. The bedroom was a catacomb, with gutters cut into the floor for drainage.

'This would make a fantastic nightclub,' said Richard. 'What was it like sleeping in here?'

'At night, there was a lot of moisture,' replied Sousath. 'And when we slept it was like being buried. You felt very tired.'

When the bombing stopped in 1973, the government built a house for Soth Phetrasy. But after living there briefly during his period as re-education commissar, Sousath's father was sent to Moscow as ambassador. Sousath left for Vientiane in 1976. The house remained vacant until March 1977, when the former king, his queen and the crown prince moved in. Sousath stood at the mouth of the cave and pointed to a small, fenced slope directly opposite. There were some banana palms growing there, and the rest of the ground looked to be taken up by vegetable gardens. On the far side of the block were two brick buildings without roofs, obscured by vegetation.

Lao officials in Vientiane at the time of the king's arrest had defended the government's treatment of him while not allowing even family visits. Said one: 'Our government gave him a special allowance, double the minimum, as well as other benefits in his new position in his family life. In order to guarantee his security and permit him to make a lasting contribution to the national government of the Lao PDR, it was decided to invite him, his wife and his son Vong Savang to travel by air to a safe place. There the government has continued to give him special advantages for his material and political position: a solid house with running water, electricity, and adequate comforts, a radio receiver and servants.'

Said another: 'A new stone or brick home was built especially for the royal family to provide a minimum standard of comfort in their exile.'

The solid house, it appeared, was near the Pathet Lao radio station, and the radio could pick up only one frequency. The servants were guards. Security was strict, and nobody was allowed to go near the buildings except on official business. Other sources gave conflicting information as to who owned the houses—some said Soth Phetrasy, others Souvanna Phouma—but the description of the royal prison as a 'solid house' was not disputed. Another informant had been even more specific, referring to 'two brick houses'. Before leaving, I photographed the two houses from our vantage point in the cave. The canopy of vegetation had already made them invisible from the air. One more wet season and they would probably be fully camouflaged by nature. As far as Sousath was concerned, that was as it should be. The royal family was best forgotten.

'The one on the right was the house,' said Sousath. 'The one on the left was a kitchen and guard house. When the king came back to Viengsai in 1977, he stayed first at the Number One Guest House. But after a short time, they moved him and his family here. The guards stayed in the second house and did the cooking. When I came back here for the first time in 1992, I saw the roof was missing. Somebody stole the wood.'

'How long did the king's family stay in your home?'

'I don't know exactly. But some months. The king even looked like a European—tall, with a big nose,' he said. 'He sold the country to foreigners.'

We spent the rest of the afternoon poking around the caves of various leaders including Kaysone Phomvihan. His cave was spacious and airy, and its huge family and meeting rooms, with their sunny aspects, would have provided quite comfortable living. On a tattered map on the wall, Hanoi was marked with a large red dot. Sop Hao was also marked, and there was the obligatory gas-attack room. The third member of the leadership troika, President Nouhak Phoumsavanh, was still alive and, together with his Vietnamese wife, was a regular visitor to the pretty bougainvillea-covered bungalow which stood outside the entrance to his cave.

Back at the Number One Guest House, they were preparing a party, not for us, but in honour of a fraternal delegation from neighbouring So'n La province in Vietnam. The dried-mud top of the large earthenware *lao lao* jar had been lopped off with a machete and 30 cm straws, capable of drawing the more potent brew on the bottom, had been placed in it. As the wine is drunk from the bottom, the jar is topped up with water, which turns to wine as the rice mash continues to brew. In the macho culture of *lao lao*, visitors are often challenged to prove themselves by consuming large quantities of the stuff. The hosts can tell how much they have drunk by how much water it takes to top up the jar. The only way to survive the ordeal is to drink alongside a Lao friend and fake it.

'You must drink carefully,' Sousath said to me.

Hoping he would not take his own advice, I produced the beer case and the whisky, placing them with a flourish on the long dining table in the seminar room.

'Uh-oh,' said Sousath. 'Look like we're going to have a big night.'

The tables were laid with an impressive spread: chopped chicken, sticky rice, scallions, strips of marinated beef, *laap*, cut chilli in soy, and other treats. But the smorgasbord didn't impress vegetarian Richard.

'I really wonder about these people sometimes,' he said. 'What do they do with the rest of the stuff? I mean, you go into the market in the morning, and it's absolutely crawling with all kinds of mushrooms, and bean sprouts, and vegetables. Yet all you ever get for dinner is fucking noodle soup and meat!'

One member of the kitchen staff kept sidling up to Richard, winking and suggesting there might be women on offer that night. Apparently the Number One Guest House had descended from palace to prison to brothel.

I went upstairs to rest before dinner, and had fallen asleep when Richard came in and woke me.

'Your friend is here to see you,' he said.

'What friend?'

'The guy from Sam Neua. Lamphan, is it? Wants to see you?'

A shiver went through me.

'Richard.'

'Yes?'

'I'm not feeling too well. Do you think you could find me a couple of aspirin?'

'Sure. What have you got? A migraine?'

'Yes. Something like that.'

Since being told about the Vietnamese party, I'd been worrying that the guests might be the men Lamphan had had in tow that morning. Now he'd caught up with me, and I was on his territory, but there was no point panicking. On the one hand, Lamphan might have come in the normal course of escorting the Vietnamese, who were staying at the hotel. On the other hand, if he had come to arrest me, there was little I could do about it except to prepare my defence. And perhaps there was a third possibility: that he suspected me of being up to no good but, having insufficient evidence, wanted to know more about what I was doing in Viengsai. As I lay fully clothed, wrapped in a blanket under the mosquito net, I heard noises from downstairs. The party was under way. At the sound of footsteps approaching down the corridor, I braced for the worst, but it was only Richard.

'Are you OK?' he asked.

'Not great,' I groaned. 'My head's splitting.'

'You don't think it's malaria, do you?'

'Maybe. Might get a check-up at Sam Neua hospital in the morning.'

'Well, I'd stay put if I were you. They're making a real racket down there. You can hear that godawful music. It's the same tape going over and over. It's like some sort of Lao rave! And your friend Lamphan—he's a shifty-looking fellow isn't he—he's bitching about you. He reckons you lied to them when you came here last time.' And he left me to my worst imaginings.

In the seminar room of the Re-education Guest House, the alcohol had flowed freely as Lao and Vietnamese officials competed to consume the most. The men from Xieng Kho district were getting familiar with the waitresses, who kept on smiling while picking up the empties. At one point, a particularly drunk Vietnamese accidentally head-butted one of the waitresses as he leaned across to tell her how gorgeous she was, and knocked her out. Another poorly executed confidence sent a mugful of beer cascading over Richard. More chaos ensued in the rush to clean up the mess.

'There must have been fifteen people in my lap,' he told me the following morning.

Sousath had been 'drinking cleverly' with the others. A singing competition had ensued in which Richard was prevailed upon to take part. He had chosen as his contribution William Blake's 'Jerusalem'.

And did those feet in ancient time
Walk upon England's mountains green?
And was the holy Lamb of God,
On England's pleasant pastures seen?
And did the Countenance Divine
Shine forth upon our clouded hills?
And was Jerusalem builded here
Among these dark Satanic Mills?

I had heard the discordant voices swirling through the stair wells and corridors. From the staff quarters under the cliff face behind, I had heard a baby's cry. The wind rattled the window frames, howling like the drunken officials in the seminar room below. They had given Richard and me the largest bedroom, and it occurred to me that it was probably the royal suite.

Towards dawn, Richard had returned, fumbling around the room. 'God! I'm shit-faced,' he said. 'Do you know, I've spent the past two bloody hours teaching the bloody district commissioner of bloody Xieng Kho how to speak bloody English. He now knows how to say, "I have got bad breath!" Sousath is blind.'

'What about Lamphan?'

'Oh, God, he left hours ago. I saw his jeep heading back to Sam Neua. Jesus, I'm covered in beer! Never again, I tell you. Not with that local fire water.'

And he drifted off to sleep, his expostulations losing coherence and eventually subsiding. When he began to snore, I got up and started packing. At 6 a.m., a dark-green Russian jeep came crunching along the drive. The hotel corridors were deserted and grey, heavy snores spilling from every room, and I slipped away unseen. Sir John's son pushed open the door of the jeep and in a few minutes I was inside a warm thatched house, enjoying fried eggs, baguettes and cheese wedges with hot, strong coffee, which Sir John, still in his cardigan, boasted he had grown himself. In the light of day I noticed he had a condition which turned his skin white in patches, but he was in fine spirits, hugging the owner of the house and introducing him as his best friend. The man seemed deferential, sitting on the floor throughout our breakfast along with Sir John's son.

I began by asking what Viengsai had been like during the late 1970s, when the campaign of re-education had been at its height. Sir John said the population had mushroomed, with thousands of people being processed for seminar. The Re-education Guest House had been busiest immediately before and after the revolution in 1975, when thousands of former royal government officials had stayed there. A centre of activity in Viengsai had been the so-called Elephant Cave, a huge cavern where public lectures were given and movies were shown.

There had also been a media cave, bristling with radio transmitters and typewriters.

'The initial assessments were done at the guest house,' he said. 'The arrivals were given initial instruction in Marxism–Leninism and the history of the revolution. Depending what they had done, and how they responded to instruction, they were classed into different categories and sent to the three main camps.'

The re-education syllabus began with the history of the Indochinese revolutionary movement from the 1920s to the revolution of 1975. Prisoners learned about the careers of the different leaders and the individual battles of the war, and were expected to memorise the name of each battle, why it was fought and how many died. There was also tuition in the fundamentals of Marxism–Leninism, and the history of the party down to the last Central Committee decision. In the mornings, the teacher would hand out documents, and in the evening there would be discussion and a written test. To do well, a seminarist had to not only pass the test but also convince the tutor that he accepted the correctness of the party's line. An excellent student might be allowed to return home within five years. But most stayed at least a decade, and many thirteen years or more. All were required to work in the labour camps in various parts of the province.

The highest-security camp was at Sop Hao, at the confluence of the Ma and Hao rivers. The camp had been fenced and consisted of four barracks buildings made of timber. Every province had at least one such high-level camp, but far more numerous were the labour camps, which were mobile, unfenced and which the prisoners had to build for themselves using bamboo and thatch. Residents of these camps were used to perform public works including road building, fencing and agriculture. Some worked on the maintenance of the leaders' caves or, after 1975, on construction of their new houses and civic buildings. Prisoners were given Sundays free, and some formed themselves into tightly managed, high-performance teams capable of doing private jobs in their free time to earn additional income. Some of the men married local women, others had brought their wives and children with them or were visited by them. But these privileges were not extended to the royal family. Management of the camps was overseen by the Lao military, at first assisted and advised by both Russian and Vietnamese specialists who regularly visited the camps. But eventually they were transferred to the control of the Interior Ministry, and discipline and standards declined to such an extent that guards, as well as prisoners, went hungry. So desperate did the guards become that they would lend their guns to prisoners and send them to hunt for food. A few people who took the opportunity to flee were later caught and executed. Families were allowed to send food and medical parcels to prisoners provided the contents were put into a common pool and shared equally. Hundreds, possibly thousands, died of disease, malnutrition and unaccustomed hardship. Burial was the usual method of disposing of the bodies, as cremations used valuable firewood.

I told Sir John of the various theories in the west—some published as fact—regarding the fate of King Savang Vatthana, Queen Khamphoui and Crown Prince Vong Savang. There had been the exposé published in *The Bangkok Post* in 1987, which painted a melodramatic picture of their last days in the camp at Sop Hao. A student picked up off the street in Vientiane in 1975 and for some reason kept in the highest-security prison in Laos for the next ten years, claimed that the king had willed himself to die soon after the death of his son. He claimed Savang Vatthana's parting words were: 'I am going to sleep. Now I give all my soul, my blood and my body to the fertile soil and beauty of Laos, and for the well-being of all the Lao people.'

The student, 'Thongpoon', claimed to have pieced together his story from what he'd heard in the camps and what he'd seen for himself. He said the king and crown prince had died within eleven days of each other in May 1978. Queen Khamphoui wasted away about three and a half years later. Thongpoon said the bodies had been buried at the base of a big *kok leung* tree, 180 m north of Camp One perimeter, along a small stream called Houy Nok Kok, a tributary of the Houy Path River. The king's body was on the north side of the tree, the crown prince's on the south, along with that of the last commander of the Royal Lao Army, General Bounpone Makthepharak, who died in July 1978 after guards withheld his rations. None of the graves was marked, and Khamphoui was not allowed to attend the burials. However, her grave was near those of her husband and son.

Then there were the documents produced by Prince Sisouk Na Champassak, which purported to show that the queen also had died in 1978, and yet other accounts which said Khamphoui had been transferred to an even more remote camp with a single Pathet Lao female guard. I had never heard two versions that didn't contradict each other.

Sir John laughed and shook his head.

'No one person who was in seminar would have been in a position to know the full story of what happened to the royal family,' he said. 'The only people who know that are the Pathet Lao. And because these matters were never discussed, even we as individuals do not know exactly. But I can tell you the crown prince died first, in Viengsai, not Sop Hao, and he did not die in the same year as the king. When they came here in 1977, they stayed in the Number One Guest House. But soon there were fears that China might try to rescue the king. He had visited Beijing in the 1960s, and Laos was taking Vietnam's side in its dispute with China and the Khmer Rouge. Also there were problems with the crown prince. He refused to accept his situation and was always speaking harshly to the staff and other seminar people. So in that atmosphere, it was decided to move Savang Vatthana and his family to the smaller brick houses behind the headquarters of Military District Five. The guards cooked and grew vegetables, although the king also liked gardening, so he helped. But the crown prince continued to cause problems. One night at dinner, he stood up and turned over the dining table. He said, "Why are we being forced to eat this terrible food? We are the kings of this country." His mother the queen was not happy at this outburst. She said to him, "What are you saying? If the soldiers did not cook this food we would starve." But Vong Savang refused to apologise. So the government ordered the troops not to cook for the family any more. They said to the king, "If the food we prepare for you is not sufficient, the family can cook for itself." So then the crown prince took charge of the food supply, and their situation got worse. About this time, the crown prince began to suffer from mental problems. He really could not accept being in detention. He began to go crazy, and developed dysentery and a brain fever. He was the first one to die, and he died here in Viengsai. A cremation was held for him and his ashes were buried in the cemetery behind the airfield. I'm not sure of the exact date, but I think it was in about 1978.'

Lao exile groups had claimed that the crown prince was shot dead by the Pathet Lao after leading an escape bid by 22 inmates of a re-education camp in Sam Neua.

'No,' said Sir John. 'But there were several uprisings after Vong Savang's cremation. There was one at Muang Et. More than 30 high-ranking officers of the old regime were transferred to Sop Hao after that. Most of them were killed. The biggest rebellion was at the camp at Sam Tai. About twenty people were killed there. They had no arms.'

'So there were executions?'

'There were. No bullets, just a club to the head.'

'Did anyone ever escape?'

He laughed bleakly.

'There was one prisoner who used to make excellent pâté. They sent him down to Vientiane because all the best cooks had left the country, and the leadership had trouble entertaining their guests from Vietnam and the Soviet Union. So that fellow was taken to Vientiane to make them his special pâté. That man escaped across the Mekong to Thailand.

'After the crown prince died, the king and queen were moved again. This time they moved them to Sop Hao, which is less than 10 km from the Vietnamese border. This happened at the time that relations were getting worse with China. But also, they felt that after the difficulties with the crown prince, the presence of the royal family here had become a focus of attention, and it would be better to move them to a more isolated place like Sop Hao.

'Conditions at Sop Hao were worse than in Viengsai. Because it was a camp, everybody had to eat the same food, which was just a handful of rice and some salt and water per day. The king and his other son, Sisawang, were given a small patch of land and told to cultivate it. Queen Khampoui was separated from them. The style of life was very different. Viengsai was like a family home compared to Sop Hao, which was an actual prison camp. I was told the queen died first, and the king six months later. He always had stomach problems, even before coming to Viengsai. I heard it was in 1980.'

'What did the king die of?'

'If you are a king, and you live alone without any wife, what do you think?'

'Where is he buried?'

'Behind the camp. The area is probably rice paddies now. But the grave is near a couple of large trees.'

'Is there anybody still in seminar?'

'There are a few. One general and one major are still not free to leave Houaphan. In fact they are living in the village of Sop Hao. The three ministers sentenced in 1991 are in the camp at Sop Hao.'

Was there anything else he wanted to say, I asked, that had not been covered by my questions?

'Yes,' he said directly. 'Yes, there is. You must wonder why I am willing to talk about these things. So, I will tell you. I am Issara. Believe me when I tell you that the Lao people supported the revolution. We were grateful for Vietnamese support, but afterwards they behaved like new kings. Had it not been for the collapse of the Soviet Union, they would still be on top of us. They still have too much power to decide what happens here. But we are still fighting for our independence. There are two types of independence leaders, the communists and the Issara. And still today there is conflict between those who want true independence, the Issara, and those who do things differently.'

The sun had risen and it looked like being a nice day. Sop Hao, with its secrets and prisoners, seemed so close again, a few hours drive down the road. But I knew I'd had my chance there. My responsibility now was to get out of Viengsai before implicating anybody. We shook hands.

'Sorry about the scotch,' I said.

'It's OK,' said Sir John, smiling ruefully. 'It was for a good cause.'

His son dropped me at the war memorial at the northern end of the main square in the middle of Viengsai. The wind had dropped and it was a beautiful morning. I felt a momentary surge of elation, strolling past the lake and football ground to the Number One Guest House, where Richard and Sousath were still sleeping soundly. The official delegation had slipped away, taking their hangovers back to Vietnam.

Sousath steadfastly resisted all efforts to wake him, and would have slept until sunset unless something was done. So after packing up and paying the bill, Richard and I carried him to the jeep. Fishing the keys from his pocket, I took the wheel and set off for Sam Neua, discovering at the first turn that the vehicle which had brought us across the Annamite Mountains had no brakes.

Stretching his long limbs in the passenger seat, Richard pushed his mousy, tousled hair back over his forehead. 'Yep,' he said. 'It's definitely the way to get in with the locals. Forget the hammer and sickle. Just hammer the alcohol.'

9

Many happy returns

In Vientiane, the twentieth-anniversary celebrations were under way, culminating with a revolutionary ballet in which pirouetting soldiers in slippers danced with bayonets.

The performance in the main hall of the National Assembly was an exclusive affair for the party and military leaders—those imbued with 'the spirit of Sam Neua'—and the diplomatic corps; 'the cave men meet the cocktail set,' as one observer put it. The Politburo members perched on brand-new, over-stuffed pink sofas. The old men were offered cognac but declined. On stage, the strident voice of a Defence Ministry diva commanded diminutive Lao soldiers to throw their grenade launchers in the air like Cossacks. Women in knee-length black boots goose-stepped across the stage. I checked for signs of excitement, or even recognition, in the front row. There were none. The American ambassador, Victor Tomseth, looked like a man in denial, longing for a GI in mufti to mount the stage and inform the gathering, 'You have not been here, you have not seen anything, and you will not talk about this to anyone!' To be fair to Tomseth, he had spent 444 days in captivity in Teheran as one of the American hostages taken by Iranian students in November 1979, certainly the longest official call of his career. And when he'd returned home, his first public engagement—a speech at the University of Oregon—had been disrupted by hundreds of demonstrators who were convinced that, as political officer in the Teheran embassy, he had encouraged the late Shah of Iran's repressive policies.

As the guerrilla–ballerinas segued into the graceful *lam vong*, the line between the official and the popular began to blur. The *khene* pipes buzzed and the dancers' hands flowed rhythmically and hypnotically, as they have done in the villages for centuries. Women still wore the *sin* in Vientiane, rather than jeans, and the *lam vong* was still more popular than disco, both largely thanks to the party's moral crusade. But the royal puppets no longer danced in Luang Prabang, their restless *phi* still imprisoned in a box.

Earlier in the day, the frail President Nouhak had needed assistance to mount the modest staircase at the nearby Memorial to the Unknown Soldier to a chorus of drum rolls, bugles and crowing roosters. Vientiane had been alive with rumours of bomb blasts and conspiracies by 'Vang Pao's people' in the weeks leading up to the event, and police checkpoints were posted on all approaches to the city. But fears of an outrage proved unfounded or, if something did happen, it went unreported. The government had decided against holding a military parade and ordered that only the national flag, not the party's, be flown, leaving the twin flagpoles all over the city strangely lopsided.

At the Lan Xang hotel, an island of good old-fashioned bad service, Foreign Minister Somsavat Lengsavad was deputed to play cat and mouse with foreign correspondents flown in for the occasion. It was the sole media conference to be held during the anniversary celebrations, and Somsavat was blinking furiously. Big houses and cars were, he said, among the achievements of the past twenty years. Overseas Lao who loved their country and wished to participate in national development were welcome to return. During question time, a correspondent from the BBC asked what the government had done with the royal family. Had they been cremated in accordance with Buddhist rites?

The foreign minister balked, no doubt pausing to check his recollection of Buddhist funeral rites, in which the body is bathed in warm water, then in cold water, before being embalmed, massaged with fragrant oils and dressed in two sets of the deceased's favourite clothes, one donned back to front. All these rites—the hot and cold water, the two sets of clothes—represent the balance of death and life. The hair of the deceased is dressed with a comb with missing teeth, which should not be used again, and the body is bound hand and foot with an unbroken length of white cotton, to ensure that the dead do not disturb the living. After this, the body is wrapped in a shroud and laid in the family home. Money is placed in the mouth lest greedy spirits wander. Before crema-tion or burial, the face of the deceased is washed with coconut water and perfume. Handfuls of lemons or banana leaves, coins and roasted rice may be thrown by mourners, and the body is carried three times around the pyre. The day after cremation, the bones are collected from the ashes for washing, thrown into the nearest river, or buried in a *stupa*. Then begin the drinking and dancing, designed not to express joy but to fool evil spirits.

Was that the kind of funeral that was held for the royal family?

There was a stirring in the room. The four or five ministers at the head table looked at their hands, or at the ceiling. A few throats were cleared, amid some whispering. The trans-lators held their breath, and suddenly the room had the atmosphere of a courtroom. We had come with our facts and allegations to a fair trial. Somsavat, smiling and blinking, prepared to answer for his party's history.

'I'm not responsible for this affair,' he said. 'Birth and illness and death is the common lot of people . . . human beings . . . and Laos is composed of many ethnic minorities, who have different customs concerning the cremation or the burying of dead people.'

Then Somsavat did an extraordinary thing. He giggled, a constricted, terrible giggle which was quickly joined by the giggles of his fellow ministers. Then one of the senior Press Department officials leaned into a microphone and said: 'Five more minutes.'

Before what, I wondered? I could almost feel Colonel Boun Kham's fevered breath on the back on my neck.

'You see!' he was hissing. 'Communist liars.'

Yet whose hands were clean in that forgotten conflict? There were at least 36 Lao political parties operating in exile, a testament to the civil war they'd continued to fight amongst themselves since 1975. Some had even accepted the help of the Khmer Rouge. Prince Sauryavong Savang, the last king's sole surviving son, who'd escaped across the Mekong in the last week of November 1975, now acted as head of the royal family in exile. A sort of regent, he advised the heir to the throne, Mahneelai's eldest son, Soulivong Savang, who'd fled Laos in 1981. Some months after leaving Laos I was able to contact Sauryavong by telephone. During our conversation he frankly admitted there was no royal government-in-exile worth the name.

'However, the flame is being kept alive by some of the former ministers in the last government,' he said from Paris, where he worked as a manager at the Citroën factory. 'We are trying to encourage them to get together, harmonise their thinking and present a coherent front, but the task is not easy. We're always ready to assist within the limits of our means.'

Prince Sauryavong had only recently returned from the US, where he had met several Republican congressmen. However, members of the Clinton administration, then heading for re-election, were unavailable. Prince Soulivong Savang was studying law in Clermont-Ferrand. Sauryavong described the heir to the throne as 'intelligent and psychologically balanced, very calm and mature', but said it was up to those who'd met him to determine whether he would be a good king.

'Believe me, we shall return some day,' he said, 'together with our fellow citizens living around the world, to participate in the organisation of a free and democratic election which in the not too distant future will be decided on by the world community. The present communist system is totally alien to our culture.'

'When will you go back?' I asked.

'It's not very easy to predict. That will depend on the support we receive from the international community. In the end, the Lao people will decide after free and fair elections.'

The royal family in exile maintained a lofty contempt for the Lao government and had made no direct contact with it, either in person or by correspondence, since 1975.

The regent's confidence in the international community was slightly surreal in the context of the Lao PDR's impending acceptance as a member of the Association of South East Asian Nations. But he insisted this would 'not make any difference to the legitimate aspirations of the Lao people for freedom and a democratic political system'. I realised he was doing the only thing he could do; waiting. Given enough time, in politics anything is possible.

'We do not think it's practical to seek the remains of our parents for the time being,' Sauryavong said. 'Let them rest in peace for now, until the day when our homeland will return to democracy and respect for human rights and fundamental freedoms. I shall do whatever is necessary, together with the Lao people, to honour their memory and sacrifices.'

Twenty years on since the abdication, delegates from all over Laos gathered at the National Assembly to hear a morale-boosting speech by the president. Pear-shaped Lao ladies with handbags on their arms sat beside heavily decorated military officers as a North Korean Kaysone bust stared back at them from the stage. Nouhak, intoning like a shaman at a *baci* ceremony, stressed the continued need for social order and party dominance in the political system. In the audience, Sisana Sisane checked his watch and apparently resisted the temptation to burst into song. Khammouane

Boupha was seated two rows back from him, near the foreign minister, who'd mastered the art of automatic nodding. Even the Phia Luang of Palavek had come, dressed up in his black pyjamas for the occasion. We were all actors in this play, including me, the nosy *felang*.

Leaving the National Assembly, we passed the Thai embassy, which sported a large banner bearing the words 'Long Live the King'. But what at first appeared like a diplomatic elbow in the ribs was in fact a 68th-birthday greeting for Thailand's King Bhumibol Adulyadej. In 1995, to mark the king's 50th year on the throne, the *Asian Wall Street Journal* editorialised that the monarch's presence 'has been like an umbrella over the country, providing the shade of security in which the Thai people could develop a sense of their own wisdom.' Was it being overly romantic to speculate that the one symbol capable of uniting Laos—the 600-year-old monarchy—had perished in the lush wilderness of Houaphan?

My last few days in Laos were spent in the south, awash with tamarind and sunshine. The Mekong at Pakse is a carefree stream, broad and shallow. On the streets of the provincial capital, men with sandwich carts sold baguettes filled with bacon and hot sauce; women roasted chicken and sweet potatoes and told me not to stand in the sun lest my brains boil; and cafes served rich black coffee from the old French plantations on the Boloven Plateau. The party's directive on removing its flags had yet to filter down, so the colonial streets were a riot of red and gold, and green palm trees.

The palace of the ancestral prince of Champassak, Prince Boun Oum, incomplete when he'd fled across the river in 1975, had been finished off by the Pathet Lao with Vietnamese tiles and military motifs; six storeys of pure architectural gall, a wedding cake melting in the sun. According to one story, probably apocryphal, it was cursed by the monks of Wat Tham Fai, who prophesied that the prince would never live in his palace after he shifted their *wat* to build it. The right-wing Boun Oum was not an old-school prince like the ones in

Luang Prabang. The most powerful feudal landowner in the south, he had tried to turn Pakse into a Lao Las Vegas, a rich, corrupt town which kept him in courtesans until he made the transition from satyr to hypochondriac.

'He was very human,' said a former National Assembly member. 'With very human appetites. He loved the good life. Wine, women and song. But then his lungs gave out.'

The son of King Ratsadanay of the Royal House of Champassak, Boun Oum had renounced his royal title to allow Laos to be reunited at the end of the French protectorate. In return he'd been given the title of inspector-general of the kingdom, but by 1973 he tired of politics, which he preferred to leave to right-wing generals. He complained constantly that Souphanouvong had '*perdu son âme Lao*'—lost his Lao soul—and that the 'Red Prince' was an intellectual, a member of a class that governments should employ but never allow to rule. 'He is so taken with Marxist ideas and his Annamite friends that he has altogether lost touch with what the Lao village people understand and want,' he once said.

Boun Oum himself believed that village people wanted the certainty provided by the old hierarchies, at the top of which he had been placed by birth. Yet apart from women, his energies had been devoted mainly to his multifarious business interests in smuggling, timber and casinos, his many houses and his health. He knew he might not live to see his palace finished, and that conditions might not favour its eventual occupation by the family. For him it had become just something an old man might hope to be remembered by.

Now the teak panelled walls of his pleasure dome had been painted over, the murals altered to put proletarian hard hats on the elephant mahouts, and the rooms partitioned with plywood to create a 70-room hotel with satellite television and portraits of the Pathet Lao leaders behind the reception desk. Boun Oum himself, after fleeing in 1975 and being sentenced to death in absentia, had died of natural causes. I toasted the old bastard anyway as I reclined in a planter's chair on the vast rooftop terrace, catching the breeze that rolled off the Bolovens and enjoying the 360-degree view.

In the evening I talked to Luang Sai, an old man happy to be working as the doorman at the Champassak Palace. Luang Sai was 60 and had no time for brass-buttoned uniforms and glad-handing for tourist tips. He just sat in a Buddha pose beside the front door, brown hands folded in his lap, or clasped behind his back as he strolled the lawns with an inspector's gait. On each wrist he wore a single, weathered *baci* string, and on his head a brown felt hat tilted at a rakish angle. His smile revealed stumpy teeth, thick and even. Pointing to an old bunker with gun turrets beside the driveway, he said it had been built by the French to defend Pakse against the Thai. In the 1960s, he said, he'd worked as a security guard at several of the princely homes, and Boun Oum used to slap him if he didn't work well.

On my last day in Laos, I boarded a pirogue for the journey further south to Champassak town and the old royal monuments at Wat Phu, 80 km from the Cambodian border. Soon we were motoring along a channel defined by numbered concrete markers, past a point where the Japanese government planned to spend $100 million to bridge the Mekong. Pakse needed a road link to Thailand for its development, but this was such a gorgeous stretch of water that I hoped the authorities might change their plans and build it a few kilometres north, out of sight of the town. A big road-building effort also was under way to complete Route Thirteen in the south, although the Cambodian border remained an effective dead end so long as the Khmer Rouge continued to roam on the other side.

Rounding the first bend in the river south of Pakse, we saw a great mountain in the shape of a mesa with a sharp peak on top. Phou Malong rose 1300 metres from the banks of the Mekong, its sheer cliffs resembling battlements. As we approached the daunting, impregnable mountain, the boat was hit by strong winds. Soon the river began to squeeze between the mountain and the island of Don Pakho, where I held it up briefly to visit another princely palace of old, Sala Boun Oum, a purpose-built holiday home now used as a police school. The dilapidated compound was deserted except for a few goats and chickens grazing in the overgrown grass. Corn sprouted from the bank and women bathed in the river, clad in wet sarongs and dunking themselves repeatedly in a motion that called to mind bathers in the Ganges in India.

As we pulled in to shore at Champassak town, women paddled out in canoes selling cooling turnips and barbecued chicken with sticky rice wrapped in palm leaves. Taking the only available *tuk-tuk*, I made my way to the tiered mountain slope of Wat Phu, where black butterflies rode the warm air currents rising from the plain. Nagas and Shivas covered the walls of the ancient stone monuments, older than Angkor. This was a rain-watching pavilion overlooking the valley of the Mekong, with the Bolovens in the distance. In the mouldering moss, the great stone blocks tumbled in disarray, little visited by tourists and unprotected by guards. A stone mahout rode high atop a triple elephant in embroidered *dupatta*; a stone rat sheltered between its curling trunks and tusks; oriental demons poked pointy tongues between their fangs. I found the holy spring—now collecting in 44-gallon drums. After three months on the road my clothes felt like they owned me, so I took them off and plunged my head beneath the water, then walked to the edge of the escarpment and let the breeze dry me.

An old car ferry took me back across the river. It was actually three aluminium dinghies lashed together, with a timber deck nailed over them and a cactus in the cabin. We made landfall 30 km south of Pakse, and I hitched a ride in a timber truck. There were about twenty people, mainly children, in the back, and we sat gingerly on the branches to avoid splinters. The air rushed through the truck, carrying my lonely thoughts away.

At the Chongmek border crossing into Thailand, blind singers busked. Presenting your passport seemed entirely optional. The Lao immigration officer looked over his shoulder at a clock which had stopped hours, possibly years ago, and a uniformed woman, seeing me watching him, giggled. Then everyone started laughing and wishing me *sogdee*—good luck—and I began, for the first time, to feel the wrench of leaving. The lutes of the blind buskers piped a gypsy song.

On the Thai side of the border I caught a taxi to Ubon Ratchathani. The road felt like a steel ribbon beneath us compared to the back-breaking ditches of Laos. In Ubon, election fever was in full swing, and posters of candidates— most of them in military uniform—were stuck to power poles along kerbed and guttered streets. There was also something Laos didn't have—a railway line—but I had to pay a bribe to the conductor to get a sleeper berth.

In Bangkok, the taxi's tyres thumped the ridges of the freeway as the sun drowned at birth in the smog. The driver turned out to be from Issan, the Lao-majority area of Thailand's north-east. He said he wished life in Thailand could again be slow and simple like that in Laos, but it was too late.

At a musty Sukhumvit hotel, the television beamed live pictures of King Bhumibol standing ramrod straight and mournful-faced in a cream Rolls-Royce convertible as he took the salute of troops in grenadier helmets. The queen followed him along a red carpet as he mounted a podium and sat on a canary-yellow throne.

In the hotel cafeteria, the attention of the waitresses was fixed on the television. But as the national anthem—announcer of coups and commercial breaks—welled up, one by one they drifted away.

Epilogue

The fate of the royal family members exiled to Houaphan province in 1977 remains a state secret in Laos.

Why?

After months of travel and hundreds of interviews, I believe one reason is that the only people with sufficient knowledge and authority to reveal the truth—Kaysone Phomvihan, Prince Souphanouvong and their ilk—are dead. Those who survived at the time this was written, like President Nouhak Phoumsavan, were well-insulated from demands for full disclosure from the Lao diaspora. In addition, as Asia reshapes and enriches itself, Western governments are less interested in contemporary human rights problems there—let alone old ones—than in doing business, futile as that sometimes may seem in a place like Laos.

As researchers plough through the vast documentation of the former Soviet empire, no doubt they will eventually reach the broom closet marked 'Lao PDR'. Therein may lie more clues. But while Russia seems willing for domestic political purposes to reveal the fate of its own royalty, the details of what happened in the satellite states remains classified, largely because disclosure could compromise Moscow's relations with former allies.

Mine was a personal journey more than an investigative or political one. At one point, I fantasised that the Lao government would seize the opportunity provided by my curious interest to make a clean breast of the past and be done with it. Towards the end of my time there, I sent a letter to the foreign ministry asking if the government would cooperate, but received no reply. Aware from the beginning that this would likely be the case, I had gone ahead anyway, expecting to find less than I did, but hoping to find more. Some questions should be asked, even if answers are unlikely to be forthcoming.

Many people believe that the echoes of the civil war are slowly fading with the people who fought it, but that ignores the way old scores are passed down from generation to generation, to be settled when history deems it appropriate—witness the war in the former Yugoslavia. There is a door separating Laos from its future. Some wait for the hinges to rust and the door to fall down, but the fate of the Lao royal family is a key which can either keep the door to the country's future locked, or open it. Unfortunately, the Lao People's Revolutionary Party has been unable to coherently address the past in a way which takes the country beyond the locked door. Disclosure is risky for those in power. The detention of Savang Vatthana and his family, like tens of thousands of others, was done without legal sanction, under the fictitious cover that 'samana' was voluntary. Transparency on the part of the government would be seen by expatriate Lao as an important symbol of goodwill, and they would return in a rush, instead of the current slow trickle. But as long as the party remains above the law, returning Lao are vulnerable to the loss of their money and liberty. Despite progress on legal reform, this is still fundamentally the case.

Most informed observers have detected an actual reverse in political and economic reforms since 1995, countering the rapid progress of the early 1990s. The 'communist' regimes of

Indochina have weathered the storm since the collapse of the Soviet Union, have found a prospective new home in the Association of South-East Asian Nations (ASEAN), and now are concerned to entrench their political domination in a more lucrative and benign period.

After leaving Laos, I met a man who had been a senior official in the royal palace at Luang Prabang in the 1960s. Like many of the older generation of exiles, he longed to return, but felt he could not, and was eager for any scraps of information I could share about the situation there. His excitement at my stories of Sam Neua and Viengsai was considerable, especially the idea that government officials would agree to take me to the village of Sop Hao, near the prison camp of the same name where the last king of Laos died.

'It might be a sign,' he said. 'They would not allow you to go there unless they wanted you to write your story.'

Much as I would like to have shared his view, I believe much of what happens on the ground in Laos is accidental, not the result of big policy hammered out across the Politburo table. Still, my friend's conclusion cheered me enormously, because it dovetailed neatly with my own paradigm—that the question itself is like litmus. When I dipped my litmus paper in the Lao solution, it turned red. But the fact that I was able to dip it at all indicates that not all is acid in the People's Democratic Republic.

The testimonies I obtained from people who were living in Viengsai at the time of the king's incarceration there, and who have remained, indicate that after their arrival in March 1977, the royal family spent several months there, until the death of the Crown Prince from some kind of fever. One source said Vong Savang's cremation had been held near the airfield at Viengsai in late 1977 or early 1978, but this was not confirmed by anyone else. After that, the king and queen were moved to Sop Hao, where they were held separately, fed on inadequate rations and denied proper medical treatment. Queen Khampoui died first, then Savang Vatthana, both apparently of old age hastened by the conditions of their imprisonment. The dates of their deaths are unknown, but were likely between 1978 and 1982.

This version must be put beside the various versions of events given by Lao exiles, who differ on the dates and claim the Crown Prince died either en route to Sop Hao (being bashed on the head for refusing to board a pirogue to cross the Nam Ma to the prison camp) or in the camp itself. A possible explanation for the contradictory reports may be the presence of a second prince, Sisavang, who is almost completely ignored in the exile accounts. Was he the prince who died in Viengsai, or the one who died in Sop Hao?

Talking to dozens of people who spent time in the camps of Houaphan province as prisoners, I was struck by how little they actually knew about what was going on at the time. Preoccupied by their life and death struggles for survival, they heard little more than snatches of vague gossip. Those still in Laos, especially those belonging to the administration, are better placed to know what happened, but those outside are more able to speak freely. It is also quite common for people in Laos to tell outsiders what they think they want to hear, even in the absence of full knowledge. Twenty years of one-party rule has not done much for the tradition of independent social science, or free speech. Historians serve the party, yet history is likely to outlast the party. Who then will they serve?

The Lao royal family in exile has its own struggle simply surviving in Western civilization. Like most of us, they have to earn their living now—the Prince Regent works as a manager at the Citroën factory near Paris. If they are to return, it will not be thanks to the international community, which does not take them seriously, but as a result of some internal change within Laos itself. And, as history has shown, changes within such a small, landlocked country usually happen in relation to events in their much larger and more powerful neighbours. Laos is influenced by the situation in Vietnam, which in turn must pay heed to events in China. Membership of ASEAN, or ten other regional groupings, will not change that, though it is true that the smaller neighbours do have slightly more room to move in an era of economic liberalisation and gradual political change.

Thai dominance looms as the most immediate challenge to Lao reformers. On a level economic playing field, powerful Thai companies would annex Laos as a province within a few years. Wisely the Lao government welcomes all investor interest, but actually admits very little. However, widespread and growing corruption within the administration means that even a wise policy can be undermined. The list of Thai ventures in gemstones and timber cutting, of dubious legality and slipping through the net, continues to lengthen, and the flashy new villas belonging to powerful families, which stand out in Vientiane like gold teeth in a mouthful of rot, point to more than just prosperity through free enterprise. Worryingly, the Lao army is involved in much of the extra-legal, and quite rapid, exploitation of the country's portable natural resources, and serving or former generals now occupy six of the nine Politburo seats. Another concern is the Lao government's apparent preference for mega-projects in the field of hydro-electricity production. Resettlement of indigenous peoples, and the impact on them of such aggressive development strategies elsewhere in the developing world, has not been a pleasant experience.

The threat to the Lao identity from Thailand is, however, more to do with the great similarities in language and culture shared by the two nations, and the disparities in wealth and population. Thailand has ten times as many people, and more people of Lao ethnicity live in Thailand than in Laos. As political and economic ideology subsides as a fault line, the Mekong begins to seem like a rather feeble and artificial border. For twenty years, the party in Laos has tried to construct an alternative political identity—'the unity of all ethnic groups'—to differentiate Laos from Thailand. But despite the historical enmity between them, most Lao people are avid consumers of Thai culture and other products, and such consumption is another powerful force for integration.

As I have suggested elsewhere in this account, Laos needs all the national symbols it can get, and by pretending to have snuffed out a 600-year-old monarchy denies itself one of them. But it remains a country worth saving, destined to play a tortured role as buffer between great nations, with a landscape as dramatic and beautiful as any, and people of great civility, charm and generosity, who may well in the long run be better off under a republican form of government.

My time in Laos was an adjunct to a two-year posting in Vietnam where, together with my wife, I enjoyed the gritty pleasures of a Hanoi which retained the austerity of the war, the romance of the French colonial period, and the ancient intellectual and social traditions of a thousand years' rule by the Chinese. When we left, it was with a sense of leaving forever. We might return one day, but the Vietnam we knew would no longer be there. In Laos, things are changing more slowly. I would gladly return tomorrow, but whether that is possible depends partly on how this book is received by the powers that be, and on how long those powers will be there. But a desire to return is nothing when compared to the private tragedies of thousands of Lao people, who lost husbands and fathers, sons and daughters, mothers and sisters, and have never been told how or why, and yet who still call that country home wherever they may live. When the Lao PDR recognises the rights of those people, it will truly have come of age as a nation, and the dream of national reconciliation—declared 'dead' by the *Economist* 20 years ago—may become a reality.

Bibliography

Adams, Nina and McCoy, Alfred (eds), *Laos: War and Revolution*, Harper & Row, New York, 1970

Branfman, Fred *Voices from the Plain of Jars: Life Under an Air War*, Harper & Row, New York, 1972

Champassak, Sisouk Na *Storm Over Laos* Praeger, New York, 1961

Delort, Robert *The Life and Lore of the Elephant*, Thames & Hudson, London, 1992

Dommen, Arthur J. *Laos: Keystone of Indochina* Westview Press/Praeger, Boulder, 1982

—— *Conflict in Laos*, Praeger, New York, 1971

Evans, Grant *Lao Peasants Under Socialism*, Yale University Press, New Haven, 1990

Fall, Bernard B. *Anatomy of a Crisis: The Laotian Crisis of 1960–61*, Doubleday, New York, 1969

Gunn, Geoffrey *Rebellion in Laos*, Westview Press, Boulder and Oxford, 1980

Halpern, Joel *Economy and Society of Laos: A Brief Survey*, South East Asia Studies, Yale University, New Haven, 1964

Hamilton-Merritt, Jane *Tragic Mountains*, Indiana University Press, Bloomington and Indianapolis, 1993

Le Bar, Frank and Suddard, Adrienne (eds), *Laos*, Hraf Press, New Haven, 1967

Manich, M.L. *History of Laos*, Chalermnit Books, Bangkok, 1967

Murdoch, John B. (trans) and Wyatt, David K. *Iron Man of Laos: Prince Phetsarath Ratanavongsa*, Cornell, Ithaca, New York, 1978

Newman, Bernard *Report on Indo-China*, Robert Hale, London, 1953

Ngaosyvathn, Mayoury and Pheuiphanh *Kith and Kin Politics: The Relationship between Laos and Thailand*, Journal of Contemporary Asia, Manila and Wollongong, 1994

Phomvihan, Kaysone *Revolution in Laos: Practice and Prospects*, Progress, Moscow, 1981

Pym, C. *Henri Mouhot's Diary—Travels in the central parts of Siam, Cambodia and Laos during the years 1858–1861* (abridged and edited), Oxford University Press, Kuala Lumpur, 1966

Rantala, Judy Austin *Laos: A Personal Portrait from the Mid-1970s*, McFarland, Jefferson, NC, 1994

Robbins, Christopher *The Raven's Crown*, New York, 1987

—— *Air America*, Putnam, New York, 1979

Stieglitz, Perry *In a Little Kingdom*, M.E. Sharpe, London, 1990

Stuart-Fox, Martin *Historical Dictionary of Laos*, The Scarecrow Press, New Jersey and London, 1992

—— (ed), *Contemporary Laos*, University of Queensland Press, St Lucia and London, 1982

Viravong, Maha Sila *History of Laos*, Paragon Books, New York, 1964

Zasloff, Joseph and Unger, Leonard (eds), *Laos: Beyond the Revolution*, Macmillan, Basingstoke and London, 1991